MEDIA
AND
MOMENTUM

The New Hampshire Primary
and Nomination Politics

Edited by
GARY R. ORREN
and
NELSON W. POLSBY
John F. Kennedy School of Government
Harvard University

CHATHAM HOUSE PUBLISHERS, INC.
Chatham, New Jersey

CHATHAM HOUSE SERIES ON CHANGE IN AMERICAN POLITICS

SERIES EDITOR: Aaron Wildavsky
University of California, Berkeley

MEDIA AND MOMENTUM
The New Hampshire Primary and Nomination Politics

CHATHAM HOUSE PUBLISHERS, INC.
Box One, Chatham, New Jersey 07928

PUBLISHER: Edward Artinian
JACKET AND COVER DESIGN: Lawrence Ratzkin
COMPOSITION: Chatham Composer
ILLUSTRATIONS: Adrienne Shubert
PRINTING AND BINDING: Bookcrafters

LIBRARY OF CONGRESS CATALOGING-IN-PUBLICATION DATA

Media and momentum.

    (Chatham House series on change in American politics)
    Includes bibliographies and index.
    Contents: Introduction, New Hampshire / Gary R. Orren
and Nelson W. Polsby -- The New Hampshire primary /
William G. Mayer -- As New Hampshire Goes -- /
Williams C. Adams -- [etc.]
    1. Primaries--New Hampshire.   2. Presidents--United
States--Nomination.   3. United States--Politics and
government--1945-   . I. Orren, Gary R.
II. Polsby, Nelson W.   III. Series.
JK2075.N42M43 1987   324.5'4   87-13224
ISBN 0-934540-67-5
ISBN 0-934540-66-7 (pbk.)

Printed in the United States of America
10 9 8 7 6 5 4 3 2 1

Contents

Acknowledgments

The Joan Shorenstein Barone Center at Harvard's Kennedy School of Government takes as its special mission the study of the relations between the news media and the world of politics. Because these relations take on special complexity and significance during the presidential nomination season, we have devoted our first book-length collaboration to probing the mysteries of the New Hampshire primary. It is our good fortune that so many of our academic colleagues not only understand the intricacies of that primary but have been willing to explain them here.

We therefore thank each of the contributors and our highly responsive publisher, Edward Artinian, for helping us put this book together. Our staff here at the Center, Maura Barrios, Christine Mattson, Bill Mayer, and Peter Yu, did what needed to be done and did it well. For moral support we relied, as usual, on Merle M. Orren and Linda O. Polsby.

We also wish to thank the following publishers for their permission to reprint from copyrighted works. Several paragraphs in chapter 1 originally appeared in *Boston Magazine,* © 1984, reprinted with permission. Several pages in chapter 5 originally appeared in *Party Democracy: The Politics of National Conventions,* ed. G.C. Perlin (Scarborough: Prentice-Hall Canada, 1987), and are reprinted by permission.

INTRODUCTION

New Hampshire: Springboard of Nomination Politics

GARY R. ORREN AND NELSON W. POLSBY

To those observers who think about, or worry about, the impact of the news media on American politics, the New Hampshire primary must rank as Exhibit A. Every four years during the primary election season, the ninth-smallest state in the union captures the attention of the national press and television to a degree unmatched in vastly more populous locales. Here, increasingly, judgments are formed and transmitted that determine the menu of choices left to the rest of the country on the pivotal issue of who will occupy the White House.

All this occurs because of enormous changes that have taken place over the past 20 years in how we choose Presidents—in particular, changes in party rules for selecting delegates, in federal regulations governing the raising and spending of money during campaigns, and in the role of the media, especially television.[1]

Rules, Money, and Media

Most crucial, perhaps, has been the way in which party rules have evolved since 1968, that year of domestic political strife in which the seeds of party reform were sown that Americans have harvested ever since. New Hampshire emerged as a decisive battleground in the presidential nominating process because party reform elevated the status of primary elections, and because New Hampshire's was, and is, the first primary of the election year. Before reform, most primary elections did not even select delegates to national party conventions. They were "beauty contests"—at best, occasions where presidential hopefuls who for one reason or another had no better way to get into the game could try out their popularity with voters. Such a demonstration might or might not be persuasive to the state party leaders who controlled the bulk of actual delegate votes at national party conventions. As late as 1960, Hubert Humphrey could say that a candidate had to be crazy to enter a primary. In 1968, in fact, he won his party's nomination without entering a single one. In any event, primaries were one element in the overall scheme, contributing more or less valuable information to a complex deliberative process that rested mainly with state party leaders.

Then came party reform. Commissions of the Democratic party issued new rules, and officials of the Democratic National Committee enforced them. Primary elections in consequence took on an entirely new importance. Party leaders in state after state came to realize that the most expeditious way to conform to the new rules was to establish primary elections as the preferred mode of delegate selection. Where this required changes in state law, the Republican party was dragged willy-nilly into the same pattern of delegate selection.[2]

Shortly thereafter came campaign finance reform. As party reform had been spurred by the shattering divisions caused by the Vietnam war that culminated in 1968, so too were the new finance regulations largely a reaction to a domestic political trauma, in this case Watergate. Congress, under growing public pressure to counteract the weight of private wealth in elections, devised an elaborate set of regulations to control the way candidates raise, spend, and account for their campaign funds. In addition to instituting a system of federal matching funds for the nomination period, the new laws put a ceiling on individual and group donations and restricted candidates' spending, both in each state and in total.

As a result of these finance rules, candidates now pour more of their resources—money, time, and effort—into the early stages of their campaigns. Where once candidates could depend on large contributors to get their campaigns off the ground, bail them out when they were broke, and translate later electoral success quickly into financial reward, today they must start their fundraising well before the first balloting in order to amass the relatively small contributions allowed under current law in sufficient aggregate amounts to support an increasingly expensive campaign. Then, to solidify their financial base, they must perform well in the early primaries and caucuses in states like New Hampshire and Iowa. If they do poorly, they can no longer turn to a small group of generous backers for salvation.

The new finance regulations have made these early battlegrounds more attractive to lesser-known candidates. Because of the contribution limits and low spending ceilings in New Hampshire and Iowa, as well as the availability of federal matching funds, better-connected or more established candidates can no longer count on overwhelming the dark horses in these states.

The Democrats' post-1968 delegate selection rules, especially the substitution of proportional representation for winner-take-all procedures, encourage candidates to wage strong efforts in nearly every state. A candidate who anticipates winning 40 percent of a state's vote in a losing cause will be disinclined to make an effort there if the rules give the winner all the delegates and the loser none, but might be more inclined to compete if the delegates are to be divided in proportion to the percentage of the popular vote each candidate wins. However, spending and contribution limits require that the candidates pick and choose. They must decide to mount only partial efforts in certain states and bypass others altogether. But most candidates concentrate on the early states, such as New Hampshire. Indeed, in recent years, some have nearly exhausted their legal spending allowance halfway through the primaries.

These transformations in the party and financial ground rules have given the power to decide who wins the nomination into the hands of voters in primary elections, especially voters in early primary states. Among the chief beneficiaries of this shift—and a contributor to the shift as well—have been the news media in general and television in particular. To learn about the choices they must make at the polls, voters depend almost entirely on public sources of information. Consequently, most presidential contenders believe that the public media—particularly television—determine their fate at the polls. That belief shapes the way they allocate their campaign resources, plan their schedules, define their themes, and select their strategies.

In the post-1968 system of presidential nominations, then, the news media are of commanding importance. Contribution and spending restrictions may force campaigns to cut back on canvassing or rallies, but rarely does a campaign substantially reduce its investment in the mass exposure afforded by television and radio ads. And restrictions make the campaigns more eager than ever to take advantage of the publicity from "free" media (i.e., news coverage).

As the number and importance of primaries has grown since the adoption of party reforms, so has the public's reliance on the media. In fact, the news media probably exert more of an influence on the nomination process—where party preference cannot be used as a means of differentiating among contestants—than on the general election. The reason is that, compared with the straightforward two-person contest in November, the primary season is relatively baffling. Several primaries occur on the same day, state contests may have many candidates, candidates run in some states but not in others, different states have different rules and procedures, and so on. To make matters worse, the voters' political knowledge in the primaries is often scant, and the cue that helps them interpret political information in other situations—their partisan allegiance—is missing. Thus, far more than during the general election, the public needs the media to keep score, to define the standards of victory, and to interpret the results. Accordingly, voters are more susceptible during the primary season than in the fall both to the candidates' paid advertising and to the stories that the media choose to emphasize in their news coverage.

News coverage, like party rules and finance laws, increases the influence of the early states. Success in New Hampshire often spells the difference between basking in media attention and languishing in obscurity. As Morris Udall, who ran in the 1976 Democratic primaries, put it: "It's like a football game in which you say to the first team that makes a first down with ten yards, 'Hereafter, your team has a special rule. Your first downs are five yards. And if you make three of those you get a two-yard first down. And we're going to let your first touchdown count twenty-one points. Now the rest of you bastards play catch-up under the regular rules.' "[3] Furthermore, because primary contests are so confusing, the media allow themselves wide latitude in their treatment of the candidates—especially in the early states, where the field is often crowded and many of the competitors are unknown. For example, Lyndon Johnson in 1968 and Edmund Muskie four years later both won in New Hampshire; yet because they failed to win by the margin that some journalists deemed appropriate for an incumbent President and a front-runner from New England, the media declared them losers.

Thus, with the rise of primaries accompanied by the decline of state party leaders and the adoption of campaign finance laws, the news media have assumed new importance in nomination politics. This has been especially true in the case of New Hampshire, the first opportunity in each election season for Americans to assess presidential candidates' ability to attract the votes of an electorate in a contest where the outcome is directly determined by the voters.

Myth and Reality

The New Hampshire primary, which every President elected since 1952 has won, is by now an established ritual of American politics. And like most rituals, it requires the repetition of familiar incantations, chants, and tenets of faith, some of them grounded in fact and others more mythical.

Every four years we hear that the tiny state of New Hampshire garners a disproportionate share of candidate and media attention. Indeed, in recent presidential elections the New Hampshire primary has been far and away the most heavily covered delegate selection event. Between 15 and 20 percent of national television and newspaper coverage of the primaries and caucuses as a whole is devoted to the Granite State.[4] The claim that the spotlight is focused too brightly on New Hampshire rests on two familiar arguments. The first is that the state is too small to warrant all this hoopla; by almost any measure—overall population, or size of the primary electorate, or delegates at stake—New Hampshire's share of the nationwide total is minuscule. The second argument is that the state's voters are unrepresentative of the rest of the country. Of the two, the latter argument presents the bigger challenge to the primacy of New Hampshire.

To begin with, we know that no primary electorate anywhere is terribly representative of a state's overall population or even the partisans for whom the voters claim to speak.[5] The question is whether the New Hampshire Democratic and Republican primary voters are out of line or in step with their counterparts nationwide. By and large, the demographic profile of New Hampshire primary voters is fairly close to that of primary voters across the country. Polls have shown that in attitudes as well, New Hampshire primary voters are not far removed from the national rank and file of each party.

Yet, there are some noteworthy discrepancies. Take, for example, the Democrats. In terms of political ideology, liberals and conservatives are well represented in New Hampshire's Democratic primary electorate. Moderates, however, seem to be missing in New Hampshire.[6] Other Democratic primary voters underrepresented there include blacks and members of industrial unions. These three constituencies—moderates, blacks, and union members—share membership in a single wing of the national Democratic party. The party can be thought of as a coalition of four ideological factions or wings: a New Politics wing of middle-class liberals, a Regular wing of blue-collar liberals, a Conservative or Backlash wing of blue-collar conservatives, and a small Centrist wing of middle-class conservatives.[7] The Granite State has an ample supply of New Politics, Conservative, and Centrist Democrats—and these voters have rewarded such candidates as Eugene McCarthy, George McGovern, Jimmy Carter, and Gary Hart. However, New Hampshire has fewer black, union, and moderate constituents, who probably would have added to the vote totals of Regulars such as Lyndon Johnson, Edmund Muskie, Birch Bayh, and Walter Mondale.

The Regular wing is the home of the Democrats' traditional establishment. It is no accident, then, that the New Hampshire primary has been fertile ground for "outsider" candidates—mavericks, insurgents, relatively weak partisans. These outsiders thrive in a place where Regular Democrats are relatively few. It also helps that New Hampshire is small and manageable logistically. If we add the factors mentioned earlier—party rules that have elevated primaries over caucuses and conventions; campaign spending ceilings, contribution limits, and federal matching funds; and news media eager to interpret and clarify the early balloting—we can see why New Hampshire has become a significant launching pad for lesser-known candidates. Especially when the field is crowded, the New Hampshire primary has been able to turn them overnight into national contenders.

Another ritual incantation we hear every four years is that victory in the New Hampshire primary requires good old-fashioned "retail politics." The argument is that the contenders cannot simply campaign through the mass media, but must—and because of the state's small size, can—meet the voters face to face in their homes and social clubs, pass out campaign literature, and organize a grass-roots army of volunteers. The voters have come to expect this personal treatment, and reporters and analysts assume that only those candidates who engage in retail politics have a chance of winning.

It is true that a large number of New Hampshire residents have the chance to meet the candidates. Fully one-third report that they have met at least one of the candidates. Still the claim of retail politics may be overblown. Eugene McCarthy's and George McGovern's meteoric rises in New Hampshire in 1968 and 1972 probably owed far more to intense antiwar sentiment and events like the Tet offensive and Muskie's crying incident than to face-to-face campaigning. Jimmy Carter may have owed his 1976 victory in large measure to retail politics. But since 1976, stories in the local and national press and on television seem to have been more decisive than local campaigning. For example, campaign events reported in the press, such as the Republican debates in Nashua and the *Union Leader*'s relentless attacks on George Bush, were crucial in 1980; national issues like the Iran hostage crisis figured prominently in the Carter-Kennedy contest in 1980; and the results of the Iowa caucuses have carried important weight in the last three primary elections.

Like other states, New Hampshire has become a "media state." New Hampshire voters learn about the campaign in their state by watching television, listening to the radio, and reading newspapers and magazines. These same sources tell them how candidates have fared in earlier states. New Hampshire voters are not immune to prior media verdicts. Increasingly, the candidates' standings in New Hampshire depend on how the media interpret the candidates' performance in Iowa. Momentum or bandwagon effects, where a candidate portrayed in the media as viable and improving begins to attract more support, are now crucial to the New Hampshire primary. Indeed, one study found that expectations of the likely success of candidates—which are shaped largely by media exposure—have a dramatic effect on the preferences of voters only in early primary states, and the effect is strongest for little-known candidates, the type who find New Hampshire friendly terrain.[8]

Envoi: 1988

As we write this, nearly a year before the 1988 New Hampshire primary, the campaigning has begun in earnest and the pundits are hawking their wisdom — conventional and otherwise. According to that wisdom, New Hampshire's influence either will be more powerful than ever or less powerful.

The candidate fields for both parties, especially the Democrats, are crowded with relatively unfamiliar faces who are new to the national stage. Public attitudes are mostly unformed toward these little-known candidates. Therefore the media should have wider discretion in setting expectations, since the more uncertain and confusing the political landscape, the more the public will need and be susceptible to media interpretations. Also, since the candidates cannot afford the time or money to campaign actively in all of the 15 or 18 states that will hold primaries or caucuses on 8 March (Super Tuesday), they will have to depend more than ever on the spillover of free media coverage from the earlier contests in New Hampshire and Iowa. All of this, according to some observers, will fuel the media-momentum cycle.

But there is wisdom that suggests the opposite as well. On the Democratic side, at least, Massachusetts Governor Michael Dukakis's "favorite son" candidacy in neighboring New Hampshire may reduce the importance of that state in the eyes of the media and thereby limit its momentum effects.

If the recent history of presidential nomination politics has taught us anything, it is that winners and losers are hard to predict. The prophecies of yesteryear gave us President Edmund Muskie and President Edward Kennedy. Unpredictability and the confounding of expert forecasting is the very hallmark of the modern nomination process. That is because the process is dominated by the volatile short-term forces we discussed earlier — rules, money, and media — which magnify the unpredictable and invite surprise. Individual candidates have proven to be mere flotsam on a roiling sea of process.

Thus, we have chosen to contemplate the future by trying to understand the past better. And we have emphasized process here rather than the fate of individual candidates. Reporters gather every four years in New Hampshire to cover the first primary in the nation. During the intervening years, political scientists ponder what it all really means. Among the serious students of American political life, one can find a few close watchers of New Hampshire, and we are pleased to have collected between the covers of this book some of the fruits of their scholarly labor.

Notes

1. The impact of each of these—rules, money, and media—is probably greater during the nomination stage of presidential selection than during the general election. See Gary R. Orren, "The Nomination Process: Vicissitudes of Candidate Selection," in *The Elections of 1984,* ed. Michael Nelson (Washington, D.C.: Congressional Quarterly Press, 1985), 27-82.

2. For a fuller discussion of these changes in party rules and their consequences, see Nelson W. Polsby, *Consequences of Party Reform* (New York: Oxford University Press, 1983).

3. Quoted in Jules Witcover, *Marathon: The Pursuit of the Presidency 1972-1976* (New York: Viking Press, 1977), 692-93.

4. For data on 1980, see Michael J. Robinson and Margaret Sheehan, *Over the Wire and on TV: CBS and UPI in Campaign '80* (New York: Russell Sage Foundation, 1983), 174-78. Data on 1984 are reported in this book by Emmett Buell.

5. James I. Lengle, *Representation and Presidential Primaries: The Democratic Party in the Post-Reform Era* (Westport, Conn.: Greenwood, 1981).

6. David W. Moore, "New Hampshire: An Early Poll for the Earliest Primary," *Public Opinion,* April/May 1983, 51-52.

7. Gary R. Orren and William Schneider, "Democrats versus Democrats: Party Factions in the 1972 Presidential Primaries" (manuscript, January 1975).

8. Larry M. Bartels, "Expectations and Preferences in Presidential Nominating Campaigns," *American Political Science Review* 79 (September 1985): 804-15.

1

The New Hampshire Primary:
A Historical Overview

WILLIAM G. MAYER

It has become, over the years, almost a part of the natural order, the sort of cycle whose recurrence helps us measure the passing of time. The leaves fall, the snows melt, the swallows return to Capistrano. And every four years, the presidential candidates of the Democratic and Republican parties lay siege to the state of New Hampshire.

The locals first notice the change in season when they can no longer walk outdoors without bumping into the ready smile and outstretched hand of some would-be President. The story is often told of the woman who met George Bush (or Jimmy Carter or George McGovern, depending on which version you hear) on some anonymous New Hampshire street corner. As Bush moved on down the street, one of a pack of trailing reporters approached the woman and asked, "Are you going to vote for him?" She replied, "I don't know. I've only met him three times."

The 1980 census records that only 921,000 people live within New Hampshire's borders, making it the ninth smallest of our 50 states. The delegates it will send to the conventions — 22 to the Democratic, 23 to the Republican — represent less than 2 percent of the number a candidate needs to be nominated. Yet, by the time the nomination race is over, the presidential candidates will almost certainly have spent more time in New Hampshire than in Texas, Pennsylvania, Illinois, California, or New York. They come because the state is the site of the nation's first presidential primary, and a victory there has an importance out of all proportion to the number of delegates awarded to the winner. And the tag line, which one hears a hundred times in every election cycle, is that since 1952, no one has been elected President without first winning the New Hampshire primary.

Never a Dull Moment

Whatever else may be said of the New Hampshire primary, it has never been boring. As a small state, close to New York City and Washington, D.C., with a single statewide newspaper run by the heirs of a combative and controversial owner, and an electorate that reputedly wants to see the candidates in person, New Hampshire is the sort of state a novelist might create as the scene for a lurid best-seller. Make a list of the most exciting moments in the history of recent presidential nominating campaigns—the sudden breakthroughs, the dramatic confrontations, the moments of stark revelation—and we find that about half of them have taken place in New Hampshire.

Like many other American political institutions, however, New Hampshire's first-in-the-nation primary came about more by accident than by design. When the Granite State enacted its first presidential primary law back in 1913, the state legislature originally set the election date for the middle of May. In 1915, someone pointed out that the state could avoid the expense of an extra election if the primary was held at the same time as Town Meeting Day. Since Town Meeting Day had to be scheduled in early March, to avoid the spring thaw that made the unpaved country roads impassable, the primary was moved up two and a half months in the calendar. Thus, through a combination of mud and Yankee frugality, New Hampshire stumbled into an early election date. Since 1920, the Granite State has always been the scene of the nation's first presidential primary.

For the first 32 years, however, no one paid it too much attention because the primary was used only to choose delegates to the national conventions and offered no direct way for the voters to say what they thought about the candidates. But in 1949, the state legislature again changed the law, adding a presidential preference (or "beauty contest") line to the ballot.[1]

And then the fireworks began.

1952. Dwight D. Eisenhower was being indecisive. In the fall of 1951, he had finally agreed to start thinking seriously about a run for President—but as of early 1952, he was still thinking. While Robert Taft was actively rounding up delegates, Ike was still the NATO supreme commander, stationed over in Europe, apparently waiting to see if there really was a groundswell of support.

So a group of Republicans decided to give him a little push. In early January, they entered his name in the New Hampshire Republican primary. There was one small hitch: Eisenhower had never publicly declared that he was a Republican. Massachusetts Senator Henry Cabot Lodge, a leader of the Draft Eisenhower movement, took it upon himself to assure state officials that Ike's allegiances were with the GOP. Eisenhower was reportedly furious, but when confronted by reporters, he confirmed Lodge's statement.

On 11 March, Eisenhower rolled up an impressive 50-39 percent victory over Taft in New Hampshire. Along with strong showings in the Minnesota and Nebraska primaries, and a huge pro-Eisenhower rally in Madison Square Garden, the New Hampshire results helped convince Eisenhower to resign his NATO command and announce his candidacy.[2]

Meanwhile, on the Democratic side of the ballot, President Harry Truman was, to all outward appearances, gearing up for one more run at the Presidency. After dismissing the primaries as "eyewash" at a press conference in late January, Truman did an about-face and agreed to mount a late campaign in the New Hampshire primary. To no avail. On 11 March, he was decisively defeated by Senator Estes Kefauver of Tennessee. In his *Memoirs,* Truman insisted that he had decided not to run for reelection on the day of his inauguration in 1949, a decision he announced to his White House staff in March 1951. Perhaps — but there is also evidence that in early March of 1952, he was listening to the pleadings of friends and advisers who were urging him to run again. If so, the New Hampshire primary may have played some role in convincing him that the Democratic party needed new blood. On 29 March, he announced that he was withdrawing from the race.[3]

1956. With Eisenhower unopposed in the Republican presidential primary, the New Hampshire GOP still found a way to stir the political waters. Amid growing speculation that Ike would drop Richard Nixon from the ticket, 23,000 New Hampshirites wrote in Nixon's name for vice-president. At a press conference several days later, Eisenhower retreated from earlier statements and declared, "I would be happy to be on any political ticket in which I was a candidate with [Nixon]." As *Time* magazine summed up the political fallout: "As far as politicians were concerned, last week was the week that Dick Nixon, for all practical purposes, was nominated."[4]

1964. The two front-runners for the Republican presidential nomination were New York Governor Nelson Rockefeller and Arizona Senator Barry Goldwater. Both candidates had severe liabilities: for Rockefeller, his recent divorce and his liberal policies; for Goldwater, his blunt, shoot-from-the-hip speaking style, which was giving him a growing reputation as a trigger-happy extremist. It was in off-the-cuff remarks while campaigning in New Hampshire that Goldwater called for a voluntary social security system, a marine assault on Cuba, and repeal of the progressive income tax.[5]

In the final weeks of the campaign, four young Bostonians, off on what Theodore White later called "a madcap adventure," decided to organize a write-in campaign for Henry Cabot Lodge, by then the U.S. ambassador to South Vietnam. Remarkably, 33,000 voters wrote in Lodge's name, and he soundly defeated both Goldwater and Rockefeller.

1968. Crime, racial unrest, and the war in Vietnam had a lot of people upset, but few observers saw any chance of denying the Democratic nomination to Lyndon Johnson. His only announced opponent was a tall, soft-spoken poet and U.S. senator named Eugene McCarthy, who quickly showed himself to be a most quixotic and diffident campaigner. With various pollsters and commentators predicting that McCarthy would get 5 to 15 percent of the New Hampshire vote, on 12 March the Minnesota senator stunned the nation by nearly beating Johnson.

Twenty years later, McCarthy's showing appears a good deal less impressive than it was considered at the time. To begin with, although many contemporary accounts trumpeted McCarthy's "victory in New Hampshire,"[6] the fact of the matter was that Johnson had actually received a plurality of the votes: 27,520 (49.6 percent) to 23,269 (41.9 percent) for McCarthy. Johnson's showing looks even stronger when one realizes that while McCarthy's name was printed on the New Hampshire ballot, all of Johnson's votes were write-ins.

No matter. Through the magic of a "better than expected" showing, Eugene McCarthy had suddenly become a credible candidate, and LBJ was vulnerable. Four days later, Robert Kennedy entered the race, and on 31 March Johnson went on national television to announce that he was no longer a candidate for President.

1972. Senator Edmund Muskie of Maine was so far ahead in the polls, and had so many heavyweight endorsements, that most of the speculation on the Democratic side seemed to be about whether President Muskie would run for a second term or not. But George McGovern never quite got the word. Aided by a small army of student volunteers, he tirelessly stumped the state. Meanwhile, the *Manchester Union Leader,* the state's largest newspaper, had targeted Muskie for its unique combination of venom, vituperation, and smear. Twice it reprinted a *Newsweek* article with an unfavorable portrait of Muskie's wife; another front-page story accused Muskie of committing an ethnic slur against French-Canadian Americans, New Hampshire's largest ethnic group. Against the advice of his local campaign managers, Muskie decided to answer the smears at a press conference in front of the *Union Leader* building. There, in a heavy blizzard, exhausted from weeks of tough campaigning, Muskie three times lost his composure and cried.[7]

Despite all this, Muskie won the New Hampshire primary, but that wasn't quite the way the press reported it. His 46 percent showing was "weaker than expected" and that, plus his tear-filled press conference, sent out the first strong signals that Muskie was vincible and McGovern was a force to be reckoned with.

1980. After George Bush's upset victory in the Iowa caucuses five weeks earlier, Ronald Reagan, once the clear front-runner for the Republican nomination, was fighting for his political life. With the public opinion polls showing a dead heat, the two candidates agreed to a one-on-one debate in the city of Nashua. At the last moment, four other Republican candidates showed up, and Reagan tried to get them included in the program. Inexplicably, Bush refused. The moderator, intent on going ahead with the two-man debate, tried to cut off Reagan's microphone, and Reagan, in an inspired piece of political theater, told him off. The upshot was a massive surge of public support for Reagan, a crushing victory over Bush three days later, and Reagan was on his way to the presidency.[8]

The Logic of Momentum

The New Hampshire primary is more than a quadrennial moment of fun and high drama. As every student of presidential politics knows, New Hampshire's verdict has an enormous influence on whom the two major parties will select as their presidential candidates. It has become a cliché over the last 20 years to speak of a candidate having or seeking momentum. But cliché or not, momentum is a reality, and the New Hampshire primary is at the center of the process by which a candidate acquires it.

The most basic reason why New Hampshire is so important is because of its immense publicity value. The New Hampshire campaign is itself the focus of a large number of stories, and its results then play a major role in shaping newspaper and television coverage decisions during the rest of the primary season.

The American news media, it has often been observed, cover a presidential campaign in much the same way they cover a baseball game. The central question they ask, around which most of their coverage is organized, is: Who's winning (and correlatively, How are they doing it)?[9] Once the delegate selection process is actually under way, tracking the horse race is a relatively easy task. On Tuesday nights, you count up the votes; and for the rest of the week, you can report the latest polls and delegate tallies.

The problem comes in the period before any of the votes are cast. Trying to pick a presidential nominee before the delegates are selected is like trying to handicap a baseball team during spring training. There are, to be sure, some telltale signs: poll results, fund-raising records, crowd reactions, and so on. But a successful campaign, like a winning team, is somehow more than just the sum of these parts. The lore of sports and politics is filled with stories about teams that looked weak on paper but played far better than the "experts" predicted (like the 1967 Red Sox); or about campaigns that seemed like they could not lose, but never quite made the grade (witness Edmund Muskie in 1972).

And then, in the midst of all this uncertainty and confusion, comes the New Hampshire primary. Looked at from a detached perspective, it is unclear how much emphasis the New Hampshire results really ought to receive. It is doubtful whether the votes cast in one, arguably unrepresentative state are actually more revealing about the campaigns and the mood of the electorate than, say, national poll ratings. But no one in the media seems very interested in being detached or philosophical. Instead, they pounce on this one bare fact like starving dogs after red meat.

The result is that a win in the New Hampshire primary buys a candidate far more publicity than a win anywhere else. To cite one example, when Jimmy Carter won the New Hampshire primary on 24 February 1976, receiving only 23,000 votes, he got his picture on the covers of both *Time* and *Newsweek*. When Henry Jackson won the Massachusetts primary just one week later, with 164,000 votes, his smiling features adorned neither cover. More remarkably, Carter's victory in New Hampshire, coming at a time when he was the choice of just 4 percent of the nation's Democrats, led an astonishing number of reporters to designate him the "front-runner" in the nomination race. The following week, when Jackson came in first and Carter in fourth, the most they would concede was that the loss might "slow . . . the Carter momentum."[10]

Add up all the stories and the disproportion becomes staggering. In an often cited study of the 1976 campaign, Michael J. Robinson analyzed the content of delegate selection stories on the three nightly network newscasts and in three daily newspapers between 24 November 1975 and 27 February 1976. In the newspapers, fully 34 percent of these stories were about New Hampshire. The second-most-covered state was Florida, which received only 10 percent. On television, New Hampshire was even more dominant: 54 percent of the network stories about presidential primaries and caucuses concerned New Hampshire.[11]

Not only does a win in New Hampshire bring lots of publicity; the publicity is almost entirely positive. The victorious candidate is portrayed as popular, exciting, confident, in control: in short, a leader. His poll ratings are increasing; his organization is growing; his message is catching on; his crowds are large and enthusiastic. His opponents, by contrast, are dead, dying, or in disarray. As one study of Gary Hart's press treatment during this period concluded, "Hart's coverage was virtually free of any harsh criticism, unflattering issues, or cynical commentary."[12]

As it so happens, we can measure the direct effect of all this favorable publicity quite precisely. In every presidential nomination race since 1936, the Gallup poll has periodically asked national samples of Democratic and Republican party identifiers whom they would "like to see nominated as (their) party's can-

TABLE 1.1

EFFECT OF THE NEW HAMPSHIRE PRIMARY ON
NATIONAL VOTER PREFERENCES, 1976-84

1976 Democratic Nomination Race

2-5 January	Humphrey 29%, Wallace 20%, Carter 4%
19 January	Iowa caucuses
23-26 January	Humphrey 27%, Wallace 22%, Carter 4%
24 February	New Hampshire primary
27 February-1 March	Humphrey 27%, Wallace 19%, Carter 16%

1976 Republican Nomination Race

2-5 January	Ford 53%, Reagan 42%
19 January	Iowa caucuses
23-26 January	Ford 44%, Reagan 43%
30 January-2 February	Ford 55%, Reagan 35%
24 February	New Hampshire primary
27 February-1 March	Ford 51%, Reagan 41%

1980 Democratic Nomination Race

4-6 January	Carter 51%, Kennedy 37%
21 January	Iowa caucuses
25-28 January	Carter 63%, Kennedy 29%
1-4 February	Carter 61%, Kennedy 32%
26 February	New Hampshire primary
February-March	Carter 66%, Kennedy 27%

1980 Republican Nomination Race

4-6 January	Reagan 41%, Baker 14%, Bush 9%
21 January	Iowa caucuses
25-28 January	Reagan 32%, Bush 32%, Baker 8%
1-4 February	Reagan 47%, Bush 25%, Baker 8%
26 February	New Hampshire primary
February-March	Reagan 55%, Bush 25%, Baker 9%

1984 Democratic Nomination Race

13-16 January	Mondale 47%, Glenn 16%, Hart 3%
27-30 January	Mondale 47%, Glenn 15%, Hart 2%
10-13 February	Mondale 49%, Glenn 13%, Hart 3%
20 February	Iowa caucuses
28 February	New Hampshire primary
2-6 March	Mondale 33%, Hart 30%, Glenn 5%

SOURCE: Gallup polls.

didate for President this year." By comparing poll results from immediately before and after the New Hampshire primary, James Beniger determined that between 1936 and 1972, the winner of the New Hampshire primary increased his standing in the national polls by an average of 8 percent.[13]

The data in table 1.1 update Beniger's study for the nomination races from 1976 to 1984. Clearly, New Hampshire's influence shows no signs of diminishing. A New Hampshire victory pushed Jimmy Carter from 4 percent to 16 percent in 1976, and increased Ronald Reagan's lead over George Bush by 8 percent in 1980. Most dramatic of all are the results from the 1984 Democratic contest. A distant second-place finish in the Iowa caucuses plus a sizable win in New Hampshire turned Gary Hart from an also-ran into a contender. In less than a month's time, the percentage of Democrats who wanted Hart as the party nominee increased by 27 percent.

A closer inspection of some of the other races in table 1.1 suggests that New Hampshire's most powerful influence was its ability to elevate poorly known candidates into national contenders, especially in crowded, multicandidate races. By contrast, when a nomination fight was between two already well-known national politicians, a New Hampshire win appeared to be considerably less important. When Jimmy Carter and Ted Kennedy squared off in 1980, Carter's victory in the New Hampshire primary increased his already sizable lead by at most 5 percent. In the Ford-Reagan contest in 1976, Ford's showing in the national polls actually diminished somewhat in the first poll conducted after his Granite State triumph.

Significant as these results are, they only begin to describe the pivotal role of the New Hampshire primary in the presidential selection process. The Granite State's influence on the media lingers long after the national press corps has checked out of their Manchester hotel rooms. Faced with a limited number of stories, and a limited pool of reporters, all news organizations have a natural interest in focusing their coverage on "the serious candidates," those who have a real chance of being nominated. And how do they determine who the serious contenders are? The answer, especially since 1972, is that they look to New Hampshire.

Separate studies of candidate coverage in 1980 and 1984 suggest that the media, in effect, divide presidential candidates into three groups: the hopeless, the plausible, and the likely, with substantial differences between the three in the amount and quality of coverage. Once the nomination process begins, which category a candidate gets placed in depends very largely on his showings in two early delegate selection events: the New Hampshire primary and the Iowa caucuses. In 1980, for example, the New Hampshire and Iowa results pushed George Bush from hopeless to plausible, and demoted Howard Baker from plausible to hopeless. In January, Baker had received 2.2 times as much coverage as Bush; but in March, Bush received 2.4 times as much coverage as Baker.[14]

Are the media the real villains (or heroes) in the New Hampshire story, then? In part, yes. In certain instances—the 1976 Democratic primary is perhaps the best example—there seems little doubt that the media did blow the New Hampshire results way out of proportion. But whatever mistakes might have been committed in the past, the New Hampshire saga has now become a self-fulfilling prophecy. Because the media cover New Hampshire so much, all the candidates have to wage vigorous campaigns there; and the media, in turn, claim that the only reason they are in New Hampshire is because the candidates are there. Joseph Heller would be proud.

. . . and More Momentum

Diatribes against media coverage of New Hampshire, in any event, ignore an important reality. Since 1968, political reformers, particularly in the Democratic party, have enacted sweeping changes in the laws and party rules that govern the presidential selection process. Almost without exception, these changes have had the consequence, presumably unintended, of enhancing New Hampshire's power in the nomination sweepstakes.

The most celebrated of these changes was the wholesale rewriting of the Democratic party delegate selection rules conducted by the McGovern-Fraser Commission and slightly amended by subsequent party reform commissions.[15] The new rules have helped New Hampshire in at least two ways. In the first place, they have increased the number of delegates selected through primaries and caucuses that are open to virtually anyone who wants to participate. Before 1972, a large percentage of the delegates were chosen through methods that were largely under the control of party leaders and relatively insulated from widespread public participation. When Kefauver beat Truman in New Hampshire in 1952, he, too, had seen his national poll ratings increase—but in the end, it did not help him very much. Too many delegates were controlled by state party leaders who did not like or trust Kefauver; at the convention, they simply ignored the primaries and the Gallup polls, and handed the nomination to Adlai Stevenson. But after the McGovern-Fraser Commission had done its work, such maneuvers were no longer possible. Ex-officio delegates and closed selection processes were banned.[16] When McGovern and Carter won a string of primaries, there was no longer a powerful party leadership that could stand in the way of their nominations.

Another set of party rules that were substantially altered were those that determined how the preferences expressed in primaries and caucuses were translated into actual delegate votes. By banning "winner-take-all" primaries, abolishing the unit rule, and encouraging the use of proportional representation, the new rules made wins in later primaries less valuable, and thus made early momentum even more difficult to stop.[17]

The California primary, for example, stuck way at the end of the nomination calendar, had never had much influence on press coverage or public opinion polls.[18] But it had still been an extraordinarily important political event, largely because of the provision in California law that awarded all delegates to the candidate who won a plurality of votes in the state's presidential primary. This provision obviously made no difference to those New Hampshire losers who had long since dropped out of the race. But it might have given a significant boost to a late-starter like Jerry Brown in 1976, or to a candidate like Ted Kennedy in 1980 who was trying to rebound from a string of early losses. But by 1976, the winner-take-all provision no longer existed. Both Brown and Kennedy won the California primary, the former by a huge margin, only to see a sizable bloc of delegates accrue to Jimmy Carter.[19]

A final set of "reforms" that enhanced the position of the New Hampshire primary was the campaign finance laws of 1974. A candidate's ability to raise money has always been linked to his performance at the ballot box. Before 1974, however, a candidate who struggled in the early stages of the nomination race might still hang on financially if he could convince a few wealthy supporters to give or lend him the necessary funds. In 1972, for example, large contributions and loans played a key role in sustaining the long-shot candidacy of George McGovern, who did not win a primary until 4 April. After McGovern started winning, it was large contributions from a very small number of supporters that allowed Hubert Humphrey to wage a serious campaign all the way to the end of the primary season.[20]

But the 1974 laws ushered in a very different era. With any one individual now prohibited from contributing more than $1000, a candidate's financial health depended on mass marketing his candidacy to a large number of contributors. Every candidate, of course, had a small core of relatives, friends, and die-hard supporters who would contribute the maximum amount. But after this source had been exhausted—and that usually occurred long before New Hampshire—the remaining money was all pragmatic money: pragmatic, at least, in the sense that it was only going to be contributed to a candidate whose campaign was doing well.[21]

A close examination of any number of recent campaigns shows that financial troubles force candidates to withdraw a lot earlier than they otherwise would, before they have a chance to test their appeal in more than one or two unrepresentative states. In 1984, for example, Ernest Hollings and Reubin Askew

both counted on a southern base to give them a big boost to the nomination —
yet both candidates withdrew before a single southern delegate had been selected. Under a different set of financial arrangements, it is hard to believe that
at least one of these men would not have stuck around for Super Tuesday. James
T. Bacchus, Askew's press secretary and issues coordinator, confirmed precisely this point in a retrospective comment on the campaign:

> We believed that we could go on and head south and win the Florida primary
> despite [Askew's poor showings in Iowa and New Hampshire], in part because
> of the loophole primary. But it would have cost us half a million dollars to do
> so. We could have borrowed that money, but that would have begun running up
> a deficit. Some of the other candidates are still in debt and very much so. Governor
> Askew has a debt now of $61,000. His decision was based on avoiding a deficit.[22]

Thus, a poor showing in New Hampshire deals a candidate a double blow.
Finding himself largely excluded from newspaper and television coverage, he
naturally wants to overcome this disadvantage by mounting an extensive field
organization or a large media blitz. But now he can no longer raise the money
that these other forms of communication require.

As a result of changes such as these, the modern New Hampshire primary
appears to have gone through two distinct stages. From 1952 to 1972, New
Hampshire was regarded as a useful but not essential step on the road to the
White House. Seven of the 12 major-party nominees during this period won
the New Hampshire contest; but in only 3 of the 12 races (Eisenhower, McCarthy, Muskie) could one say that the New Hampshire results played a major
role in shaping the final outcome. More striking is how many serious candidates
decided to bypass the New Hampshire primary (Humphrey in 1960, Humphrey
and Wallace in 1972, Wallace and Jackson in 1976) or announced their candidacies after it had taken place (Kennedy in 1968, Brown and Church in 1976)
or did not enter any primaries at all (Stevenson in 1952, Johnson in 1960, Humphrey in 1968).

But 1976 was a turning point. That was the last year in which one can
say that a variety of different strategies were used in pursuit of the nomination. Henry Jackson bypassed the early primaries and tried to show strength
in the big industrial states. Frank Church and Jerry Brown entered late. George
Wallace seems to have believed that he had a hard-core following that would
rally behind him regardless of when or how he campaigned. About half the
Democratic contenders, however, developed an early-state strategy: organize
heavily and campaign personally in New Hampshire, and rely on a victory
there to provide momentum through the rest of the primaries. Jimmy Carter,
of course, was the best known of the early-state organizers, but he was far from

being the only candidate to make regular pilgrimages to the Granite State in the year before its primary. Morris Udall, Birch Bayh, and Fred Harris had much the same idea. Carter simply executed it better than his rivals.[23]

Carter's victory in New Hampshire, as we all know now, was the sine qua non of his march to the White House. By 1980, almost every other candidate was doing exactly the same thing.[24] The results in both 1980 and 1984, in any event, only reinforced the lessons of 1976: Come in first or second in New Hampshire, or by late March you'll be out of the race entirely. As Elaine Kamarck, an adviser to Walter Mondale in 1984 and Bruce Babbitt in 1988, commented: "The difference between now and the past is that now there is only one strategy. It doesn't matter whether you are a Walter Mondale with deep ties to the party or whether you are a newcomer—you both do the same things."[25]

Enter Iowa

Just when analysts thought New Hampshire had established a position of unrivaled influence in the presidential sweepstakes, they were blindsided. New Hampshire is still the first presidential primary—but since 1972, it has not been the first public delegate selection activity. That distinction now belongs to the Iowa precinct caucuses, and today no assessment of the New Hampshire primary is complete without considering the impact of its midwestern rival.

Iowa had been using a caucus system to select its delegates to the national conventions ever since 1920, with the first stage usually beginning in late March or early April. After the announcement of the McGovern-Fraser guidelines, however, the state Democratic party was forced to restructure the process substantially. In the end, the state committee approved a plan that added an extra level of caucusing, allowed for proportional representation of candidate preferences, made the whole process more open and participatory—and set the date of the first-round, precinct caucuses for 25 January.[26]

Why did the Iowa Democrats decide to start selecting their delegates so early in 1972? The principal factor, according to then state chairman Clif Larson, was the need to allow for five or six weeks between each stage of caucusing so that participants could be notified well in advance of the times, places, and pending issues. Counting back from the state convention, which had traditionally been held in mid-May, that put the precinct caucuses in mid-January. There was some appreciation that the Iowa caucuses were now early in the nomination calendar and that this might bring them more media coverage. But no one in the Iowa Democratic party seems to have had any intimation of the media monster they were creating.[27]

Nor did anyone in New Hampshire. By 1972, as we shall see, New Hampshire was just beginning to fend off the first intruders who were trying to challenge its status as the first primary in the nation. Had the Granite State appreciated what Iowa was doing, perhaps they would have tried to schedule their primary even earlier in the year. But in 1972, few people in New Hampshire (and for that matter, few in the media or among the candidates) understood what postreform caucuses were or how they operated. Where the old caucuses had been small, closed, poorly publicized affairs, the new Democratic rules required that caucuses be well publicized and open to any Democrat who wanted to participate. In a high-visibility situation like Iowa, such caucuses would soon evolve into, in Howard Baker's words, "the functional equivalent of a primary."[28] The result is that New Hampshire and Iowa now compete for preeminence in the nomination race.

In 1972, New Hampshire was the clear winner in the battle for influence, candidate time, and press attention. Iowa did not even have the first delegate selection event that year: The Mississippi caucuses were held two days earlier. But in 1972, the Mississippi Democratic party was still holding separate caucuses for blacks and whites, and so was written off as unrepresentative of the national party.[29] It was the Iowa caucuses that the media marked off as, in the words of the *New York Times*, "the first direct confrontation between presidential candidates in 1972." That appellation notwithstanding, the Iowa caucuses were largely ignored in 1972. The *Times*, for example, did a total of three stories on them; not one was on the front page.[30] Only at the very end of the year, when the campaign histories were being written, did reporters notice that Iowa had, in fact, been an early demonstration of exactly the same "lessons" later drawn from New Hampshire: that Muskie's support was soft and that George McGovern had both a good organization and a loyal following of anti-war activists.

New Hampshire won again in 1976, but this time the battle was somewhat closer. Having misreported the Muskie bandwagon, the national press corps was now determined not to overlook a single early indicator of candidate strength. Iowa, as it turned out, provided two of these: a straw poll taken at a Jefferson-Jackson Day Dinner in late October 1975, and then the actual caucuses on 19 January. Carter "won" both of them (in the caucuses, he actually came in second to an uncommitted slate), and as a result, the national media finally began to take him seriously.[31]

But in 1976, Iowa was still largely an elite-level affair. The media, financial contributors, and political junkies all took notice, but there is no evidence that the mass public did. When Michael Robinson counted up the newspaper and television coverage of state delegate selection activities from 24 November 1975 to 27 February 1976, he found that Iowa had received only 6.6 percent of the newspaper stories and 5.9 percent of the television reports, as compared to 34.3 percent and 53.5 percent, respectively, for New Hampshire.[32] As a result, Carter's early "victory" in Iowa seems to have made little dent in public opinion. A Gallup poll conducted immediately after Iowa showed Carter still the nomination choice of only 4 percent of national Democrats, exactly where he had been in early January. Carter's real breakthrough in public support would come only after his victory in New Hampshire.

By 1980, however, Iowa had clearly arrived. The same sort of crazy logic that had once sent the candidates flocking to New Hampshire now compelled them to mount a major campaign in Iowa. One could even hear New Hampshire residents complaining to reporters about how a single state with such a low turnout was getting more attention than it deserved.

Which state was more influential in the 1980 and 1984 nomination contests? In the race for press attention, the two states finished in a virtual dead heat. In Michael Robinson and Margaret Sheehan's study of media in the 1980 campaign, Iowa received slightly more coverage on CBS television (2940 news seconds vs. 2815 for New Hampshire), and slightly less from United Press International (679 column inches vs. 774 for New Hampshire). In both media sources, Iowa and New Hampshire each got at least 40 percent more coverage than any other state.[33]

Which state had more impact on public opinion, and on that elusive quest for momentum, is more difficult to answer. In 1980, it was a win in Iowa that allowed George Bush to break out from the rest of the Republican pack and start whittling away at Ronald Reagan's massive popularity among the party faithful. Whatever momentum Reagan lost in Iowa, however, he regained by his triumph in New Hampshire. Bush stayed in the race until the final week of primaries, but his only real chance to deny Reagan the nomination came to an end in New Hampshire.

Gary Hart's rise to national prominence in 1984 came about in two steps. By any reasonable standard, his showing in the Iowa caucuses must be rated as unspectacular. He was the choice of only 15 percent of the caucus participants, fully 30 percent behind Mondale and only 2 percent ahead of George McGovern's symbolic candidacy. But while it did not win him many delegates, Hart's finish in Iowa had a dramatic effect on his press coverage. By convincing the news media that he, and not John Glenn, was the principal alternative to Mondale, Hart actually received more coverage than Mondale did in the week after Iowa.[34] This, plus a good local campaign, allowed him to achieve a substantial victory in New Hampshire. In retrospect, it seems clear that *both* Iowa and New Hampshire were essential to derailing the Mondale juggernaut. Hart would never have won the Granite State primary without the substantial fall-out from his second-place finish in Iowa.[35] But Hart's distant second in Iowa probably would not have meant as much if it had not been immediately followed up by a substantial, high-visibility victory in New Hampshire.

It is dangerous to generalize on the basis of only two cases, but if the 1980 Republican and 1984 Democratic races are any indication, it appears that Iowa and New Hampshire now serve distinct functions in the nomination race. The "winnowing" function—the process by which a large, multicandidate field is narrowed to two (or at most, three) top contenders—is now performed almost entirely by the Iowa caucuses. New Hampshire propaganda still likes to portray itself as the Great Winnower, but in fact, there is no evidence that it has actually played this role in any election since 1976. By the time Iowa was over, the 1980 Republican race was effectively a contest between Bush and Reagan; and in 1984, Gary Hart had emerged as the principal alternative to Walter Mondale.

The New Hampshire primary, in contrast, has become the first major test of strength between the two candidates who will, in all probability, fight it out through the rest of the primary and caucus season. Clearly, this represents an important reduction in New Hampshire's influence. Where New Hampshire was once the key event that gave a candidate momentum, increasingly analysts may find, as they did in 1984, that the New Hampshire results are determined in large part by the momentum that candidates have already acquired in Iowa. This sort of scenario becomes even more likely now that the time between Iowa and New Hampshire, once five weeks, has been cut to eight days.

But the weight of tradition—plus an extraordinary amount of press coverage—guarantees that New Hampshire will be more than just one in a long series of head-to-head encounters. There is little doubt that both Reagan and Hart got a lot more mileage by winning New Hampshire than they would have from a triumph in Massachusetts or Vermont. Although less important than it used to be, New Hampshire still has a formidable capacity to reshape the political landscape.

However one decides to rank-order these two events, it is clear that, together, the Iowa caucuses and the New Hampshire primary play an extraordinarily powerful role in selecting American presidential candidates, a role that appears to grow ever greater with each passing election. Perhaps the best way to appreciate this fact is to look at when candidates who lose in Iowa and New Hampshire have withdrawn from recent presidential elections.[36] As table 1.2 shows, in 1972, candidates who did poorly in New Hampshire and other early primaries, even those who were widely regarded as long shots, could stay in the race for a month or two longer, to test their appeal in other states and regions. Since 1976, however, the life span of a New Hampshire loser has grown

TABLE I.2

SELECTED WITHDRAWAL DATES IN

MULTICANDIDATE PRESIDENTIAL RACES,

1972-84

1972 Democratic Nomination Race

7 March	New Hampshire primary
4 April	John Lindsay withdraws
27 April	Edmund Muskie withdraws
2 May	Henry Jackson withdraws
22 May	Eugene McCarthy withdraws

1976 Democratic Nomination Race

24 February	New Hampshire primary
4 March	Birch Bayh withdreaws
12 March	Milton Shapp withdraws
22 March	Sargent Shriver withdraws
8 April	Fred Harris withdraws
1 May	Henry Jackson withdraws

1980 Republican and Democratic Nomination Races

26 February	New Hampshire primary
5 March	Howard Baker withdraws
9 March	John Connally withdraws
15 March	Robert Dole withdraws
1 April	Jerry Brown withdraws
17 April	Phil Crane withdraws
22 April	John Anderson announces intention to run as an independent

1984 Democratic Nomination Race

28 February	New Hampshire primary
29 February	Alan Cranston withdraws
1 March	Ernest Hollings and Reubin Askew withdraw
14 March	George McGovern withdraws
16 March	John Glenn withdraws

SOURCE: Compiled from stories in the *New York Times*.

progressively shorter. For the majority of recent candidates, New Hampshire and Iowa were no longer just the first inning; they were the entire ballgame.

Contemporary presidential campaigns, it appears, can accommodate only two competitive candidates. One gets designated the front-runner; the other provides a rallying point for his opponents and gives the media some kind of continuing story to report. In 1984, everybody else had withdrawn from the race by two and a half weeks after New Hampshire. (The only exception was Jesse Jackson, who defied most of the rules of conventional politics.)

Should New Hampshire Be First?

To paraphrase an old political axiom, in America power revealed is power attacked. Not surprisingly, New Hampshire had not been throwing its weight around for very long before a lot of other states began to get jealous. After all, if there is a small battalion of presidential candidates tripping over one another to get to the voters, and an even larger army of drooling press people waiting to report it all, it is hard to keep a thing like that secret.

Initially, most of the New Hampshire criticism was not about the *amount* of publicity the primary received but about the peculiar way in which its results were often interpreted. In 1968 and 1972, Lyndon Johnson and Edmund Muskie had been seriously wounded by the New Hampshire results, in spite of the fact that both men had received more votes than any of their opponents. They had not actually *lost* the primary, but they had done "worse than expected." Muskie, in particular, often complained that he was judged, not in relation to his actual opponents, but according to some kind of ideal, mythical, "front-runner" standard that no candidate could meet in the highly fragmented political environment of 1972.

The American media are often accused of ignoring their own shortcomings, but in this case, they really do seem to have taken the criticism to heart. Prior to the 1976 New Hampshire primary, a number of candidates devoted considerable effort to manipulating media expectations, to defining the standard against which they wanted the media to judge them. Ronald Reagan, for example, continually said that since he was running against an incumbent President, he would regard it as a victory if he could get at least 40 percent of the vote in New Hampshire. To no avail: In 1976 and subsequent New Hampshire primaries, a win was a win. When Gerald Ford beat Reagan by an exceedingly narrow margin—50.1 percent to 48.6 percent— the result was nevertheless interpreted as a victory for Ford. (Old habits die hard, however; recall that in 1984, Hart received more press coverage than Mondale after running 30 percent behind him in Iowa.)

As the "worse than expected" problem has grown less salient, however, the controversy surrounding New Hampshire has simply shifted ground. New Hampshire's pivotal role in determining who gets to sit in the White House necessarily raises two closely related sets of questions. First, what difference, if any, does it make that New Hampshire is the site of the nation's first primary? What would the selection system be like if a different state, or some combination of states, were given the opportunity to lead off the process? Second, *should* New Hampshire be first? Is the country better or worse off for having New Hampshire at the head of the primary calendar?

These questions, in turn, have led journalists, politicos, and academics to focus on three distinctive features of the New Hampshire political environment. If New Hampshire has put a special stamp on recent presidential candidates, that imprint probably arises from (1) the extent to which the New Hampshire population is or is not representative of the national electorate; (2) the quality and fairness of the New Hampshire media, particularly the *Manchester Union Leader*; or (3) New Hampshire's size.

The question of New Hampshire's representativeness is often raised—and very rarely answered in the proper way. Taken as a whole, New Hampshire is clearly not representative, being considerably more conservative and more Republican than the United States as a whole—but this is not the relevant comparison. New Hampshire's policy outputs and general election results are determined largely by the relative sizes of its Democratic and Republican parties. The key question in a primary, by contrast, is whether the state Democratic (or Republican) party, whatever its size, is representative of the national Democratic (or Republican) party.

The sort of data necessary to answer this latter question is arrayed in table 1.3.[37] For Republicans, the survey evidence suggests that the New Hampshire electorate is reasonably representative of national party identifiers. A few differences emerge: New Hampshire Republican registered voters are better educated, more Catholic, and more middle income than their counterparts in the rest of the country; and they are less likely to live in a large city. But most of these differences are fairly small; equally important, it would be difficult to argue that any of these groups constitutes a distinct "faction" within the Republican party, with its own separate policy agenda and voting history. Although it has its share of internal disputes, the Republican party remains a fairly homogeneous group[38]—white, middle class, Protestant, rural and suburban—both in New Hampshire and in the country as a whole.

For Democrats, however, there are some sizable and important discrepancies between the New Hampshire party and the national party. The most obvious difference is in racial composition. Nationally, 19 percent of all registered

TABLE I.3

COMPARISON OF REGISTERED VOTERS
IN NEW HAMPSHIRE AND NATIONALLY
(IN PERCENT)

	Republicans		
	New Hampshire Registered Voters	National Registered Voters	National Adult Population
Education			
Less than high school	7	14	18
High school graduate	34	32	32
Some college	22	29	28
College graduate	36	24	21
Age			
18-29	20	20	21
30-44	29	33	34
45-64	30	26	24
65 and over	20	21	22
Race			
White	99	97	96
Black	0	1	2
Religion			
Protestant	60	73	74
Catholic	33	21	20
Jewish	3	1	1
Income			
Under $10,000	8	12	14
$10,000-25,000	27	34	37
$25,000-40,000	36	26	24
Over $40,000	28	27	25
Location			
City with 100,000 population	0	15	17
N	(156)	(462)	(606)

TABLE 1.3 *(continued)*

	Democrats		
	New Hampshire Registered Voters	National Registered Voters	National Adult Population
Education			
Less than high school	15	24	27
High school graduate	25	34	35
Some college	20	25	23
College graduate	39	17	14
Age			
18-29	10	20	21
30-44	37	31	28
45-64	30	31	30
65 and over	21	18	20
Race			
White	98	78	78
Black	2	19	19
Religion			
Protestant	33	59	60
Catholic	56	31	30
Jewish	3	4	4
Income			
Under $10,000	12	25	28
$10,000-25,000	29	32	34
$25,000-40,000	32	27	24
Over $40,000	28	16	14
Location			
City with 100,000 population	0	28	28
N	(107)	(603)	(828)

NOTE: In all three columns of this table, Democrats and Republicans were determined by answers to the standard party identification question.

SOURCE: New Hampshire data taken from September 1986 poll by Market Opinion Research. Used with permission. National data taken from American National Election Study, 1984.

voters who think of themselves as Democrats are black; in New Hampshire, only 2 percent of Democratic registered voters are black. The New Hampshire electorate is also significantly better educated, wealthier, more Catholic, and less urban than the national Democratic party is. And in the highly factional-ized Democratic party, many of these groups have distinctive and passionately held ideas about what direction the party should go, and what kinds of candi-dates it should nominate.

In one of the best analyses of ideological factions within the Democratic party, Gary Orren and William Schneider, using data from the 1972 presiden-tial primaries, argued that the Democrats were divided into three major wings. The New Politics or Liberal wing supported George McGovern in 1972 and consisted primarily of white-collar liberals, the college educated, and younger voters. The Regular wing, which had backed Hubert Humphrey and Ed Mus-kie, included blacks, union members, and blue-collar workers who were liberal on economic issues. The Conservative or Backlash wing, which voted for George Wallace, drew on blue-collar conservatives.[39]

If this analysis still holds, and I think it does, then it should be clear that New Hampshire's demographics have important implications for the kinds of candidates who do well in Granite State primaries. Simply put, there is a hole in the center of the New Hampshire Democratic electorate. It has New Politics and Conservative voters aplenty, but is conspicuously short of Regulars. The result is clearly reflected in the history of the New Hampshire primary. Of the candidates who have been seriously hurt in a New Hampshire primary—John-son in 1968, Muskie in 1972, Mondale in 1984—all can plausibly be described as coming from the Regular wing of the party. All had strong ties to labor and black leadership, and sought to portray themselves as representing the party's traditional establishment. In contrast, the candidates who have been helped by a strong New Hampshire showing—McCarthy in 1968, McGovern in 1972, Carter in 1976, and Hart in 1984—have all been insurgents and were ideologi-cally aligned with one of the non-Regular wings of the party.

Mondale's campaign organization certainly appreciated this problem. As his pollster commented in a campaign retrospective, "We always found New Hampshire to be the most unfriendly state to the Mondale candidacy. Com-pared to Alabama, Georgia, Florida, and every place else we were polling, Mon-dale did a lot less well."[40]

Another important criterion that an early primary state ought to meet is that it have a good media system, to keep the voters informed and the candidates honest. Those who think and write about such issues would undoubtedly dis-agree about just what a "good media system" might look like. But on one point there would be wide agreement: It would look nothing like New Hampshire.

The New Hampshire news system is dominated by the presence of the *Manchester Union Leader*, a newspaper that has virtually become a synonym for some of the most questionable practices in all of American journalism. For many years, the driving force behind the *Union Leader* was its owner and publisher, William Loeb. A man of strong conservative convictions, Loeb used his newspaper to espouse his views in a forceful, blatant way, both through his signed, front-page editorials and in the selection and content of news reports. But to call the *Union Leader* "conservative" really misses the point. The *Union Leader* practices a kind of journalism and descends to a level of intemperance and incivility that go far beyond the bounds of ideology and that no self-respecting conservative journalist could possibly approve of.

Consider, for example, how the *Union Leader* has described the following major American public figures:

☐ Dwight Eisenhower: "Dopey Dwight"; "that stinking hypocrite"; "Playboy president"; "fatuous—fat-headed"

☐ Henry Kissinger: "Kissinger the Kike?"; "Tool of the Communist conspiracy"

☐ Robert F. Kennedy: "the most vicious, vindictive, egotistical man on the face of the earth"

☐ Reverend Martin Luther King, Jr.: "really asked for what happened to him".[41]

Or consider the *Union Leader's* coverage of the 1972 Democratic presidential primary. First, there was the matter of coverage. In the last five weeks of the campaign, Loeb saw fit to allocate 420 column inches to Muskie, 262 inches to McGovern—and somehow allotted 870 inches to Sam Yorty, the erratic Los Angeles mayor whom Loeb was supporting and whose candidacy nobody but Loeb took seriously. Yorty's coverage, of course, was almost entirely favorable: lengthy accounts of routine speeches; pictures of him with nuns and cardinals; reprints of articles that had originally appeared in Yorty's own campaign newspaper.[42]

Coverage of Muskie, by contrast, was savage. Year-old columns critical of Muskie were reprinted. Misleading headlines sought to link Muskie with communists or accused him of taking New Hampshire for granted or implied that a scientific examination had found the senator vague and confused. It is no accident that when Nixon's dirty tricks' squad decided to sabotage Muskie's campaign, they did it by sending a forged letter to the *Union Leader*, accusing Muskie of insulting French-Canadians. It is difficult to believe that any other paper in America would have printed the letter on the front page without being able to verify its authenticity.[43]

Loeb died in 1981, but the *Union Leader* has not changed much since then. It is still run by the people who were Loeb's top deputies in his last years (Loeb's widow, Nackey, has assumed the publisher's duties), and they clearly learned their trade from the master. The consensus of New Hampshire politicos and academic observers is that the new leadership lacks a little of Loeb's instinct for the jugular but that the basic tone of the paper has remained the same.[44]

Yet, somehow, this newspaper thrives. The altogether remarkable fact is that the *Union Leader* is the largest paper in New Hampshire and dominates the state's media to an extraordinary degree. Its 60,000 circulation is three times that of any other paper in New Hampshire; surveys show that about 40-45 percent of all Granite State voters read it regularly. Moreover, because it has such a lion's share of the New Hampshire market, the *Union Leader* also has a major influence over the wire-service copy that is fed to the state's other newspapers.[45]

It is difficult to avoid the conclusion of Neal Peirce, probably the country's leading journalistic chronicler of state politics and government: "If there is any American state in which the public dialogue is more distorted or polluted, this writer—having interviewed extensively in all 50 states in the past few years—is unaware of it."[46]

There is no simple way to summarize the effect that the *Union Leader* has on a New Hampshire election. According to Jules Witcover, "a political folklore" has developed which claims that a Loeb endorsement can make a difference of about 15 percent in most elections[47]—but undoubtedly the effect of the *Union Leader* varies a lot from election to election. One can point to Loeb-endorsed candidates (like Sam Yorty in 1972) who fared very poorly at the ballot boxes, as well as to candidates (like former Governor Meldrim Thompson) whom Loeb plucked out of obscurity and after years of support got them elected to major state offices.

The worst aspect of the *Union Leader's* influence, however, is the way that it makes an informed, effective discussion of the issues nearly impossible in many New Hampshire elections. As an aide to former Governor Walter Peterson put it, "A campaigner spends all his time putting out brush fires started by Loeb and never has time to speak to the issues." Said another public figure who had been pilloried in Loeb's paper and had tried to respond, "I discovered that there is just no vehicle for another view. Everything is so fragmented that it is always a fight on [Loeb's] terms and in his field."[48]

A third distinctive feature of the New Hampshire political environment often claimed to affect the presidential selection process is the size of its population. New Hampshire is not *the* smallest state to hold a presidential primary, but the number of votes cast in a typical New Hampshire contest is considerably smaller than in most other primaries. The 1984 results are typical in this respect. When New Hampshire held its Democratic presidential primary on 28 February, 101,000 votes were cast. By comparison, 1,659,000 votes were cast in the Illinois Democratic primary, 960,000 in North Carolina, 322,000 in Tennessee, and 2,970,000 in the five states that held primaries on Super Tuesday. The point is made even more dramatically when posed in terms of the number of votes needed to win in New Hampshire. When Jimmy Carter achieved his great breakthrough in the 1976 New Hampshire primary, he did so on the basis of receiving slightly more than 23,000 votes. Gary Hart received 37,000 ballots in 1984; and George McGovern slowed Ed Muskie's bandwagon by getting 33,000 New Hampshirites to put their mark next to his name.

New Hampshire's size, it is asserted, has several effects on the presidential selection process. Most significantly, it makes it possible for candidates without national reputations and large war chests to enter the presidential sweepstakes with better prospects of succeeding. Instead of having to sell themselves to millions of voters across the country, New Hampshire allows long-shot candidates an opportunity to win an early contest in a smaller, less expensive arena — one where face-to-face communication and grass-roots organization are supposedly more important — and then parlay that into a national campaign.

To be sure, the New Hampshire primary is far from the only factor working in this direction. The delegate selection reforms, the campaign finance laws, the behavior of the media, the growth of television, and the decline in partisan allegiances have also served to undermine traditional party leadership and spurred on the fortunes of insurgent and outsider candidates. But New Hampshire probably still has some independent effect. If one doubts this, think of how different the process would be if it began with the California primary, or with the five primaries and four caucuses that took place on Super Tuesday in 1984. Gary Hart might still have emerged as the principal opponent of Walter Mondale, but it is difficult to believe that Jimmy Carter in 1976 would have fared half so well.

Over the last 15 years, New Hampshire's size has become the principal selling point of those who defend its influential position in the nomination calendar. As Charles Brereton phrases the argument in his history of the New Hampshire primary:

> The end of New Hampshire's first-in-the-nation distinction would not ensure an increased "democratization" of the election process. . . . If New Hampshire's role were greatly diminished, the potential for many candidates — the long shots, the poorly financed and those not blessed by the national press corps as "serious contenders" — to break through the barrier of obscurity and begin to gain national reputations would be greatly reduced.[49]

The first thing that should be said about this argument is that it may be 12 years out of date. From 1952 to 1976, face-to-face campaigning and grass-roots organizing may have played a key role in the New Hampshire primary. But in elections since then, the locus of retail politics has increasingly shifted to Iowa. Gary Hart had, by all accounts, an excellent organization in New Hampshire in 1984; but as David Moore has shown, the increase in Hart's support in the eight days between Iowa and New Hampshire, and the decline in John Glenn's vote, occurred far too rapidly to be explained by organization or face-to-face campaigning.[50] The 1984 New Hampshire results were determined largely by a media event (Hart's showing in Iowa), as for that matter were Reagan's triumph in 1980 (the Nashua debate) and Carter's victory that same year (the crisis in Iran).

But whether it applies to New Hampshire or Iowa, this argument stands up very poorly to closer scrutiny. For it all rests on a very dubious premise: that we would *want* to give an unknown, inexperienced person a good chance of becoming President. The American Presidency is commonly called the toughest job in the world. Yet New Hampshire defenders argue that some great national interest is served by conferring the position on a person whom we knew nothing about a year before the election, and whose capacity for national leadership and decision making is usually untested. Surely, the entire experience of Jimmy Carter's Presidency speaks to the contrary. The presidential nomination system works best when it is an occasion for the two parties to select candidates from among their recognized leaders. It is definitely not a time to be worried about the fates of obscure and untried hopefuls.

The Prospects for Reform

Many commentators over the years have argued in favor of reducing New Hampshire's role in the presidential selection process. Their reform proposals range from a national primary to a series of regional primaries, to simply finding some other state in which to hold the first primary (presumably one that is larger and a little more diverse and does not have the *Union Leader*). Somewhere in between the extremes is my own preference, which would be to start off the nomination calendar with primaries or caucuses in four or five different states on the same day, from different regions and with different problems and constituencies. Candidates would then have the option of contesting all four primaries, or if their time and finances were limited, just one or two. Thus, unknown and underfinanced candidates would still have some chance to organize a single state intensively; but a victory there would only make them contenders, not front-runners. Having four separate contests on the same day might also reduce somewhat the ability of the media to declare a clear early winner.

When it comes to the New Hampshire primary, however, the most intractable question is not, What do we put in its place? but rather, How can we create and enforce some new alternative?

One point is clear: New Hampshire will not surrender its privileged position without a fight. Although the Granite State stumbled into its first-in-the-nation status largely by accident, it did not take long before residents recognized that this position had real advantages. Every Rotary and Kiwanis Club in New Hampshire discovered that it could hold a Candidates' Night—and actually get three U.S. senators and a former Cabinet officer to attend. And, of course, all those candidates—and the campaign aides and press people who followed them around—spent lots of money.

So, after a while, New Hampshirites began to speak of their holding the first primary as if it were the very Pillar of American Democracy. And just in case anyone did not get the message, when Massachusetts and Vermont tried in 1975 to schedule their primaries on the same day as New Hampshire's, the New Hampshire legislature not only moved its primary up a week; it also wrote into state law an explicit provision that *requires* New Hampshire to hold its primary at least one week before any other state does.

A somewhat more likely source of relief is the political parties or, more accurately, the Democratic party, since the Republicans have consistently taken a laissez-faire posture toward delegate selection and basically leave the states free to do whatever they want. The Democrats, in contrast, have created a major party reform commission every four years since 1968, many of which have demonstrated a remarkable zeal for issuing national rules and guidelines that every state was expected—and often compelled—to follow.

The last three of these commissions, concerned about the excessive length of the nomination race, established a definite time period (the so-called window) during which all delegate selection activity had to take place. But on all three occasions, before the ink on that provision was dry, the Democrats turned around and specifically exempted New Hampshire and Iowa from it, in effect sanctioning their claim to a privileged position in the presidential selection process.

To be fair about it, the Democrats' options were distinctly limited. If the national party ever does pass a rule including New Hampshire within the window, New Hampshire state officials and party leaders have made no secret of the fact that they would go ahead and hold their primary anyway. The national party has no authority to prevent them from doing so. What it *could* do is refuse to seat the delegates selected at that primary at the national convention—but obviously this is a clumsy enforcement mechanism, coming months after the actual primary and arguably hurting the Democrats' chances in that state in the fall.

The Democratic party has shown an occasional willingness to go to the mat on such issues: to compel nondiscriminatory delegate selection processes in the South; and to end Wisconsin's crossover primary.[51] But even in the Democratic party, the days of centrally imposed reforms seem to be waning. When the latest Democratic rules panel, the Fairness Commission, was organized in June 1985, the predominant sentiment was that it was time, in the words of one commission adviser, "to stop mucking around with the nomination process." The commission made, as a result, only three very slight modifications of the rules—one of which, ironically, was to let Wisconsin go back to holding its crossover primary. The prospects for party-initiated action against New Hampshire, in short, appear to be exceedingly slight for the foreseeable future.[52]

For those worried about the influence of the New Hampshire primary and the Iowa caucuses on the rest of the nomination race, then, a more productive tack than trying to reschedule them may be to think about ways of limiting their effects. Three possibilities present themselves. One is for the media to exercise a little more restraint in covering and interpreting them. Granted that New Hampshire is the first primary and that the candidates do spend a lot of time there—still, was it really necessary to declare Jimmy Carter the "front-runner" on the basis of 23,000 votes? And was it necessary to underplay so severely the results of the following week's Massachusetts primary—a primary which actually had more candidates and nine times as many voters? And granted that Hart deserved somewhat more coverage after Iowa than he had received before it. But was it necessary to give him *more* coverage in the next week than Mondale, who had beaten him by three to one?

A second way to stem New Hampshire's momentum would be to liberalize the campaign finance laws, to make it easier for candidates to raise money and thereby stay in the race after a poor New Hampshire showing. Whatever may be said about the problematic role of money in *congressional* elections, it seems difficult to believe that contributions of $10,000 or $20,000 can "buy" a presidential candidate.

Finally, the best single antidote for momentum is time. When a relative unknown wins a breakthrough primary like New Hampshire, there is a definite cycle of aftereffects. The initial fallout is all positive: increased press coverage, almost all of it favorable; disarray and indecision in the opposition camps; the public intrigued by a fresh face. But after a few weeks, a reaction begins to set in. The press gets over its fascination, begins to do its own investigating—and may discover, for example, that the candidate has unaccountably changed his name, his age, and his signature. The public becomes bored as the great new hope starts to look more and more like just another politician. The fresh face develops blemishes.

A good example of this phenomenon was the early stages of the 1980 Republican nomination race. Since 1977, the national polls had shown that Ronald Reagan was the clear choice of most Republican identifiers to be their party's candidate in 1980.[53] Immediately after Bush's dramatic victory in the Iowa caucuses, however, there was a sizable surge in Bush's direction. A Gallup poll in late January showed Bush and Reagan tied, each favored by 32 percent of Republicans. Fortunately for Reagan, there were five weeks between the Iowa caucuses and the New Hampshire primary; and during that time, even before Bush's gaffe at the Nashua debate, the Republicans' natural affection for Reagan reasserted itself. In a poll conducted between 1 and 4 February, Gallup found Reagan back comfortably ahead of Bush, 47 percent to 25 percent. As a result, most accounts of the 1980 election claim, Reagan would probably have won New Hampshire even without the Nashua incident.[54]

This suggests that if delegate selection activities were more widely spaced—if there was a three- or four-week interval between Iowa and New Hampshire and the rest of the state primaries and caucuses — there would be considerably less risk of an ill-advised, headlong bandwagon for a candidate about whom too little was known. After an initial week or two of euphoria and hoopla, we might finally get to learn more about Hart's convoluted personal history, or about what kind of governor Jimmy Carter really was; and then, with that information available, decide if we still wanted such men as our presidential candidates.

Unfortunately, the presidential selection process appears to be headed in precisely the opposite direction. The five weeks that once separated Iowa and New Hampshire have now been reduced to eight days. Many other states, jealous of these two states and anxious to increase their own influence over the nomination, have moved their primaries or caucuses near the beginning of the delegate selection process. As of early 1987, the campaign calendar for 1988 was shaping up as follows: Six states would begin selecting their delegates before the start of the Democratic window—four with the approval of the party, two without approval. Then, on 8 March, the first day of the window, 17 states were scheduled to hold their primaries or caucuses.[55] A state that moves its delegate selection earlier in the year increases the likelihood that it will cast its votes while the nomination race is still undecided—but it also increases the influence of New Hampshire and Iowa, and the momentum those states provide.

This furious outbreak of "front-loading" also illustrates the peculiar vulnerability of New Hampshire's position. For if there is no agency that can authoritatively tell New Hampshire when to hold its primary, neither is there anyone to protect it from the scheduling decisions of other states. The events of the last 12 years have clearly made a mockery of the Democratic window. Once the Democrats decided not to enforce it against New Hampshire and Iowa, a sizable number of other states gradually realized that they could violate its provisions with impunity. Eventually, political leaders in some state, fed up and jealous, will recognize that they, too, can hold the first primary in the nation, if only they are willing to be as stubborn and unyielding about the issue as New Hampshire politicians have been. Just as New Hampshire now has a law requiring that its primary be the first in the nation, this other state will pass a law requiring that its primary be held on the same day as New Hampshire's. To appreciate the absurd lengths to which such a competition might go, one need only observe the recent actions of the Michigan Republican party, which started selecting its 1988 delegates at precinct caucuses held on 5 August 1986.

In the meantime, as the delegate selection process becomes more and more compressed, the danger increases that one of the parties might nominate a candidate with a serious, overriding flaw that becomes public only after he has effectively sewn up the nomination. A system that is already low on deliberation, information, and rationality may, it appears, have even less of these qualities in the future.

Notes

1. This history and many of the histories of individual campaigns rely heavily on Charles Brereton, *First Step to the White House: The New Hampshire Primary 1952-1980* (Hampton, N.H.: Wheelabrator Foundation, 1979); and Neal R. Peirce, *The New England States* (New York: Norton, 1976), 315-23.

2. For Eisenhower's own discussion of his decision, and the role New Hampshire played in it, see Dwight D. Eisenhower, *Mandate for Change 1953-1956* (Garden City, N.Y.: Doubleday, 1963), 16-24.

3. For Truman's account, see Harry S Truman, *Memoirs* (Garden City, N.Y.: Doubleday, 1956), 2:488-89. On his March 1952 reconsideration, see Donald R. McCoy, *The Presidency of Harry S Truman* (Lawrence: University Press of Kansas, 1984), 301-2. Most Truman biographers, it should be noted, draw no connection between his loss in New Hampshire and his decision to withdraw. See, for example, McCoy, *Presidency of Harry S Truman;* and Robert J. Donovan, *Tumultuous Years: The Presidency of Harry S Truman 1949-1953* (New York: Norton, 1982), 392-96.

4. Brereton, *First Step to the White House,* 10.

5. On Goldwater's mistakes, see Allen J. Matusow, *The Unraveling of America* (New York: Harper & Row, 1984), 135.

6. For a particularly good illustration of this, see the 25 March 1968 issue of *Newsweek.* The second paragraph in the article on New Hampshire begins, "[McCarthy's]

victory in New Hampshire can hardly be disputed." Then, one sentence later: "He came within six percentage points . . . of defeating his own party's incumbent President" (p. 22).

7. A detailed account of this campaign, and the *Union Leader*'s coverage of it, can be found in Jules Witcover, "William Loeb and the New Hampshire primary: A Question of Ethics," *Columbia Journalism Review*, May/June 1972, 14-27.

8. For a more detailed account, see Jack W. Germond and Jules Witcover, *Blue Smoke and Mirrors* (New York: Viking Press, 1981), chap. 6.

9. The literature on this point is voluminous. As one good discussion puts it, "To our knowledge, no systematic study of any national medium has ever uncovered a campaign in which the modern press, during the course of an election year, emphasized anything more heavily than it emphasized 'horse race.' " See Michael J. Robinson and Margaret A. Sheehan, *Over the Wire and on TV* (New York: Russell Sage Foundation, 1983), 147-48, and chap. 6. See also Thomas E. Patterson, *The Mass Media Election* (New York: Praeger, 1980).

10. For some examples, see F. Christopher Arterton, "The Media Politics of Presidential Campaigns: A Study of the Carter Nomination Drive," in *Race for the Presidency: The Media and the Nominating Process*, ed. James David Barber (Englewood Cliffs, N.J.: Prentice-Hall, 1978).

11. Michael J. Robinson, "Media Coverage in the Primary Campaign of 1976: Implications for Voters, Candidates, and Parties," in *The Party Symbol*, ed. William J. Crotty (San Francisco: Freeman, 1980).

12. The quotation is from William C. Adams, "Media Coverage of Campaign '84: A Preliminary Report," *Public Opinion*, April/May 1984, 11.

13. James R. Beniger, "Winning the Presidential Nomination: National Polls and State Primary Elections, 1936-1972," *Public Opinion Quarterly* 40 (Spring 1976). See especially table 5.

14. For 1980 results, see Robinson and Sheehan, *Over the Wire and on TV*, 69-82; the statistics cited appear on p. 81. For analogous results in 1984, see Henry E. Brady and Richard Johnston, "What's the Primary Message?" in this volume.

15. A detailed history of the McGovern-Fraser reforms is Byron E. Shafer, *The Quiet Revolution: The Struggle for the Democratic Party and the Shaping of Post-Reform Politics* (New York: Russell Sage Foundation, 1983). For a good discussion of their aftermath, see Nelson W. Polsby, *Consequences of Party Reform* (New York: Oxford University Press, 1983).

16. In 1981, the Hunt Commission restored a small number of ex-officio delegates — about 550, or 10 percent of the total — to the Democratic selection process. Republican party rules make no allowance for ex-officio delegates.

17. On the general effect of the shift to proportional representation, see James I. Lengle and Byron E. Shafer, "Primary Rules, Political Power, and Social Change," *American Political Science Review* 70 (March 1976): 25-40.

18. See, for example, Beniger's ranking of it in "Winning the Presidential Nomination," 33.

19. Both of these changes, it will be noted, occurred as a result of rules reforms undertaken by the *Democratic* party. The Republican party was also affected quite significantly, however. Many Democratic-dominated state legislatures, required by party rules to change their delegate selection procedures, passed laws that also applied to

the Republicans. Thus, the number of Republican presidential primaries increased from 15 in 1968 to 20 in 1972 to 26 in 1976 and then to 34 in 1980. The GOP was also affected by changes in media expectations and coverage patterns.

20. On the role of large contributions in the McGovern and Humphrey campaigns, see Herbert E. Alexander, *Financing the 1972 Election* (Lexington, Mass.: Lexington Books, 1976), 121-24, 126-27, 151-56.

21. On this point, see Gary R. Orren, "Fundraising in the Primaries: An Analysis of Contributions to Presidential Campaigns," in *Financing Presidential Campaigns* (Cambridge, Mass.: Institute of Politics, John F. Kennedy School of Government, Harvard University, January 1982), 34-37.

22. Jonathan Moore, ed., *Campaign for President: The Managers Look at '84* (Dover, Mass.: Auburn House, 1986), 69-70.

23. For a detailed discussion of 1976 prenomination strategies, and why Carter succeeded, see Jules Witcover, *Marathon: The Pursuit of the Presidency 1972-1976* (New York: Viking Press, 1977). Carter, it should be said, was also very lucky: In New Hampshire he had the conservative vote all to himself, while the liberal vote was split among four of his rivals.

24. There were a few partial exceptions, like John Connally. Even Connally's strategy was premised on the necessity of winning an early primary: For reasons having to do with Connally's background and appeal, however, his campaign targeted South Carolina, the first *southern* primary. By that time, Reagan's momentum proved unstoppable.

25. Rhodes Cook, "In '88 Contest, It's What's Up Front That Counts," *Congressional Quarterly Weekly Report*, 23 August 1986, 1997.

26. As a subject of journalistic and scholarly inquiry, the Iowa caucuses still lag far behind the New Hampshire primary. The only good discussion of the development of the Iowa caucuses I know of is Steven E. Schier, *The Rules and the Game: Democratic National Convention Delegate Selection in Iowa and Wisconsin* (Washington, D.C.: University Press of America, 1980). My account draws on Schier and on interviews with several of the key participants.

27. Interview with Clif Larson, February 1987.

28. For a good account of the growth of the Iowa Republican caucuses between 1976 and 1980, which includes the Baker quotation, see Germond and Witcover, *Blue Smoke and Mirrors*, chap. 5.

29. *New York Times*, 24 January 1972, 17.

30. One on the day of the caucuses, two on the day after. The "first direct confrontation" quotation appears on 25 January 1972, 20.

31. It was after Carter's victory in the October straw poll, for example, that R.W. Apple, Jr., the highly influential national political correspondent of the *New York Times*, first called attention to Carter's lead in Iowa, and the "dramatic progress" his campaign was making nationally. See Witcover, *Marathon*, 202.

32. Robinson, "Media Coverage in the Primary Campaign of 1976," 182-84.

33. Robinson and Sheehan, *Over the Wire and on TV*, 176-77. I have not been able to locate comparable data on the 1984 race.

34. This is the conclusion of several studies, looking at a variety of news sources. For UPI data, see Brady and Johnston, "What's the Primary Message?" For NBC data, see Adams, "Media Coverage of Campaign '84," 11. On CBS, Hart's coverage quintupled

in the week after Iowa, though his total still lagged slightly behind Mondale's. Ibid.

35. On the post-Iowa shift to Hart, see the data in David Moore, "The Death of Politics in New Hampshire," *Public Opinion*, February/March 1984; and in Nelson W. Polsby, "The Democratic Nomination and the Evolution of the Party System," in *The American Elections of 1984,* ed. Austin Ranney (Washington, D.C.: American Enterprise Institute, 1985).

36. Withdrawal is defined here as the day on which a candidate publicly announced that he was suspending active campaigning for his party's presidential nomination. A few of the candidates in table 1.2 claimed that they were not completely withdrawing from the race and might get back into it at a later time. But their statements were usually interpreted as withdrawals by the media and other politicians, and not one of them actually did resume active campaigning.

37. As this table indicates, there are actually a number of additional complications, the most important of which concerns the sampling universes being compared. Too often, the comparison is made between a national sample of all Republicans (or Democrats) in the adult population, and an exit poll of those who voted in the New Hampshire Republican primary. See, for example, Scott Keeter and Cliff Zukin, *Uninformed Choice: The Failure of the New Presidential Nominating System* (New York: Praeger, 1983), 35-43. The problem with such a comparison is that primary electorates are widely recognized as unrepresentative of party identifiers. See James I. Lengle, *Representation and Presidential Primaries: The Democratic Party in the Post-Reform Era* (Westport, Conn.: Greenwood, 1981).

Hence, if a discrepancy arises between the national and New Hampshire party profiles, it could derive from one of two sources: *(a)* the discrepancy between national Republican identifiers and New Hampshire Republican identifiers; or *(b)* the discrepancy between New Hampshire Republican identifiers and voters in the New Hampshire Republican primary. The first of these sources of bias is an important concern; but the second source is likely to exist *regardless* of what state, or combination of states, holds the first primary.

Obviously, the best way to test New Hampshire's representativeness would be to compare a sample of the national adult population with a sample of the New Hampshire adult population. Unfortunately, I have been unable to locate a single survey of the full New Hampshire population conducted within the last seven years that also includes a party identification question. Another possibility is to compare primary voters in New Hampshire (as measured by exit polls) with those respondents within a national sample who say that they voted in a presidential primary. Both the 1976 and 1980 American National Election Studies asked respondents if they had voted in a presidential primary; but the discrepancy between the national primary vote totals and the ANES sample distribution is so large as to raise serious questions about the reliability of this variable.

Accordingly, in table 1.3, I have settled for the best available alternative: a comparison between a survey of registered voters in New Hampshire, and that part of the 1984 ANES sample which said that they were registered voters. The third column in the table shows the demographic composition of party identifiers in the entire ANES sample, for those who are concerned about what bias may be introduced by limiting the comparison to registered voters. On the whole, it appears the bias is very small indeed.

38. For a good discussion of the differences in factionalization between the Republican and Democratic parties, and the difference that makes in intraparty politics, see Polsby, *Consequences of Party Reform*, especially 64-71 and 211-15.

39. Gary Orren and William Schneider, "Democrats versus Democrats: Party Factions in the 1972 Presidential Primaries" (manuscript). Orren and Schneider actually found a fourth wing, consisting of white-collar conservatives, but argued that this faction was a good deal smaller than the other three, since outside the South, white-collar conservatives tend to be Republicans.

40. Peter Hart, speaking in Jonathan Moore, ed., *Campaign for President,* 59.

41. These and similar epithets may be found in Kevin Cash, *Who the Hell Is William Loeb?* (Manchester, N.H.: Amoskeag Press, 1975), appendix A; and in Peirce, *The New England States,* 299.

42. Witcover, "William Loeb and the New Hampshire Primary."

43. Ibid.

44. See David Moore, "The Legacy of William Loeb," *Public Opinion*, December/January 1983, 43-44.

45. For further details, see the discussion in Peirce, *The New England States,* 298-307.

46. Ibid., 301-2.

47. Witcover, "William Loeb and the New Hampshire Primary," 15.

48. Both quotations appear in Peirce, *The New England States,* 301 and 303-4.

49. Brereton, *First Step to the White House,* 3.

50. See David Moore, "The Death of Politics in New Hampshire."

51. For details on these issues, and the legal battles that followed in their wake, see Leon D. Epstein, *Political Parties in the American Mold* (Madison: University of Wisconsin Press, 1986), chaps. 6 and 7.

52. See *Congressional Quarterly Weekly Report,* 24 August 1985, 1687-89; 1 March 1986, 509-10; and 15 March 1986, 627.

53. Reagan had a clear lead, that is, as among those candidates who actively sought the nomination. Gerald Ford ran even with Reagan through most of this period.

54. Germond and Witcover, for example, say that Reagan had a pre-Nashua lead of 7 or 8 percent (though they add that it might have leveled off). See *Blue Smoke and Mirrors,* 124-25 and 130. Similarly, in a campaign retrospective, both Reagan's pollster and the national political director of the Bush campaign say that the "axial event" was not the Nashua debate but the Manchester debate held three days earlier. See the discussion in Jonathan Moore, ed., *The Campaign for President: 1980 in Retrospect* (Cambridge, Mass.: Ballinger, 1981), 116 and 121-23.

55. On front-loading in 1984, see Polsby, "The Democratic Nomination and the Evolution of the Party System." On developments since then, see Maxwell Glen, "Front-Loading the Race," *National Journal,* 29 November 1986; and Cook, "In '88 Contest, It's What Up Front That Counts."

2

As New Hampshire Goes . . .

WILLIAM C. ADAMS

New Hampshire towers over the nation when a map of the United States is drawn in proportion to the share of news coverage in presidential nomination races. Figure 2.1 shows a 1984 map of the states, based on ABC, CBS, NBC, and *New York Times* campaign stories from 1 January to 10 June.* Rising like a mountain over the New England corner is an enormous New Hampshire.

Everyone knows the importance of the New Hampshire primary is exaggerated. That comes as no surprise. But the magnitude of that exaggeration is startling. New Hampshire is not just mildly disproportionate; on the map, it dwarfs all other states. Consider the following comparisons using the 1984 data:

☐ By itself, the New Hampshire primary received more attention than was given all the contests for delegates in the 17 southern and border states (including Texas and Florida) and the 7 Rocky Mountain states combined.

☐ New Hampshire's primary received 125 times as much coverage per Democratic primary voter as the large Ohio primary.

☐ The 8,403,000 Democratic primary voters in Pennsylvania, Ohio, Illinois, North Carolina, and California, combined, did not receive as much media attention as the 101,000 people who turned out for the Democratic primary in New Hampshire.

This chapter begins with a review of the factors that may explain the distortions illustrated above and goes on to examine the impact of New Hampshire's high-volume coverage on the electorate.

*The content data from 1 January through 10 June 1984 are calculated from all early-evening network newscasts summarized in Vanderbilt's *TV News Index and Abstracts* (using seconds of air time per state and proportionately allocating the time of multiple-state stories) and from the *New York Times* using column inches.

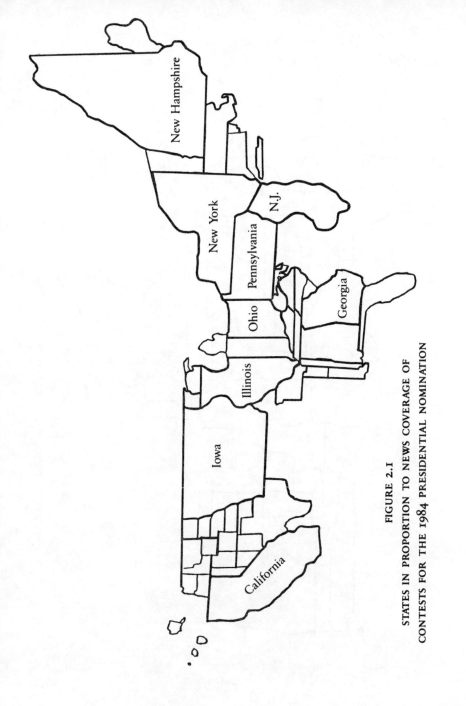

FIGURE 2.1

STATES IN PROPORTION TO NEWS COVERAGE OF
CONTESTS FOR THE 1984 PRESIDENTIAL NOMINATION

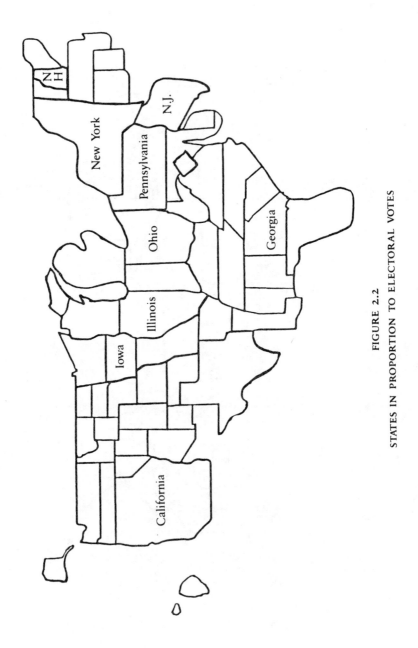

FIGURE 2.2

STATES IN PROPORTION TO ELECTORAL VOTES

New Hampshire Uber Alles

Figure 2.2, a map of the United States showing a shrunken New Hampshire and Iowa, presents the states in proportion to their electoral votes, which approximate their actual populations. This map dictates tactics and travel during the fall general election campaign. But geography for the nomination campaign in the previous winter and spring is vastly different. Figure 2.1 reflects those priorities. New Hampshire may have little weight when the general election comes around, but it is enormously powerful in the campaign for party nominations.

TABLE 2.1

MEDIA COVERAGE OF THE PRESIDENTIAL NOMINATION CAMPAIGNS,
1 JANUARY–10 JUNE 1984

State	Percentage of Total Coverage	Percentage of U.S. Population
New Hampshire	19.2	.4
Iowa	12.8	2.5
New York	11.1	7.5
California	6.9	10.8
Pennsylvania	5.5	5.0
New Jersey	5.0	3.2
Illinois	4.1	4.9
All other states	35.4	65.7

SOURCE: Calculated from ABC, CBS, NBC, and *New York Times* coverage.

As shown in table 2.1, four states—New Hampshire, Iowa, New York, and California—garnered half the media coverage during the 1984 nomination races. Seven states together received nearly two-thirds of the coverage. New Hampshire, with one-fifth of all coverage, is by far the least populated of the top seven states.

Is there any pattern in these priorities? What factors are likely to predict a state's volume of media coverage? What can explain New Hampshire's remarkable role? Likely explanations include primary date, delegation size, disance from media centers, drama involved, and displacement by other primaries.

PRIMARY DATE

Americans treasure "firsts." Journalists put a premium on a "new" story and become bored with an old, somewhat repetitive story. Timing would seem to be a probable determinant, with the earliest states profiting most. Nevertheless, the date of each state's contest (Iowa = Day 1; California = Day 100) shows only a minor correlation of −.21 with the relative amount of media attention allocated to each state. Not all early contests were highlighted, and not all later races were ignored.

DELEGATION SIZE

The size of a state's delegation to the party convention may also be a factor. Certainly at the level of pure logic a contest for several hundred delegates would seem more newsworthy than one for several dozen delegates. Yet delegation size had only a .38 correlation with a state's media share. (Only 14 percent of the variation in media visibility can be statistically explained by knowing the number of convention delegates at stake.) While no one would expect a perfect journalistic equivalent of "one man, one vote," the discrepancy is substantial.

DISTANCE FROM MEDIA CENTERS

Proximity to media headquarters is often a major factor in international news priorities,[1] and evidence shows that it is also a factor in domestic news. Proximity to New York City, headquarters for the major networks and leading print outlets, accounts for some variations in coverage. For example, New York State garnered 18 percent of all network news time, although it had only 9 percent of the population.[2] And members of the 96th Congress representing districts in the New York area were significantly more likely to make an appearance or be cited on the nightly network news than were other members.[3] In the nomination campaign, however, distance from New York accounted for only a small portion of media priorities. The correlation coefficient was −.27; more miles from New York meant only a little less coverage.

ELEMENT OF DRAMA

Primaries are easier to cover than complex caucuses. The results of primaries are usually known sooner, and primaries have more *vox populi* excitement. One might hypothesize that caucuses and conventions would attract the least coverage, with nonbinding primaries ("beauty contests") getting more coverage and binding primaries receiving the most coverage. Type of delegate selection had a −.28 correlation with coverage (scoring binding primaries as 3, nonbinding primaries as 2, and strictly caucus states as 1). Primaries have a slight advantage, but several primaries were essentially ignored and the Iowa caucuses were spotlighted.

DISPLACEMENT BY OTHER PRIMARIES

Perhaps a state that selects its delegates on the same day as several other states receives proportionately less attention because it is somewhat "displaced" by the competition. A Super Tuesday may gain in overall hype, but any one state's treatment may be diluted. To have the entire day, or week, alone may be a bigger advantage. But the displacement factor did not make much difference in 1984. More contests on the same date only mildly depressed (−.18) a state's visibility.

If all five factors are examined simultaneously, how successfully do they predict coverage? In some instances, they appear to perform well. For example, South Dakota and New Mexico select delegates in June, at the end of the selection process; their primaries are on the same day as four other primaries (including California); they select only a few delegates; and the two states are remote from Manhattan or any other network bureau. For all practical purposes, they are invisible.

For all 50 states, the five factors do not predict as well. A multiple regression using the 1984 Democratic data produces a multiple R^2 of only .35. That is, barely more than one-third of the variation in coverage can be attributed to a state's having more delegates, deciding earlier in the season, having few or no other contests on the same day, and holding a primary rather than a caucus. ("Distance from media center" has almost no additional explanatory power once these other factors are held constant.)

As shown in table 2.2, a separate examination of the coverage of caucus states only and primary states only shows little improvement in the explanatory power of these variables. Overall, roughly two-thirds of the variation in coverage from state to state is left unexplained.

TABLE 2.2

PREDICTING STATE MEDIA COVERAGE,

1984

	Correlation Coefficients		
Relative Media Coverage	All States	Primary States	Caucus States
Number of Democratic delegates	.38	.34	.22
Date of contest	−.21	−.28	−.18
Number of same-day contests	−.18	−.26	−.28
Distance from New York City	−.27	−.22	−.15
Mode of selection (caucus or primary)	−.28	—	—
Multiple R^2	.35	.41	.37

Inspection of the residuals shows two states as extreme outliers with far more coverage than predicted by the regression equation. The states are New Hampshire and Iowa. If these two cases are excluded, relationships change enormously.

TABLE 2.3

PREDICTING STATE MEDIA COVERAGE,

EXCLUDING NEW HAMPSHIRE AND IOWA,

1984

	Correlation Coefficients		
Relative Media Coverage	All States	Primary States	Caucus States
Number of Democratic delegates	.82	.84	.71
Date of contest	−.07	−.22	.35
Number of same-day contests	−.03	−.11	−.32
Distance from New York City	−.29	−.17	−.20
Mode of selection (caucus or primary)	−.42	−	−
Multiple R² with all variables	.73	.78	.57
Simple R² with number of delegates only	.67	.71	.50

Table 2.3. shows the correlates of coverage of the 48 other states. Usually, news coverage is apportioned with considerable weight to the number of delegates at stake in each contest; the correlation is .82. Thus, excluding Iowa and New Hampshire, the purely objective element of delegation size can, by itself, statistically explain two-thirds of the variations in coverage ($R^2 = 67$). Moreover, once size is taken into account, the other factors offer little additional explanation.

Without the first two contests in the equation, several important findings emerge:

☐ When New Hampshire and Iowa are excluded from the prediction, nothing matters more than the number of delegates at stake. The apportionment of coverage has an imprecise but unexpectedly strong correlation with delegation size.
☐ Since most of the heavily populated states have primaries, primaries are covered more than caucuses. But the mode of selection contributes little (less than 2 percent in predicting coverage) after delegation size is accounted for.

☐ Minus New Hampshire and Iowa, even the date of the contest makes little difference. News coverage is fairly proportional considering what is at stake, and stays with the race on a surprisingly sustained basis.

☐ Contrasting figures 2.1 and 2.2 shows that the South has been somewhat neglected given its share of the U.S. population. Southerners intend to change that with a huge regional primary early in 1988.

☐ Overall (omitting New Hampshire and Iowa), the nomination campaign is reported in a way that keeps most contests in rough perspective.

Nevertheless, the exceptions, New Hampshire and Iowa, consumed more than 30 percent of 1984 nomination campaign coverage. To put matters in perspective, one could say that if one-third of all European media coverage were about Luxemburg and Portugal, it would be small consolation that the balance of the coverage was apportioned more sensibly. The saturation emphasis on New Hampshire and Iowa overwhelms the other 48 states. Figure 2.3 shows the relationship between Democratic delegation strength and 1984 media attention. Hovering far from the regression line (based on the 48 other states) are New Hampshire and Iowa.

This review has focused on coverage by ABC, CBS, NBC, and the *New York Times*. The exact rankings of the states will vary somewhat from year to year and from outlet to outlet. Most newspapers naturally emphasize campaign activities in their market area. In a year when the nomination is wrapped up earlier than it was in 1984 (when Hart vigorously fought Mondale until the end), New Hampshire and Iowa would receive an even larger proportion of nomination campaign coverage.

The "secondary" primaries have varied over the years depending on the unique circumstances of each race. In 1972, Florida ranked second in coverage.[4] In 1976, Massachusetts came in second, and journalists discovered the early Iowa caucuses. In 1980 and 1984, Iowa was firmly entrenched in second place. Illinois and Pennsylvania were the runners-up in 1980; New York and California had that distinction in 1984. Thus, the prominence of the states that follow New Hampshire has varied, but New Hampshire's extraordinary domination has not.

Dynamics of the Pivotal Primary

All of the New Hampshire media coverage has political clout not only because of its volume. It is doubly powerful because of its content. Leading journalists use the New Hampshire results as the basis for restructuring their coverage of the candidates and issuing political obituaries for those who do poorly. New

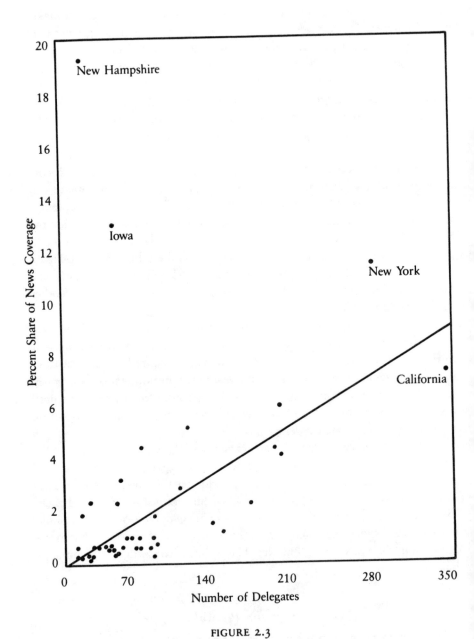

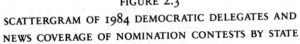

FIGURE 2.3
SCATTERGRAM OF 1984 DEMOCRATIC DELEGATES AND
NEWS COVERAGE OF NOMINATION CONTESTS BY STATE

Hampshire is not treated as simply an interesting preliminary contest. It is made into a definitive test, which means disqualification for those candidates who do not pass with sufficiently high marks. A review of the race for the 1984 Democratic nomination shows how this works.

As 1983 began, candidates who were high in the polls were those who had received the most prior media attention: Walter Mondale (a former vice-president), John Glenn (a former astronaut), and George McGovern (a former Democratic nominee). Most people had never heard of Alan Cranston, Gary Hart, Reubin Askew, or Ernest Hollings, and no more than 2 percent of the Democrats polled preferred any one of these candidates.

These early poll standings were an almost perfect barometer of candidate news attention throughout 1983. As shown in table 2.4, rankings of the volume of coverage on the nightly network news and stories in both the *Washington Post* and *New York Times* closely duplicated early standings in the polls. (The only candidate with any discrepancy between his poll ranking and news ranking was George McGovern, who did not announce his candidacy until late in the year.)

Allocations of 1983 coverage let the rich get richer. The only candidates to improve significantly in the polls during 1983 were those who had dominated print and broadcast journalism: Walter Mondale and John Glenn. Conversely, those who were "poll poor" at the start stayed "media poor" during most of the year and went nowhere in the polls. There were a few minor instances in 1983 when media did more than just reinforce the preexisting pecking order.[5] But, by and large, journalists followed the lead of poll standings.

TABLE 2.4
RANKING IN POLLS AND 1983 COVERAGE

Candidate	December 1982 Gallup Poll		1983 Television News Time	1983 *Washington Post* and *New York Times* Stories	December 1983 Gallup Poll	
Mondale	1	(32%)	1	1	1	(40%)
Glenn	2	(14%)	2	2	2	(24%)
Jackson	–	–	3	3	3	(10%)
McGovern	3	(6%)	8	7	4	(8%)
Hart	4[a]	(2%)	4	4	5[a]	(3%)
Cranston	4[a]	(2%)	5	5	5[a]	(3%)
Hollings	4[a]	(2%)	6	6	7	(2%)
Askew	7	(1%)	7	8	8	(1%)

a. Tied for this placement in polls.

This early nomination process, before the primaries, is circular: Prior visibility produces high poll ratings, which ensures media coverage/legitimacy, which sustains poll standings, which ensure media coverage/legitimacy. For those with a low standing initially, the situation is fairly static. Low visibility produces less than 5 percent in the polls, which means little media attention/credibility, which ensures continued low standings in the polls. This cycle depresses or stimulates the other key elements in campaign dynamics: money and volunteers. The next stage, however, undergoes a radical transformation.

Starting with the first caucus, journalists change their entire perspective on the nomination race. They abandon reliance on national polls to rank the candidates. They reorder candidate status by the nomination results in Iowa and New Hampshire. Though they are small and unrepresentative, the first caucus (Iowa) and the first primary (New Hampshire) are used to winnow out candidates who fail to do well in those two states and boost candidates who do well.

In 1984, during the week before the Iowa caucuses, airtime allocations[6] still mirrored national polls, with Mondale way out front, and Glenn and Jackson coming in second and third. Most of the rest of the pack were essentially ignored. Hart received 4 percent of the candidate coverage that week, as did McGovern. Hollings and Askew each received less than 2 percent.

On 20 February the Iowa caucuses changed all that. The Democratic caucuses were attended by about 85,000 people, less than one-sixth of the number who regularly vote Democratic in presidential elections in Iowa. Total caucus turnout constituted only 17 percent of the half-million Iowa Democratic votes cast, for example, in 1972 for McGovern.

This one-sixth segment of the party resides in a state that has gone Democratic only one since siding with neighbor Harry Truman in 1948. But no matter how inconsequential Iowa Democrats are in November, thanks to the news, they are powerful in February. As shown earlier, enormous attention is given to the Iowa caucuses—the networks often devote over one-third of their entire newscast to Iowa.

Although no candidate came close to Mondale's 45 percent of the vote, measured against expectations, two outcomes attracted the most interest: (1) Glenn did poorly, winning only 5 percent; and (2) Hart unexpectedly placed second to Mondale, though he had only 15 percent (12,600 votes), less than 2,000 votes ahead of McGovern.

Despite the tiny segment of the electorate that participated, the media verdict was unequivocal, and the self-fulfilling power attributed to the caucuses was monumental. Said Tom Brokaw of NBC News on 21 February: "Senators Hart and Glenn traded places in Iowa. Hart moved up to number two. Glenn became an also-ran. The effect of this surprising reversal already is being felt in their campaigns."

Iowa produced far-reaching transformations of news priorities. Broadcast journalists awarded newfound status to Gary Hart and drafted preliminary obituaries for John Glenn. Hart gained most on NBC, where Hart's airtime actually equaled that of Mondale after Iowa—each received almost 30 percent of candidate airtime. Hart also gained substantially on CBS. Hart's relative share of coverage the week after Iowa was ten times what it had previously been on CBS.

Walter Cronkite had said in 1980, "Iowa has replaced New Hampshire as the place we start the elimination process." One victim of that practice in 1984 was John Glenn. Viewers were told that the events in Iowa were almost fatal for Glenn, who "tried to put on a brave front" and whose new goal was "simply surviving" (NBC), hoping for "some emergency oxygen for his badly shaken campaign" (CBS).

Taken together, the Iowa "surprises" raise another issue. Some might argue that the Iowa outcome refutes the entire theory that the media confer status; after all, Glenn did much worse, while Hart and McGovern did better, than national media coverage would have predicted. Actually, Iowa only proved (via John Glenn) that prior media attention does not guarantee a constituency but only offers an opportunity to assemble one; it does not indefinitely compensate for weak speeches and poor organization.

Iowa also demonstrated that it is possible for a candidate (Gary Hart) portrayed as a dark horse to mobilize 3 percent (12,600) of the Iowans who regularly vote Democratic in presidential elections (500,000) to attend caucuses one evening in February. That little feat does not demolish but only qualifies the role of media status conferral when it comes to small subsets of activists early in a presidential campaign.

After Iowa, Hart was depicted as the leading alternative to Walter Mondale, and Hart's coverage was nearly free of harsh criticism, unflattering issues, or cynical commentary. In contrast, John Glenn was "trying desperately to recharge his batteries" (Brokaw), and Jesse Jackson was "spending a lot of time . . . defensively fielding questions about . . . alleged remarks about Jews" (Rather). McGovern continued to be dismissed, and the rest hardly existed in the world of the networks. This left Gary Hart enjoying his Iowa windfall of coverage and not yet ripe for network scrutiny of his name change, age, and "new ideas."

Next came the New Hampshire primary on 28 February.[7] Hart beat Mondale by a margin of 37,702 to 28,173 out of 101,131 votes cast. Glenn received 12,088 votes, and the remaining 23,168 were divided among six other candidates.

David Broder has commented:

> The safest bet you can make, in advance of any presidential year, is that the winner of the out-party's New Hampshire primary will be on all three networks' early-morning and evening news shows the next day, that he will be featured in long profiles in the next Sunday's newspapers, and that he will be on the covers of the three news magazines the following week."[8]

Indeed, Hart was the recipient of priceless "free media." Following his triumph in New Hampshire, CBS and NBC presented viewers with a two-man race. Hart's share of coverage continued to rise dramatically. After only two contests, the networks had winnowed the nomination race to two candidates.

As ABC's Harry Reasoner said, years earlier: "For some, New Hampshire will be fatal to their ambitions." And in the two weeks after New Hampshire, Glenn, with 4 percent of the candidate airtime on CBS and 7 percent on NBC, joined McGovern (5 percent on CBS and 1 percent on NBC) in relative obscurity. Askew, Cranston, and Hollings finally got some coverage when they dropped out of the race.

Coverage in the wake of New Hampshire is extremely potent because it hits many voters who are just "tuning in" to the campaign. The peak for following the 1984 nomination campaign on television and in the newspapers came

TABLE 2.5

PUBLIC ATTENTIVENESS TO THE NOMINATION CAMPAIGN

	Pre-N.H. Primary (11 January- 28 February)	Post-N.H. Primary (29 February- 10 April)	Post-Penn. Primary (11 April- 8 May)	Post-Ohio Primary (9 May- 6 June)
Follow campaign on television	28%	45%	39%	37%
Follow campaign in newspaper	17	29	24	19
Attempt to persuade others	14	25	28	26
Interested in campaign	46	46	44	48
Approximate sample size	(488)	(468)	(310)	(305)

SOURCE: Calculated from data presented by Henry Brady and Richard Johnston, "What Is the Primary Message: Horse Race or Issue Journalism?" herein, based on the National Election Studies' "rolling cross-section" weekly surveys. Weeks combined to create sample sizes of at least 300 total.

in the days and weeks just after the New Hampshire primary.[9] At that time, nearly half said they were regularly following the campaign on television, and nearly one-third were doing so in newspapers (see table 2.5).

The number of people who had a favorite candidate whom they recommended to others also increased in March and stayed fairly steady at around 25 to 28 percent. The segment expressing an interest in the campaign was stable in the 44 to 48 percent range throughout the season. Yet active monitoring of the campaign clearly peaked during the post-New Hampshire through post-Super Tuesday period.

Thanks to 2000 Iowa and 9500 New Hampshire voters (Hart's margins), and the way in which these votes were amplified by the media at a time when the audience was especially primed and ready, the new question was, "Can Hart be stopped?" In a replay of Jimmy Carter's 1976 media momentum, Hart was suddenly a contender or even a favorite in states where he had not had any organization and virtually no support just two weeks earlier. The big difference between Carter in 1976 and Hart in 1984 was that the media's honeymoon with Hart ended before he had a chance to lock up the nomination.

Starting on 8 March, barely one week after the New Hampshire primary victory, and running for two crucial weeks until Mondale's victory in Illinois on 20 March, Hart was subjected to an extraordinary barrage of criticism.[10] When Ed Fouhy, then a producer at ABC news, was asked about this rush to critique Hart, he said, "We try and learn from past mistakes, so we made a real effort to dig as deep as we could as quickly as we could."

After laboring under the accusation of having propelled unscrutinized "unknowns" (McGovern in 1972 and Carter in 1976) with dubious talents into positions of power, journalists had the instinctive reaction not to let it happen again. They would not sell the Republic another untested hinterland visionary. This time there would be no sustained excitement over a conquering dark horse, no gullible faith in the promise of "new ideas," no long ride on New Hampshire's momentum.

While the post-New Hampshire honeymoon was in its full glory, Hart was catapulted from being the choice of 7 percent to the choice of 38 percent of the nation's Democrats. Meanwhile, Mondale plummeted from 57 to 31 percent.[11] That 31 percent jump for the winner and 26 percent fall for the loser was the largest national opinion shift on record after a New Hampshire primary. The average surge for nonincumbent victors is 14 percent, while the average decline for their major opponent is 11 percent.

Table 2.6 is a compilation of national poll standings before and after contested New Hampshire primaries since 1964. During these six presidential election years, there have been nine contested primaries.

TABLE 2.6

BEFORE AND AFTER THE NEW HAMPSHIRE PRIMARY

Year and Party	"Winner" of New Hampshire Primary	Nationwide Support in Own Party		"Winner's" Change	Major Opponent's Change
		Pre-N.H.	Post-N.H.		
1964-R	Henry Cabot Lodge	12%	42%	+ 30%	− 5%
1968-R	Richard Nixon	49	60	+ 11	− 5
1968-D	Eugene McCarthy[a]	18	29	+ 11	− 12
1972-D	George McGovern[a]	6	5	− 1	− 12
1976-D	Jimmy Carter	4	16	+ 12	− 4
1980-R	Ronald Reagan	32	39	+ 7	− 9
1984-D	Gary Hart	7	38	+ 31	− 26
Winning Incumbent Presidents					
1976-R	Gerald Ford	55	51	− 4	+ 6
1980-D	Jimmy Carter	61	59	− 2	− 1

a. Media-awarded "moral victory."

SOURCE: Figures are based on the last Gallup poll before the New Hampshire primary and the first Gallup poll after the New Hampshire primary, except for the 1980 Republican race (ABC News/Harris polls) and 1984 Democratic race (CBS/New York Times). One other 1972 primary and three other 1976 primaries were held before the post-New Hampshire surveys were conducted.

In two instances, incumbent Presidents won over their challengers. But neither of these New Hampshire victories improved their popularity ratings. Neither President Ford in 1976 (against Ronald Reagan) nor President Carter in 1980 (against Ted Kennedy) enjoyed a post-N.H. boomlet. An incumbent President who is so weak as to prompt a within-party challenge benefits little from holding off the challenger. Incumbent Presidents already have a well-established—perhaps too well-established—image and scarcely need extra publicity. A defeat or a perceived defeat may hurt (as it hurt Lyndon Johnson in 1968), but a victory does not seem to help.

In contrast, all nonincumbent winners have found their relative standing improved by the New Hampshire results. In every instance, their major opponents suffered, although none more than Mondale's 26-percentage-point slide. And, in all cases but one, the winner's poll rating shot upward. Henry Cabot Lodge, who was not even in the country at the time, raced ahead 30 points. Gary Hart holds the record with his 31-point gain.

Two of those classified here as "winners" actually lost the primary. Yet, because they did unexpectedly well against the front-runners, journalists granted them "moral victories." In 1968, Eugene McCarthy was proclaimed the "winner" when he surpassed expectations and lost to the front-runner (President Lyndon Johnson) by 8 percent. In 1972, George McGovern was declared the "winner" when he beat expectations and lost to the front-runner (Edmund Muskie) by 9 percent.[12]

McGovern was the only winner (or pseudo winner) who failed to translate a positive media verdict out of New Hampshire into an immediate popularity gain. Nevertheless, his chief opponent was damaged. Edmund Muskie, previously considered the likely nominee, was hurt by the interpretation of his winning margin as a disappointment. Twelve percent of his Democratic fans departed soon after New Hampshire, and his downward slide began.

Some analysts have speculated that Democrats are more vulnerable to these vicissitudes than Republicans are. While it is true that the most recent and most dramatic case (Hart-Mondale) did occur among Democrats, there are no examples of Republican (nonincumbent) winners who failed to chalk up a post-New Hampshire improvement as well.

Most people vote for the candidate they like the best (or dislike the least) among those who appear to be viable. Henry Brady's analysis of weekly surveys conducted throughout the 1984 campaign confirms the heavy degree to which voters' choices are not only a function of candidate policy positions and traits but of perceived candidate viability and electability as well.[13] Tom Patterson for 1976 and Tom Marshall for 1980 have shown how, for those nomination campaigns, coverage was keyed to candidates' early performances;[14] again, positive media verdicts produced public opinion payoffs. Protest votes and other special cases excepted, most people do not want to waste their votes on a lost cause. Preferences swing toward the most tolerable candidate who has a chance — hence, the devastating impact of being branded "hopeless" in the aftermath of New Hampshire.

Who Reforms Whom?

Before an election, candidates dare not acknowledge the oddities of the system. They cannot afford to alienate voters in Iowa and New Hampshire, on whom so much depends. They cannot solicit votes while publicly admitting the absurdity of those same voters having de facto veto power over the nomination.

After an election, candidate complaints are dismissed as "sour grapes." After Iowa, John Glenn tried to point out how unrepresentative its caucuses were. He was right, but who listens to a "sore loser?"

To skip Iowa or New Hampshire implies weakness. That option is too dangerous for most candidates to attempt. Morris Udall had intended to skip

Iowa in 1976, until he discovered how heavily the media planned to cover Iowa.[15] Then, like almost every candidate since, he felt compelled to make Iowa a high priority.

If candidates have no standing, critiques of the system revert to party leaders and party committees. Iowa and New Hampshire are such historically Republican states that one would think the process would be of special concern to the Democratic leadership. Considering the persistently dismal performance of Democratic presidential nominees, there seems to be some basic flaw in a nominating system that regularly produces tickets that produce landslide rejections. In four of the past five presidential elections, the Democrats have not exceeded 43 percent of the popular vote. At least for the Democrats, more meditation over Nelson Polsby's *Consequences of Party Reform*[16] is in order.

So much for politicians and parties; what about the press? The apportionment of campaign coverage is not easy or obvious. That journalists must make such decisions is unavoidable, but that fact does not make their decisions any less powerful or any less influential.

Some writers have argued that the obsession with Iowa and New Hampshire is unavoidable, their gravitational pull is too strong to resist. That "the press and television would give exaggerated importance to those early contests" was "inevitable," wrote David Broder.[17] But is the exaggeration of the New Hampshire and Iowa results inevitable? It is not fair to journalists to say they will not or cannot put the early contests into a more restrained perspective.

Both broadcast and print journalism has grown steadily more sophisticated in the coverage of campaigns. Extensive surveys are conducted to help interpret voting results more insightfully rather than rely on guesswork. Increasingly, efforts are made to provide the public with reviews of where candidates stand on the issues—often despite the efforts of candidates to remain artfully vague. There is every indication that journalists' sensitivity to the unfairness of calling primary winners "losers" has been responsible for the decline of this practice in recent years.[18] The unfortunate experiment with a viewer call-in ersatz poll to declare who won the presidential debates was never repeated. There is nothing inescapable or irreversible about the rush to anoint two semifinalists based on the first tentative tests.

What, then, is the wisest way to winnow candidates based on New Hampshire and Iowa? That may be the wrong question. Why should the nomination race be reordered at all, based on such laughably minuscule electorates?

Notes

1. William C. Adams, "Whose Lives Count?: Television Coverage of Natural Disasters," *Journal of Communication*, Summer 1986.

2. Joseph R. Dominick, "Geographical Bias in National TV News," *Journal of Communication* (Autumn 1977): 94-99.

3. Timothy E. Cook, "House Members as Newsmakers," *Legislative Studies Quarterly* 11 (May 1986): 203-26.

4. For a review of early 1972 and 1976 coverage, see Michael J. Robinson and Karen McPherson, "Television News Coverage Before the 1976 New Hampshire Primary: The Focus of Network Journalism," *Journal of Broadcasting* 21 (Spring 1977): 177-86. For 1980 CBS and UPI coverage, see Michael J. Robinson and Margaret Sheehan, *Over the Wire and on TV* (New York: Russell Sage Foundation, 1983).

5. William C. Adams, "Media Coverage of Campaign '84," *Public Opinion*, April/May 1984, 9-13; "The Power of 'The Right Stuff,' " *Public Opinion Quarterly* 49 (Autumn 1985): 330-39.

6. Starting one week before the Iowa caucuses, early weeknight CBS and NBC newscasts were coded for the amounts of airtime devoted to each Democratic candidate. Calculated as a percentage of the total time given to all Democratic candidates, this measure shows the relative share of attention assigned each candidate.

7. Unlike the Iowa caucuses, New Hampshire's primary draws as many as four-fifths of the people who vote Democratic in November. Their numbers are still small, however; New Hampshire has gone Democratic only once since the presidential election of 1944.

8. "Braking the Bandwagon," *Washington Post*, 11 March 1984.

9. These findings are calculated from data presented by Henry Brady and Richard Johnston, "What's the Primary Message: Horse Race or Issue Journalism?" in this volume. Since single-week samples were relatively small (only about 75 usable interviews per week), to reduce sampling error, weeks were combined to create sample sizes of at least 300 total.

10. Adams, "Media Coverage of Campaign '84."

11. Based on national CBS/ *New York Times* polls, 21-25 February and 5-8 March.

12. In 1976, however, Ronald Reagan was said to have lost when he came within 2 percent of the front-runner (President Gerald Ford).

13. See Brady and Johnston, "What's the Primary Message?"

14. Thomas E. Patterson, *The Mass Media Election* (New York: Praeger, 1980); Thomas R. Marshall, "The News Verdict and Public Opinion during the Primaries," in *Television Coverage of the 1980 Presidential Campaign*, ed. William C. Adams (Norwood, N.J.: Ablex, 1983), 49-67.

15. F. Christopher Arterton, "Campaign Organizations Confront the Media-Political Environment," *Race for the Presidency*, ed. James David Barber (Englewood Cliffs, N.J.: Prentice-Hall, 1978), 17.

16. New York: Oxford University Press, 1983.

17. David S. Broder, "Braking the Bandwagon."

18. See Michael J. Robinson, "TV's Newest Program: The Presidential Nominating Game," *Public Opinion* 1 (May/June 1978): 41-46.

3

"Locals" and "Cosmopolitans": National, Regional, and State Newspaper Coverage of the New Hampshire Primary

Emmett H. Buell, Jr.

Were it not for the media, the Iowa caucuses and the New Hampshire primary results would be about as relevant to the presidential nomination as opening-day baseball scores are to a pennant race.
— Paletz and Entman, *Media Power Politics*

Here come the animals.
—Walter Mondale, announcing the arrival of his press entourage to a New Hampshire audience

Anyone reading an account of the contemporary presidential nominating process is likely to find news media coverage of the New Hampshire primary characterized, if not denounced, as out of all proportion to the votes cast or the delegates chosen. According to Doris Graber, proportionate to the number of delegates selected, New Hampshire generally gets ten or more times the media coverage of any subsequent primary.[1] 1984 was no different. When *Congressional Quarterly* compared 29 states and the District of Columbia according to Democratic presidential primary turnout, New Hampshire ranked twenty-fourth.[2] And of the 5255 delegates and alternates allowed to attend the San Francisco convention, New Hampshire was entitled to 29, the same number as Idaho. Aside from a few territorial outposts like American Samoa and Guam, only Alaska, Delaware, Nevada, North and South Dakota, and the nation's capital sent smaller delegations.[3] Yet in 1984, as before, the news media amplified the mouse's roar worldwide.[4]

The Ultimate Media Event

In a study of 1976 presidential primary and caucus coverage, Michael Robinson and Karen McPherson found an overwhelming preponderance of New Hampshire news during the "invisible primary."[5] In 1980, according to Robinson and Margaret Sheehan, Iowa and New Hampshire ranked first and second in airtime among 36 state caucuses and primaries covered by CBS. New Hampshire got the most and Iowa second-most UPI copy about primaries and caucuses in 46 states.[6]

How much coverage did the news media lavish on the 1984 New Hampshire primary? Although this analysis mainly focuses on newspapers, a few television facts underscore that New Hampshire is indeed the ultimate media event of each presidential election year. On NBC's half-hour "Nightly News," for example, stories solely about the 1984 New Hampshire Democratic primary consumed 2830 news seconds (over 47 minutes of viewing time) and came to 10.2 percent of that program's coverage of all Democratic caucuses and primaries from 1 October 1983 through 5 June 1984. No other contest, not even crucial southern primaries on Super Tuesday nor those in California or New Jersey, enjoyed as much coverage on NBC. And ABC was even more generous, allocating 4240 news seconds (over 70 minutes) or 16.4 percent of its total evening news time on 1984 Democratic caucuses and primaries to New Hampshire. Finally, CBS invested 5260 news seconds in telling the New Hampshire primary story (almost 90 minutes), fully 19.1 percent of its total 27,545 seconds of news about the entire Democratic race.[7]

Staggering as these statistics may seem, they actually understate the extent of New Hampshire coverage on the respective network evening news shows. "Front-loading" of caucuses and primaries now compels the news media to focus on multiple contests occurring more or less simultaneously. Only eight days separated the Iowa caucuses and New Hampshire primary in 1984, and three states voted within a week of New Hampshire. Fourteen more states held their primaries and caucuses the next week, nine on Super Tuesday. If anything, 1988 promises equally short intervals between early events and even greater concentration with a bigger Super Tuesday and a midwestern regional primary to follow.

A more telling estimate of New Hampshire primary coverage must therefore include stories partly about other contests. In 1984, the three network evening news programs together invested yet another 4610 news seconds in combined Iowa and New Hampshire coverage. They devoted 2450 news seconds more to stories about New Hampshire and subsequent contests in Maine, Vermont, Wyoming, and Super Tuesday states. Add these sums to the 12,330 news seconds of strictly New Hampshire coverage already discussed, and the total

TABLE 3.1

COVERAGE OF 1984 DEMOCRATIC PRESIDENTIAL PRIMARIES AND CAUCUSES
BY THE BOSTON GLOBE, WASHINGTON POST, AND NEW YORK TIMES,
1 OCTOBER 1983 THROUGH 5 JUNE 1984

Event	Globe	Post	Times	All 3
Early straw polls (10/83)				
Column inches	167	138	68	373
% of total	1.2	*	*	*
Iowa caucuses (2/20/84)				
Column inches	483	1089	1031	2603
% of total	3.4	7.4	7.7	6.2
Iowa caucuses/N.H. primary				
Column inches	865	1072	892	2829
% of total	6.2	7.3	6.7	6.7
New Hampshire primary (2/28/84)				
Column inches	2971	1412	1333	5716
% of total	21.2	9.7	10.0	13.6
N.H. primary and later contests				
Column inches	2736	1960	1300	5996
% of total	19.5	13.4	9.8	14.3
Caucuses and primary in Maine/ Wyoming/Vermont (3/4-10/84)				
Column inches	390	270	180	840
% of total	2.8	1.8	1.3	2.0
All Super Tuesday contests (3/13/84)				
Column inches	1929	1794	1136	4859
% of total	13.7	12.3	8.5	11.6
Alaska/Ark./Mich./Miss./S.Car./ P.R. caucuses (3/15-18/84)				
Column inches	194	243	179	616
% of total	1.4	1.7	1.3	1.5
Illinois primary (3/20/84)				
Column inches	273	323	421	1017
% of total	1.9	2.2	3.2	2.4

TABLE 3.1 *(continued)*

Event	Globe	Post	Times	All 3
Illinois and other contests				
Column inches	224	243	223	690
% of total	1.6	1.7	1.7	1.6
Minnesota caucuses (3/20/84) and other contests				
Column inches	0	38	5	43
% of total	0	*	*	*
Kansas/Montana/Virginia caucuses (3/24-26/84)				
Column inches	80	472	88	640
% of total	*	3.2	*	1.5
Connecticut primary (3/27/84) and other contests				
Column inches	121	120	176	417
% of total	*	*	1.3	1.0
New York primary (4/3/84)				
Column inches	557	334	1067	1958
% of total	4.0	2.3	8.0	4.7
New York and other contests				
Column inches	293	343	467	1103
% of total	2.1	2.3	3.5	2.6
Wisconsin primary (4/3/84) and other contests				
Column inches	61	141	172	374
% of total	*	1.0	1.3	*
Pennsylvania primary (4/10/84)				
Column inches	203	145	412	760
% of total	1.4	1.0	3.1	1.8
Pennsylvania and other contests				
Column inches	245	316	310	871
% of total	1.7	2.2	2.3	2.1
Arizona/Missouri caucuses (4/14-24/84)				
Column inches	125	247	205	577
% of total	*	1.7	1.5	1.4

FIGURE 3.1 *(continued)*

Event	Globe	Post	Times	All 3
Guam/Utah caucuses (4/16/84)				
Column inches	3	43	25	71
% of total	*	*	*	*
D.C. primary (5/1/84) and other contests				
Column inches	14	948	18	980
% of total	*	6.5	*	2.3
Tennessee primary (5/1/84) and other contests				
Column inches	58	129	150	337
% of total	*	*	1.1	*
Louisiana primary (5/5/84) and other contests				
Column inches	12	83	82	177
% of total	*	*	*	*
Texas caucuses (5/5/84)				
Column inches	130	124	407	661
% of total	*	*	3.1	1.6
Texas and other contests				
Column inches	270	285	266	821
% of total	1.9	1.9	2.0	1.9
Colorado caucuses (5/7/84) and other contests				
Column inches	0	15	13	28
% of total	0	*	*	*
Indiana/Maryland/N.Carolina/ Ohio primaries (5/8/84)				
Column inches	256	971	610	1837
% of total	1.8	6.6	4.6	4.3
Oregon/Nebraska primaries (5/15/84)				
Column inches	131	183	117	431
% of total	*	1.2	*	1.0
Idaho primary and caucuses (5/23/84)				
Column inches	0	38	16	54
% of total	0	*	*	*

FIGURE 3.1 *(continued)*

Event	Globe	Post	Times	All 3
California/New Jersey/New Mexico/S. Dakota/W. Virginia primaries (6/5/84)				
Column inches	1239	1100	1945	4284
% of total	8.8	7.5	14.6	10.2
Total column inches	14,030	14,619	13,314	41,963

* Less than 1 percent of total column inches.

time all three networks spent on the first primary, one way or another, comes to an incredible 19,390 news seconds. This was more than 5 hours of viewing time and just under one-quarter of the total volume of network evening news of 1984 Democratic primaries and caucuses.[8]

Table 3.1 (pp. 62-65) compares the primary and caucus coverage of three major newspapers—the *Boston Globe, Washington Post,* and *New York Times* —over the same period, 1 October 1983 to 5 June 1984. The data for this tabulation consisted of all news stories, news feature articles, and brief news notes about the 1984 Democratic primaries and caucuses published in the three newspapers.[9]

Once again the New Hampshire mouse got the lion's share of coverage. With newspaper column inches as the basis of comparison, New Hampshire was foremost among primary and caucus stories. The *Washington Post* and *New York Times* each allocated about 10 percent of all respective space for news of 1984 Democratic primaries and caucuses to items solely about New Hampshire. No doubt responding to its New England readership, the *Globe* was twice as generous to New Hampshire. Like the *Globe,* the *Post* and *Times* paid particular attention to primaries and caucuses nearest home. Therefore, the *Times* did much more with the New York and New Jersey primaries than the *Globe* or *Post,* and the *Post* offered much more on the Virginia caucuses, and the Maryland and D.C. primaries than the *Times* or *Globe* did. But, as the table shows, none of these local contests matched New Hampshire's coverage in the *Post* or *Times.*

The table also reflects the aforementioned calendar compression, for many items clearly were about more than one contest. Taking these data into consideration underscores once again the first primary's importance. Indeed, these major newspapers were even more preoccupied with the New Hampshire story than the networks were. Counting all items in which it figured prominently, whether alone or linked to other contests, New Hampshire got 46.9 percent of all space the *Globe* set aside for news of 1984 Democratic primaries and caucuses. It claimed 30.4 percent of all such space in the *Post* and 26.5 percent in the *Times*. And, to show how much timing determines the newsworthiness of nominating events, adding Iowa's coverage to New Hampshire's reveals that the three newspapers combined set aside about 41 percent of their caucus and primary "newshole" for the first caucuses and the first primary.

Why New Hampshire?

The foremost reason for New Hampshire's extraordinary coverage is that this primary is the first real test of ordinary voter preference in a presidential election year, impressive turnout in the Iowa caucuses notwithstanding. Voting first has given the New Hampshire primary enormous influence over all subsequent state nominating events. This is partly so because New Hampshire narrows the choice. Reubin Askew, Alan Cranston, and Ernest Hollings dropped out after the 1984 primary; Gary Hart's poll standings, financial support, and media coverage soared.

Fully aware of their clout in the present nominating system, New Hampshire officials have repeatedly demonstrated their resolve to keep their primary first. State law provides for a presidential primary on the first Tuesday in March of each presidential election year or on the Tuesday preceding any "similar election." An attempt to move the primary back one week in 1984 resulted in a prolonged struggle in which state election law ultimately prevailed over national Democratic rules. New Hampshire politicians are no less determined to be first in 1988.

Going first also means that Iowa and New Hampshire residents see more of presidential candidates than anybody else. Walter Mondale effectively began campaigning there three years early, and spent 30 days in the state during the final 12 months. John Glenn first turned up in New Hampshire to speak at a fund-raiser for the late Governor Hugh Gallen in 1981. He campaigned 32 days in New Hampshire in the year before the 28 February primary. Several dark horses virtually took up residence in the Granite State—Hart 52 days between late January 1983 and primary election day, Hollings about 60 days during the same period, and Askew over 70 days.[10] Only in Iowa did the 1984 candidates make a similar effort.

The importance of the nation's first primary to the news media virtually guarantees that every serious candidate will make nothing less than an all-out effort in New Hampshire. "A kind of circular process goes on here," Elizabeth Drew wrote in 1984; "the results of the New Hampshire contest receive disproportionate attention because of where it comes in the calendar, and, because of that attention, the candidates put a disproportionate amount of their energy and resources into the contest."[11] Held hostage to the deliberations of slightly more than 100,000 voters, no incumbent President seeking another term will likely repeat Harry Truman's "eyewash" gaffe of 1952. Sitting Presidents may not brave Manchester's icy sidewalks or navigate Nashua's slush like other candidates, but since 1968 and LBJ's narrow write-in victory over Eugene McCarthy, they have gotten their names on the ballot and sent others to campaign in their place. Even in 1984, when Ronald Reagan's chief New Hampshire adversary was Harold Stassen, Vice-President George Bush paid a visit to GOP party workers in the Granite State. Like incumbents, front-runners dare not ignore this primary, as Adlai Stevenson did in 1956. Incumbents and front-runners are alike in one other respect. They must win by enough votes to satisfy media expectations. Finally, the New Hampshire primary is no less critical for dark horses, as none is likely to break out of the "second tier" without astonishing the press in Iowa or New Hampshire. In short, since 1976, when the late Senator Henry Jackson followed some bad advice and left New Hampshire to Jimmy Carter, every serious Democratic candidate has come into this primary with money, marbles, and chalk. Republicans regard it with equal gravity; none is likely to repeat John Connally's 1980 mistake of passing up New Hampshire for a later contest.[12]

Another reason why New Hampshire is so amply covered is because it has become a venerable media tradition, "as much a staple in the national political diet as national conventions, election day in November, or a President's inauguration."[13] Scribes from the networks, wire services, news magazines, major newspapers, newspaper chains, and numerous foreign media gather in familiar haunts for what James Perry describes as "part reunion, part convention, part warm-up for what's to come."[14] In his final book the late Theodore H. White contrasted the seven reporters following Estes Kefauver during the last week of the 1956 New Hampshire primary with the 450 or so he encountered at the end of the 1980 primary. Altogether, White estimated, over a thousand media personnel were in the state for primary election day.[15] And what does the media make of this tradition? Michael J. Robinson has a succinct answer:

> The tradition? Emphasize anybody who wins in New Hampshire, especially if he wins unexpectedly. Every campaign manager, journalist, and pundit knows this convention in journalism before the game starts. Front-runners bank on it. Challengers borrow on it. This is, in the last analysis, the power of the press "convention" as much as anything else.[16]

Rivals in Conformity?

Now that we know how much coverage the New Hampshire primary gets and why it is so newsworthy, let us briefly consider how campaigns are reported. Two generalizations almost always turn up in the burgeoning academic literature on campaign journalism. First, journalists define news in ways more instinctive and subjective than objective; and, second, the news media are remarkably alike in selecting all the news fit to print or broadcast.

As to the first generalization, the absence of fixed and objective criteria should not be misinterpreted to mean there are no rules-of-thumb governing news coverage. Editors and reporters prefer action over inaction, conflict to harmony, the familiar to the foreign, and celebrities to ordinary people.[17] Applied to presidential contests, these conventions promote coverage of campaign dynamics more than discussion of issues, debates more than noncontroversial speeches, and front-runners more than conventional dark horses.

Apparent consensus on what constitutes news lends support to the second generalization positing similarity of coverage. "No matter which network or major newspaper an American voter depends on for news," Thomas Marshall concluded from his 1980 research, "that reader or viewer will likely receive a similar picture of how each candidate is faring in the nomination struggle."[18] After much analysis of election news content, Graber observed that reporters "everywhere selected the same kinds of stories and emphasized the same types of facts, despite the wealth of diverse materials available to them."[19] Findings by Robinson and Sheehan, based on UPI and CBS coverage of the 1980 presidential campaigns, affirmed this striking uniformity.[20]

There are various explanations for similar news coverage, one being an argument that common training and experience on the job develop the same news instincts in most journalists. One offshoot of this professional socialization is a general commitment to objective reporting. However subjectively facts are selected, according to Herbert Gans, journalists strive to be objective both in intent and effect. This partly consists of personal detachment from the people they write about or the consequences of what they write.[21] Objective journalism is also empirical in its documentation and corroboration of information. Yet, as nearly all journalists acknowledge, campaign reporting cannot avoid selective presentation of facts. Robinson and Sheehan pick up on this point to argue that contemporary campaign reporting is better described as "objectivistic" than objective, or "in the manner of being objective."[22] A strong professional commitment to accuracy informs factual selection, but the facts selected add up to only part of the whole truth.

Helping to standardize factual selection is that much maligned phenomenon of "pack journalism"—the close professional and social interaction among reporters following the same campaign. Timothy Crouse has argued that campaign reporting is simply pack journalism by another name. "Even the most independent journalist," he avows, "cannot completely escape the pressures of the pack."[23] The process is most obvious on press planes or buses, where reporters swap impressions, verify quotes, try out interpretations, and judge one another's work. Stories notably deviant from the general consensus will almost certainly be challenged by other reporters. Often adding to pressures for similarity as well as high standards is the presence of a David Broder, Curtis Wilkie, or another highly esteemed reporter.

Reporters are also impelled toward similar stories by their own news organizations. Lashed to deadlines, limited in news space, and lacking enough resources to cover every candidate in a crowded field equally, editors select only some of all possible stories about the campaign. In this connection, Nelson Polsby characterizes news competition as chiefly a race to report the same information and notes the discomfiture of editors with stories notably at variance with those of other news organzations. The upshot, according to Polsby, is "news convergence."[24] Or, as one of the boys on Crouse's bus put it, editors have an abiding interest "in making sure that nobody else has got anything they don't have, not getting something that nobody else has."[25]

In what specific ways is news coverage of presidential primaries similar? At least four emerge from the literature: (1) unequal treatment of candidates; (2) much more attention to the "horse race" or campaign dynamics than to substantive issues of public policy; (3) relatively little discussion of candidate qualifications for office or their personal backgrounds; and (4) much ado about candidate gaffes or campaign blunders.

Unequal Candidate Coverage

In contrast to general election coverage of the Democratic and Republican nominees, newspapers and other media do not give equal coverage to all serious contenders for their party's nomination. Robinson and Sheehan have developed this point more than anyone else with a "journalistic triage" model in which news media favor front-runners and plausible challengers while slighting seemingly hopeless rivals.[26] Unless Iowa and New Hampshire force revision of the media pecking order, coverage is allocated on the basis of national poll standings, endorsements, and evidence of successful fund raising. Polls loom largest in these calculations, indeed so much so that we have Bill Plante's "law of press scrutiny": "The degree of scrutiny a candidate receives increases in direct proportion to his standing in the polls."[27] William C. Adams found this more or less true of very early coverage of 1984 Democratic candidates in the *Washington Post* and *New York Times,* and on network evening news telecasts.[28]

If Gallup polls can be likened to cardiac screens, then the nomination support most Democratic dark horses exhibited in surveys from December 1982 until the eve of the Iowa caucuses in February 1984 must have looked to the news media like ventricular fibrillation — or that faint and likely false series of blips preceding death — however much national media inattention may have helped keep these candidates in extremis. Hollings appeared to be in worst shape during this polling period, with support for his nomination peaking at 2 percent of all Democrats sampled and 3 percent of the Independents sampled nationwide, but flattening out at 1 point among the Democrats in the final six polls before Iowa. Askew's readings were equally feeble. In October 1983 his Independent support dropped to a fraction of a percent, and he never exceeded 3 percent among Democrats in the final six polls before Iowa. Hart was hardly robust during this polling period, starting as another asterisk and topping out at 4 and 5 percent among Democrats and Independents, respectively. One week before Iowa, only 3 percent of the Democrats and as many Independents favored his nomination. Seven percent of the Democrats and Independents alike in July 1983 wanted Cranston to get the nod, but not much of this sentiment survived the summer. By February 1984, his support in each group was down to 3 percent.[29]

Unlike the aforementioned dark horses, George McGovern entered the fray in 1984 with very high name recognition, higher indeed than John Glenn. Yet no more than 10 percent of the Democrats in Gallup's polls before Iowa favored another McGovern nomination.[30] To the extent the news media followed the polls in his case, they followed the trend on nomination support.

Jesse Jackson's coverage can only be described as unique with little correlation with national poll standings or any other measure of candidate viability.[31] Already a celebrity, being "the first serious black presidential candidate" made him far more newsworthy than other candidates with comparable prospects.

Long shots are never slow to hold the press responsible for consistently poor national poll ratings. After pulling out of the 1984 race, McGovern contended that only Glenn and Mondale had gotten substantial coverage before Iowa—"not because of their records, their characters, or their convictions, but because of their high standings in early public opinion polls, their large campaign war chests, and their big campaign staffs."[32] Askew's issues coordinator ruefully recalled how seldom his candidate got on the evening news: "We were working very hard in Iowa, but being increasingly ignored. We found it hard to believe we could be ignored any more, but we were."[33]

Dark horses also often resent the tone and spin of what national press coverage they do receive. According to Robinson and Sheehan, candidates classified initially as hopeless get mostly "death-watch" coverage, consisting of stories mentioning low poll ratings, flagging finances, depressed supporters, and even rumors of quitting. More positive material is consigned to funereal stories written after these campaigns have folded.[34] "I cannot recall any other presidential contender in recent years," McGovern wrote of the news stories, columns, and editorials about his 1984 effort, "who received more scathing press coverage at the start of a campaign and more complimentary coverage at the end."[35] A former Hollings aide claimed his candidate was crippled by such coverage even before formally declaring.[36] And the co-chair of Hart's New Hampshire campaign wrote about her candidate's early treatment by the national press with some asperity:

> In New Hampshire, people were convinced of Hart's capabilities and they were attracted to his message. . . . But the national press coverage reinforced the notion that Mondale was inevitable and that Hart had no chance of winning. Because of that, people hesitated to work for Hart, to think seriously about supporting Hart, even to vote for Hart. . . . As long as the national press presented Hart's case as a futile exercise, our job was ten times more difficult.[37]

HORSE RACE VERSUS ISSUES COVERAGE

Probably the most criticized aspect of campaign journalism is its preoccupation with covering the "game" or "horse race," with trying to find out "who is ahead, who is behind, who is gaining, who is losing, what campaign strategy is being followed, and what the impact of campaign activities is on the candidate's chances of winning."[38] In his 1984 postmortem, for example, McGovern accused the press of neglecting "proper inquiry, analysis, and truthtelling as to where candidates stand on important public concerns."[39] In this he has been joined by a legion of academics. "Issue material is but a rivulet in the news flow during the primaries," Thomas E. Patterson wrote of 1976 newspaper and television coverage, "and what is there is almost completely diluted by information about the race."[40] Nevertheless, unlike watching television news, Patterson allowed readers could learn at least something from daily newspaper reading. More recently, F. Christopher Arterton pointed out that many news stories are about both horse race and issues, but conceded that most of the latter coverage was thin.[41] Robinson and Sheehan likened standard issue reporting in 1980 to Cliff Notes for undergraduate courses in public policy.[42] Rare words of praise for the media came from Henry Brady, who found news of candidate stands on issues in 16 percent of the UPI copy he analyzed about the 1984 Democratic presidential struggle.[43]

Before Iowa, of course, reporters have to make do without hard indicators (e.g., votes or delegates) of the horse race. Candidates try to sell the press scenarios of how the race will unfold, while skeptical reporters try to establish specific benchmarks.[44] Among the 1984 candidates, Mondale enjoyed the most success in selling his inevitability scenario to reporters, but, of course, New Hampshire changed all that. Yet, Mondale was careful throughout the New Hampshire campaign not to give the press a precise benchmark. Asked repeatedly to predict the margin of his impending victory in the first primary, Mondale replied that a victory of any size was enough.

SPARSE COVERAGE OF PERSONAL BACKGROUNDS AND QUALIFICATIONS
According to Graber, the news media provide substantial information about the personal and political backgrounds of major-party nominees for the Presidency. This was not true of coverage leading up to these nominations, however. In 1976, she found more discussion of "issues and events" than "presidential qualifications" despite the unfamiliarity of most potential nominees to most citizens.[45] In 1980, Robinson and Sheehan found virtually no UPI or CBS coverage of any primary candidate's "life, background, personality, family, or character."[46]

After Hart surprised them in New Hampshire four years later, however, the news media took great interest in Hart's personal affairs and family background. Initially favorable coverage soon changed after Hart could not satisfy reporters asking about his altered birthdate, name and signature change. By Super Tuesday, his television coverage had decidedly soured. Robinson compared Hart's treatment during this time to that suffered by Gerald Ford immediately after the Nixon pardon. By the end of Super Tuesday, he concluded, Hart's "electoral magic had ended."[47]

According to Jack Germond and Jules Witcover, it was the "raw material" in Hart's background rather than any media cabal that made him vulnerable to this treatment.[48] Hart's supporters have countered that this was "search and destroy" journalism out of pique for having been proven so wrong.[49] Whatever the truth, Hart's coverage after New Hampshire shows that the press can delve into candidate backgrounds when it suits their purpose.

GAFFES AND BLUNDERS
Another much-noted pattern of campaign coverage is emphasis on candidate mistakes. When candidates stumble, as in Jackson's "Hymie" reminiscences, the best hope for ending what could become a long-running and debilitating "candidate issue" or "press crisis" is prompt and public contrition. Jackson chose to dissemble and so suffered much adverse publicity in the critical week before primary election day in New Hampshire. Estimates of Hymie's impact on voters there vary, some saying 10 percentage points in local polls, but all agree it was

substantial.[50] In any event, the long New Hampshire primary campaign holds out many opportunities to blunder, as George Romney discovered after his "brainwashing" confession of 1968, and Edmund Muskie learned four years later.[51]

News Media Responses

Before determining how prevalent the above patterns were in newspaper coverage of the 1984 New Hampshire primary, we should note that journalists are hardly defenseless against such charges. Responding directly to the inequality issue, for example, David Broder argued that (1) there was no fairness doctrine for candidates seeking presidential nominations; (2) journalists were obliged to find out how much support candidates had; and (3) unequal coverage in the past had not prevented dark horses from winning early primaries. In the same article, Walter Robinson defended his and other newspapers by pointing out that unequal coverage was not necessarily inadequate coverage.[52]

This last point can be extended to coverage of issues as well. Most reporting in this vein consists of what candidates have to say on questions of public policy. During the period observed for this research, the *Boston Globe* published a substantial profile of each candidate containing some information regarding issues; the *New York Times* ran full-page transcripts of interviews setting out the policy stands of all eight candidates; and the *Washington Post* printed two series on each candidate's personal background, political experience, and platform. True, such articles were relatively infrequent, but they did set out where the candidates stood. The second *Post* series was particularly rich in detail, as is illustrated by the following account of McGovern's ideas for dealing with Cuba and Central America:

> If he were elected President, McGovern said he would immediately withdraw all U.S. troops from Lebanon and terminate American support for guerrilla fighting in Central America.
>
> In place of soldiers, he would send in diplomats—special envoys, or the President himself—to try to deal with foreign adversaries. "You just can't underestimate the value of face-to-face diplomacy to deal with these differences."
>
> McGovern said he feels strongly, for example, that the time has come to cut a deal with Cuba's Fidel Castro.
>
> "We could have him in a cooperative relationship with the United States if we'd go after him," he said, "I would begin conversations looking to the exchange of ambassadors . . . and lifting of the trade embargo . . . so that instead of fighting at every turn in Central America, we'd have at least a working relationship of some kind with him."

In return, McGovern said, the United States would have to replace financial aid that Cuba receives from the Soviet Union. Still, he argued, "you'd save a lot of money" overall because Castro would be expected, in return, to work together with the United States to diminish Soviet influence in the hemisphere and to find peaceful resolution of intra-American disputes.[53]

Even when issue coverage is shallow, the press cannot always be held responsible. Candidates are often at fault, since their interests are sometimes served by saying as little of substance as possible on controversial issues. Not for nothing was Mondale dubbed "the cautious candidate." Some candidates instinctively repeat campaign slogans with all the spontaneity of recorded messages. Alan Cranston was particularly prone to such lapses in 1984. Still others, like George Bush in 1980, much prefer campaign dynamics to issues as topics of conversation with reporters.[54] Thus thin-issue coverage cannot always be blamed on the press, nor should its presence be taken as evidence of journalistic unwillingness to probe candidates. After one of Glenn's attacks on Mondale's support of "failed policies of the past," for example, reporters pushed the Ohioan hard to name Carter-Mondale programs he had voted against in the Senate.[55]

Yet another problem is agreement on what constitutes an "issue." Graber notes a distinct candidate preference for fairly general thematic pitches such as "peace and jobs" or "new ideas," whereas reporters want candidates to commit themselves on more specific topics likely to provoke conflict.[56] Evidently this press disinclination to report general appeals informed one recent study's finding that Mondale and Hart enjoyed little success in getting their respective "fairness" and "new ideas" themes into selected newspapers.[57]

Finally, of course, members of the fourth estate generally prefer the horse race because it is news. Glenn's slippage in national public opinion polls was news; his fifteenth repetition of a five-point plan for arms control was not. Moreover, news of the horse race is easy to document with hard information consisting of poll standings, Federal Election Commission (FEC) figures, and actual endorsements. Issue reporting is not so straightforward, especially when available information is highly technical, biased, or heavily qualified. When Glenn and Mondale wrangled over deficit-reduction plans, for example, their exchange soon bogged down in a swamp of conflicting assumptions.

Some Caveats

Much of the literature reviewed above disparages campaign journalism and its practitioners. One seldom finds tough criticism of unequal coverage, horse-race reporting, or pack journalism balanced by acknowledgment of the skill, political knowledge, and high standards reporters bring to their craft. Anyone who has taken part in a presidential campaign, or followed one for an extended time, knows how brutal its demands can be. After his stint on press buses and planes, Crouse likened the requisite physical rigors of campaign reporting to those of the Long March.[58] Although each day on the bus varies in certain respects, the day itself is likely filled with repetitous, ritualistic, and often contrived events. Richard Joslyn is hardly alone in wondering how long reporters can offer new insights or fresh information under such circumstances.[59] Reporters on the press bus or plane often ask themselves the same question. News organizations can help somewhat by rotating personnel, but the basic challenge remains: Find something newsworthy in the day's events to report, write a factually accurate account under conditions allowing little privacy or opportunity for reflection, and file under a deadline. Small wonder that reporters frequently consult one another, fasten on the horse race, and promote conflict between candidates.

A second caveat is that the news media may not cover presidential primaries as similarly as the literature suggests. Robinson and Sheehan hinted at possible differences between wire services and major newspapers, for example, but did not follow up on the point. Major newspapers like the *Post, Times,* and *Globe* might also differ importantly from much smaller newspapers based in the primary states. Hart certainly saw differences in the way national and local newspapers reported the early days of his 1984 campaign:

> In Dubuque or Colorado Springs, I am treated as a viable candidate. The reporter does not feel the need to characterize my campaign as faltering, halting, stumbling, or any of the rest of those gratuitous words. Routinely, even in the tiniest papers, that is the coverage: three-quarters quotes from what I said, and they get it right, and at most a mention that I am "one of the dark horse candidates."[60]

Even if reporters working for smaller newspapers have gotten the same journalistic training as their counterparts on the *Post* or *Times,* there are at least four good reasons to anticipate significant differences in major and local newspaper coverage of the New Hampshire primary. First, local newspapers are more interested in reporting the campaign involvement of area people than out-of-state papers are. Second, dark horses in New Hampshire generally cater to the local media in hopes of compensating for what they regard as inadequate national press. Local newspapers might respond with more egalitarian coverage. Third, the pack in "pack journalism" probably does not include the local press. Reporters for New Hampshire newspapers seldom rode on campaign press buses during the 1984 primary campaign, and although covering many of the same events as the traveling press, they seemed to have little social or professional interaction with their national media counterparts.[61] Finally, national and local media cover members of Congress quite differently.[62] Why not candidates in presidential primaries as well, especially if the primary occurs at home?

Locals and Cosmopolitans

The five newspapers chosen for comparison for this study were the *Washington Post*, *New York Times*, *Boston Globe*, *Concord Monitor*, and *Manchester Union Leader*. The *Post* and *Times* are regarded as newspapers of national record and so qualify as "cosmopolitans." With its regional hegemony, national coverage, and nationally respected correspondents, the *Globe* too is a cosmopolitan newspaper. In contrast, the *Monitor's* readership is limited chiefly to New Hampshire's capital city and surrounding Merrimack County. Highly regarded in New Hampshire for its coverage of state news, the *Monitor* clearly is a "local" newspaper. And, despite its national notoriety, the *Union Leader's* predominant concern with New Hampshire affairs also deserves a local designation.[63]

The cosmopolitan-local distinction is hardly absolute, for as noted earlier, each cosmopolitan paper devoted substantially more news space to primaries and caucuses of greatest interest to local readers. Nevertheless, each cosmopolitan covered the 1984 Democratic race, from initial straw polls to Mondale's nomination in San Francisco, with its own reporters. The *Monitor* and *Union Leader* relied on wire-service reports for news of all contests outside New Hampshire.

For the *Post* and *Times*, New Hampshire was the most important contest of all those deciding the nomination. It was this plus a story of compelling regional interest for the *Globe*. And for the *Monitor* and *Union Leader*, it was the most important local news story in four years. Support for these distinctions is found in the two localism indexes of table 3.2.

TABLE 3.2

LOCALISM INDEXES

	Washington Post	New York Times	Boston Globe	Concord Monitor	Manchester Union Leader
News items[a]	51%	57%	71%	97%	96%
Editorials[b]	5	1	2	19	64

a. News items about New Hampshire primary as percentage of all 1984 Democratic primary and caucus news items, 1 October 1983-2 March 1984.
b. Editorials about the New Hampshire primary, in five newspapers, 1 October 1983-2 March 1984.

One localism measure was the extent New Hampshire primary news dominated each paper's coverage of the 1984 Democratic race. The period observed began 1 October 1983 and ended 2 March 1984, three days after the first primary. Table 3.2 shows the results of adding the New Hampshire percentage of each paper's total Democratic primary and caucus news items. The measure is straightforward: Higher percentages indicate greater localism. We would expect localism to increase with direct relevance to readers, and this was indeed the case.

A second localism measure was the number of editorials each newspaper published about the New Hampshire primary. Contrary to expectations, the *Post* published more such editorials than the *Globe,* but otherwise the cosmopolitan-local distinction remained intact. The *Monitor* editorialized about the primary more often than all three cosmopolitan papers combined, and the *Union Leader* ran three times as many of these editorials as the *Monitor.* Moreover, in keeping with tradition established by its late publisher, 11 of the 64 *Union Leader* editorials appeared on the front page.

Table 3.3 compares all five newspapers according to circulation, reporters writing regularly (five or more news stories over the entire period) about the

TABLE 3.3

FIVE NEWSPAPERS COMPARED BY CIRCULATION AND 1984 NEW HAMPSHIRE PRIMARY COVERAGE FROM 1 OCTOBER 1983 THROUGH 2 MARCH 1984

	Post	*Times*	*Globe*	*Monitor*	*Union Leader*
Monday-Saturday circulation in 1983-84	728,857	934,530	520,081	20,647	69,882
New Hampshire Monday-Saturday circulation	*	3,996	29,147	20,647	69,882
Total news items about N.H. primary	123	126	233	373	354
Reporters writing 5 or more N.H. primary news stories	7	8	6	12	7
Total column inches of N.H. primary news	3,001	2,712	4,768	7,401	4,880

SOURCE: For Audit Bureau of Circulation figures, *Editor & Publisher International Yearbook* (New York: Editor & Publisher, 1985), chap. 1.

* *Washington Post* New Hampshire circulation assumed negligible. "News items" included all stories, feature articles, and brief news notes.

New Hampshire primary, and total column inches of news and opinion copy devoted to the primary. Several points in this table are noteworthy.

One obvious disparity in 1984 was the vast difference in weekday circulation. Each cosmopolitan newspaper was a Goliath in this respect, boasting 500,000 or more subscribers, while the two locals had fewer than 100,000 between them. The *Globe* showed its regional muscle with 8500 more Monday-through-Saturday subscribers in New Hampshire than the *Monitor*, and its Sunday readership of 61,112 (not shown in the table) posed a growing threat to the *Union Leader*'s twin, the *New Hampshire Sunday News* (80,278).[64]

Despite the enormous differences in organizational resources suggested by these figures, the local newspaper with the smallest overall newshole supplied the biggest volume of primary news, whether measured in number of items or total column inches. With a dozen reporters regularly assigned to the primary, the *Monitor*'s effort was no less than prodigious.

A final noteworthy contrast in this table was between the *Union Leader* and *Globe*. On the one hand, the *Union Leader* published substantially more New Hampshire primary news items than the *Globe*: 354 to 233. Yet the difference in total column inches of New Hampshire primary news for these papers was negligible. This discrepancy is easily explained by the *Union Leader*'s extensive reliance on brief notes to report news of the primary.

Data and Findings

The unit of analysis for most of this research was the "news item," whether news story, feature news article, or brief news note, and the full dataset included 1209 such items.[65] Table 3.4 shows the breakdown of stories, features, and news notes for each newspaper and reveals the *Union Leader*'s penchant for brief news notes. These items constituted the total New Hampshire primary news coverage of each paper between 1 October 1983 and 2 March 1984.[66] Let us now enlist these data in an analysis of each newspaper's coverage of the 1984 primary.

UNEQUAL CANDIDATE COVERAGE

How unequal was the candidate coverage in each newspaper's reporting of the New Hampshire primary, and did locals treat dark horses better than cosmopolitans? Before these questions can be answered, "coverage" must be operationally defined. Since choice of indicators so often influences findings, this research made use of several.

One gauge of coverage was the number of times a candidate made news-item headlines. This was perhaps the most obvious indicator of candidate prom-

TABLE 3.4

BREAKDOWN OF NEWS ITEMS IN NEW HAMPSHIRE PRIMARY COVERAGE
OF FIVE NEWSPAPERS, I OCTOBER 1983 THROUGH 2 MARCH 1984

	Post	Times	Globe	Monitor	Union Leader	All Five Papers
Stories	85	106	144	239	217	791
Features	14	10	48	89	40	201
Notes	24	10	41	45	97	217
Total	123	126	233	373	354	1209

inence, and other things being equal, front-runners were expected to enjoy an enormous advantage. When a story was about all or most of the candidates, in other words, who should be included in the headline other than the most newsworthy? Early outcomes in Iowa and New Hampshire greatly influence such determinations, of course, and in 1984 Iowa's impact was profound. So, breaking down the headline count into before- and after-Iowa tallies made sense.

Table 3.5 shows that indeed it did, at least insofar as cosmopolitan papers were concerned. Before Iowa caucused, Mondale and Glenn led the count by comfortable margins in the *Post, Times,* and *Globe.* In contrast, McGovern did not get into a single *Post* headline. Askew made only one. He fared no better in the *Times,* which headlined Hollings only once. Except for Hart and Jackson mentions in *Globe* headlines, dark horses lagged far behind Mondale and Glenn in the Boston paper. One way in which Hart replaced Glenn after Iowa was in the headlines of all three cosmopolitan papers. Unexpectedly finishing a fairly close third in Iowa did little for McGovern in this respect. Askew, Cranston, and Hollings found their way into more *Globe* headlines in the week after Iowa than in the preceding several months, but this was because of death-watch coverage after their poor caucus performances.

Before or after Iowa, the *Monitor* appeared downright egalitarian, in contrast to the cosmopolitan papers. True, Askew, Cranston, Hollings, and McGovern did not get in as many headlines as the front-runners, but the *Monitor* still named them in twice as many as the *Post, Times,* and *Globe* combined. It also gave front-runners substantially less of an edge. Indeed, the *Monitor* featured Jackson in this way more than any other candidate before Iowa. After Iowa, the *Monitor* put Glenn and Hollings, of all people, in as many headlines as Mondale.

Before Iowa the *Union Leader* somewhat resembled the *Globe* in its headline count, although Glenn led Mondale on this measure. One interesting *Union Leader* difference from all other newspapers during this period was its treat-

TABLE 3.5

HEADLINES NAMING DEMOCRATIC CANDIDATES IN
NEW HAMPSHIRE PRIMARY COVERAGE OF FIVE NEWSPAPERS,
BEFORE AND AFTER IOWA CAUCUSES

			Before Caucuses			
Candidate	Post	Times	Globe	Monitor	Union Leader	All Five Papers
Askew	1	1	3	13	8	26
Cranston	6	6	4	21	10	47
Glenn	16	17	33	31	26	123
Hart	5	4	10	22	6	47
Hollings	3	1	4	16	13	37
Jackson	7	4	10	34	17	72
McGovern	0	3	3	16	8	30
Mondale	24	19	36	32	24	135
			After Caucuses			
Askew	1	1	5	4	0	11
Cranston	2	1	6	5	1	15
Glenn	3	7	7	10	5	32
Hart	13	13	15	12	7	60
Hollings	3	2	5	10	2	22
Jackson	4	3	9	7	8	31
McGovern	2	2	5	8	3	20
Mondale	13	11	18	10	8	60

NOTE: Many headlines named more than one candidate.

ment of Hart, whom it headlined less often than any other candidate. No other paper during this time put Askew or McGovern in more headlines than Hart or put Hollings in twice as many. After Iowa, the *Union Leader* left Askew out of its headlines and billed Hart, Jackson, and Mondale equally.

In sum, important differences between local and cosmopolitan papers surfaced when compared on who made their headlines. The *Post, Times,* and *Globe* consistently favored front-runners over dark horses, generally by whopping ratios before Iowa. This practice continued after Iowa, only with Hart replacing Glenn as Mondale's plausible alternative. If dark horses wanted to see their names in big type, the *Monitor* was their best bet.

Each candidate's coverage was also measured by counting the number of New Hampshire primary news items mentioning him before and after the Iowa caucuses. This measure happily generated more cases than any other but made no distinction between passing and prominent mentions. Even so, it affirmed

TABLE 3.6

PERCENTAGE OF NEW HAMPSHIRE PRIMARY NEWS ITEMS MENTIONING
CANDIDATES BEFORE AND AFTER IOWA CAUCUSES

			Before Caucuses		
Candidate	Post	Times	Globe	Monitor	Union Leader
Askew	29	32	39	28	18
Cranston	52	46	42	40	24
Glenn	64	67	72	45	30
Hart	44	44	52	40	24
Hollings	29	31	43	32	23
Jackson	39	42	46	37	24
McGovern	27	32	39	30	17
Mondale	73	78	73	54	40
			After Caucuses		
Askew	44	29	27	29	21
Cranston	50	38	29	36	22
Glenn	69	53	44	47	32
Hart	83	73	57	52	35
Hollings	52	40	29	39	26
Jackson	62	49	32	41	34
McGovern	58	44	31	37	27
Mondale	90	78	70	65	49
(Pre-Iowa N)	(75)	(81)	(145)	(272)	(245)
(Post-Iowa N)	(48)	(45)	(88)	(101)	(109)

the inequality of candidate coverage. Table 3.6 shows that this inequality was most pronounced in the three cosmopolitan papers.

Before Iowa, for example, 78 percent of all *Times* news items about the New Hampshire primary mentioned Mondale; so did 73 percent of all *Post* and *Globe* items. Glenn followed with mentions in 64 percent of all *Post* items, 67 percent of all *Times* items, and 72 percent of all *Globe* items. McGovern got the short end of this stick, appearing in only 27 percent of all *Post* items, 32 percent of those in the *Times,* and 39 percent in the *Globe.*

After Iowa rearranged the race, fully 90 percent of all *Post* news items about the New Hampshire primary made reference to Mondale. His *Times* and *Globe* coverage in this respect remained as preponderant as before. Hart's coverage in the *Post* and *Times* proved the value of doing better than expected. The *Post* had mentioned him in 44 percent of its New Hampshire news items before Iowa; in the week after Iowa, it referred to him in 83 percent of its items. Hart's cov-

TABLE 3.7

DID THE NEWSPAPERS DIFFER SIGNIFICANTLY IN CANDIDATE MENTIONS?

| | | Before Iowa Caucuses | | |
Candidate	Three Cosmopolitans	Two Locals	Three Cosmopolitans and *Monitor*	Three Cosmopolitans and *Union Leader*
Askew	no	yes[a]	no	yes[c]
Cranston	no	yes[c]	no	yes[b]
Glenn	no	yes[c]	yes[c]	yes[c]
Hart	no	yes[c]	no	yes[c]
Hollings	no	yes[a]	no	yes[c]
Jackson	no	yes[b]	no	yes[c]
McGovern	no	yes[c]	no	yes[c]
Mondale	no	yes[c]	yes[c]	yes[c]
		After Iowa Caucuses		
Askew	no	no	no	yes[a]
Cranston	no	yes[a]	no	yes[b]
Glenn	yes[a]	yes[a]	yes[a]	yes[c]
Hart	yes[b]	yes[a]	yes[c]	yes[c]
Hollings	yes[a]	no	no	yes[b]
Jackson	yes[b]	no	yes[b]	yes[b]
McGovern	yes[b]	no	yes[a]	yes[c]
Mondale	yes[a]	yes[a]	yes[a]	yes[c]

NOTE: Yates corrective used in test for *Monitor* versus *Union Leader*.

a. p is less than .05.
b. p is less than .01.
c. p is less than .001.

erage also took off in the *Times*. The *Globe* mentioned him more frequently after Iowa but not so often as the *Post* and *Times*. Even so, Hart's coverage in the *Globe* during this later period was second only to Mondale's.

The *Monitor* and *Union Leader* generally gave front-runners much less of an advantage over their rivals on this measure. For example, almost as many *Monitor* and *Union Leader* news items named Cranston and Hart as Glenn before Iowa. After Iowa, the *Union Leader* mentioned Jackson and Glenn in almost as many items as Hart. In sum, the two local papers put dark horses in more news items than their cosmopolitan counterparts and thereby reduced front-runner advantage.

Were newspaper differences in candidate coverage statistically significant? The academic literature's heavy emphasis on similarity of campaign coverage suggests a null hypothesis (no significant differences), at least among the three cosmopolitans. Table 3.7 reports the results of chi-square tests in comparisons of (1) all three cosmopolitans; (2) both locals; (3) the cosmopolitans and *Monitor;* and (4) the cosmopolitans and *Union Leader*—both before and after Iowa changed the media pecking order. (This statistic simply indicates whether the differences between the newspapers were big enough to rule out their occurrence through chance or error. A result indicating chance as the likely explanation in fewer than 1 out of 20 cases (*p* is less than .05) is generally said to be significant.)

As the table shows, the null hypothesis stood up in every instance of cosmopolitan coverage before Iowa. In other words, there were no significant differences in candidate coverage by the three cosmopolitan papers during this period. Except for Glenn, the *Monitor* did not significantly differ from the cosmopolitans before Iowa. Not so for the *Union Leader,* which stood out from all other newspapers in every comparison.

One clue that Hart's second-place finish in Iowa transformed reporting of the Democratic race can be seen in the breakdown of cosmopolitan consensus after 20 February 1984. Table 3.7 points up significant post-Iowa differences in *Post, Times,* and *Globe* coverage of six of the candidates. The *Monitor* and *Union Leader* differed significantly on four. As before, *Union Leader* coverage was significantly different from that of the cosmopolitan papers in every case.

A rather mechanical reason for these *Union Leader* differences was that so many of its news items made no mention of any major Democratic candidate. Table 3.8 reveals that more than one-fifth of all *Union Leader* news items about the New Hampshire primary prior to the Iowa caucuses did not include any of the eight candidates. The same pattern obtained during the brief period observed after Iowa. In short, the *Union Leader* set aside an unusually large number of New Hampshire primary items for coverage of local people.

One final inequality measure worth noting was the number of column inches for news items exclusively about one candidate. Since the length of news

TABLE 3.8

PERCENTAGE OF NEW HAMPSHIRE PRIMARY NEWS ITEMS
NOT MENTIONING MAJOR CANDIDATE

	Post	Times	Globe	Monitor	Union Leader	Differences Significant
Before Iowa	12	9	3	9	22	Yes[b]
After Iowa	0	7	3	8	16	Yes[a]

a. p is less than .01. *b. p* is less than .001.

items varied so greatly, column inches offered a more precise calibration of coverage. Unfortunately, there was no practical way to allocate this space when items mentioned more than one candidate, hence the reliance to this point on items rather than item length. Table 3.9 is based on items about one candidate only for which column inches could be tabulated. It shows that dark horses for once fared as well or better than front-runners in space set aside for solo candidate coverage. Before Iowa, for example, Cranston got substantially more exclusive coverage than Mondale in the *Post* and *Globe.* Hollings got as much. Glenn got less in the *Monitor* than Askew, Hart, Jackson, or McGovern during this time. Jackson received the lion's share of solo coverage in the *Monitor, Union Leader,* and *Globe.*

TABLE 3.9

COLUMN INCHES OF PRIMARY NEWS ITEMS

EXCLUSIVELY ABOUT ONE CANDIDATE

Candidate	Post	Times	Globe	Monitor	Union Leader
Before Iowa Caucuses					
Askew	9	0	15	101	87
Cranston	45	3	61	87	108
Glenn	0	20	44	88	166
Hart	10	4	12	179	62
Hollings	15	0	40	83	147
Jackson	10	47	120	373	266
McGovern	0	0	9	182	110
Mondale	15	57	41	230	182
After Iowa Caucuses					
Askew	0	0	17	54	8
Cranston	0	0	18	45	5
Glenn	0	19	16	145	27
Hart	0	4	5	31	56
Hollings	0	0	0	67	12
Jackson	45	19	87	86	88
McGovern	3	3	18	106	40
Mondale	35	15	45	111	110

Another pattern suggested by this table was an apparent reluctance by *Post* and *Times* editors to feature any candidate exclusively in its New Hampshire coverage. Front-runners enjoyed a distinct advantage in these newspapers, but they seldom had the limelight all to themselves. In marked contrast, the two local papers often published stories and special features exclusively about one candidate. Fully 30 percent of all column inches of *Union Leader* copy (before and after Iowa) was exclusively about one candidate or another. The *Monitor* used 27 percent of its New Hampshire primary newshole in this fashion. Corresponding figures for the *Post, Times,* and *Globe* were 7, 6, and 11 percent, respectively. Exclusive coverage, then, was yet another way in which local and cosmopolitan newspapers importantly differed in reporting the New Hampshire primary.

HORSE RACE AND POLICY COVERAGE

We turn now to the much-criticized media preference for reporting the horse race more than substantive policy stands. As in measuring unequal candidate coverage, some basic terms must be defined.

According to the academic literature, for example, campaign journalism rarely focuses on policy issues unless directly addressed by candidates. In other words, issue coverage consists mostly of what candidates say about issues. The news items in this research accordingly were coded for explicit candidate pronouncements on issues, however extensive.

As noted earlier, the horse-race concept incorporates numerous aspects of candidate and campaign performance. Aspects measured for this study were:

1. *Scenario:* Did the item indicate where a candidate expected to do well (or poorly), whose support he expected to receive, or where he planned to campaign?

2. *Endorsements:* Did the item note prominent individuals or groups formally endorsing the candidate?

3. *Relative standing in the race:* Did the item mention how well the candidate was doing in the race?

4. *Momentum in the race:* Did the item indicate a shift in the candidate's standing relative to other candidates?

5. *Campaign problems:* Did the item mention conflict between aides, poor field coordination, or other problems of this sort?

6. *Able campaign:* Did the item mention favorable assessments of the candidate's organization?

7. *Money problems:* Did the item mention campaign debts, tight budgets, or other financial problems?[67]

How much coverage of candidate issue stands was there relative to different aspects of the horse race? Owing to Iowa's early influence, a before and after comparison seemed wise. Tables 3.10 and 3.11 affirm the sensibility of this approach.

TABLE 3.10

PERCENTAGE OF NEWS ITEMS ABOUT EACH CANDIDATE'S ISSUE STANDS
AND HORSE-RACE ASPECTS OF CAMPAIGN BEFORE IOWA CAUCUSES

	Post	Times	Globe	Monitor	Union Leader	Differences Significant?
Askew						
Scenario	9	19	25	13	7	no[a]
Endorsements	4	0	4	8	9	no[a]
Standing in race	50	19	36	21	11	yes[c]
Momentum	18	0	5	4	2	no[a]
Able campaign	4	4	2	1	0	no[a]
Money problems	0	4	0	3	0	no[a]
Issue stand(s)	18	19	20	27	24	no
(N of items)	(22)	(26)	(56)	(75)	(45)	
Cranston						
Scenario	23	30	33	23	5	yes[c]
Endorsements	5	3	7	4	3	no[a]
Standing in race	38	24	39	16	12	yes[d]
Momentum	20	8	15	6	7	no[a]
Campaign problems	0	5	0	0	0	no[a]
Able campaign	3	3	2	6	0	no[a]
Money problems	3	3	3	1	0	no[a]
Issue stand(s)	31	32	26	35	16	no
(N of items)	(39)	(37)	(61)	(108)	(58)	
Glenn						
Scenario	15	30	39	21	14	yes[c]
Endorsements	4	9	9	3	1	no[a]
Standing in race	58	52	47	37	25	yes[d]
Momentum	42	22	18	11	5	yes[d]
Campaign problems	17	17	23	10	4	yes[d]
Able campaign	0	2	0	0	0	no[a]
Money problems	4	7	6	1	0	no[a]
Issue stand(s)	23	28	30	25	18	no
(N of items)	(48)	(54)	(104)	(122)	(73)	
Hart						
Scenario	24	25	28	26	10	no
Endorsements	3	3	8	6	2	no[a]
Standing in race	51	25	34	16	10	yes[d]
Momentum	30	14	16	5	3	no[a]
Campaign problems	0	0	3	2	0	no[a]
Able campaign	6	6	8	7	0	no[a]
Money problems	15	8	4	7	0	no[a]
Issue stand(s)	15	19	17	27	12	no
(N of items)	(33)	(36)	(76)	(108)	(60)	

TABLE 3.10 (continued)

	Post	Times	Globe	Monitor	Union Leader	Differences Significant?
Hollings						
Scenario	18	16	19	11	4	no[a]
Endorsements	4	0	3	0	3	no[a]
Standing in race	54	20	34	18	9	yes[d]
Momentum	27	0	11	5	5	no[a]
Campaign problems	9	0	0	1	0	no[a]
Money problems	14	0	0	6	0	no[a]
Issue stand(s)	36	32	27	32	19	no
(N of items)	(22)	(25)	(62)	(87)	(57)	
Jackson						
Scenario	31	26	31	35	10	yes[b]
Endorsements	10	3	6	4	8	no[a]
Standing in race	52	21	34	16	15	yes[d]
Momentum	41	15	12	4	3	no[a]
Campaign problems	3	3	2	9	2	no[a]
Money problems	0	0	0	2	2	no[a]
Issue stand(s)	17	21	22	21	19	no
(N of items)	(29)	(34)	(67)	(101)	(59)	
McGovern						
Scenario	15	27	19	17	10	no[a]
Endorsements	0	0	0	0	2	no[a]
Standing in race	50	27	32	19	12	yes[c]
Momentum	10	0	3	4	2	no[a]
Campaign problems	0	0	2	7	0	no[a]
Money problems	0	8	0	8	5	no[a]
Issue stand(s)	20	19	21	30	17	no
(N of items)	(20)	(26)	(57)	(82)	(41)	
Mondale						
Scenario	7	22	29	18	8	yes[c]
Endorsements	22	17	28	20	25	no
Standing in race	71	67	60	37	32	yes[d]
Momentum	24	17	22	6	3	yes[d]
Able campaign	5	16	16	7	1	yes[c]
Money problems	0	0	1	0	0	no[a]
Issue stand(s)	22	33	22	30	16	no
(N of items)	(55)	(63)	(106)	(148)	(97)	

NOTE: None of the five newspapers mentioned problems in the Askew or Mondale campaigns nor characterized the Hollings, Jackson, or McGovern campaigns as able.

a. "No" cells too small for valid test; b. p less than .05; c. p less than .01; d. p less than .001.

Table 3.10 (pp. 86-87) compares amount of issue and horse-race coverage in each newspaper's reporting of the eight Democratic candidates before the Iowa caucuses. The computational base for this table was the number of news items about a candidate in each newspaper, and each percentage indicates the number of items mentioning the candidate's policy views and the aforementioned horse-race aspects of his campaign. So, for example, half of all the *Post* items about Mondale before the Iowa caucuses noted he was the front-runner, 18 percent indicated he was either holding his lead or further outdistancing his rivals, and another 18 percent referred to his stands on issues.

Table 3.10 contains several noteworthy findings. The foremost is that newspapers usually mentioned standings (the most basic horse-race indicator) more often than views on issues. Even so, information about issues often surfaced in news items about most candidates before Iowa. Thirty-six percent of all *Post* items about Hollings mentioned his positions on the federal deficit, draft, education, or some other issue. One-third of all items about Mondale in the *Times* made some reference to his policy views, as did 30 percent of all Mondale items in the *Monitor*. Finally, local and cosmopolitan newspapers differed less systematically on these measures than in earlier comparisons. Indeed, inspection of table 3.10 reveals no consistent difference in candidate coverage other than the significantly greater mention of standings in the race by cosmopolitan papers.

By providing the first "hard" news of the horse race in 1984, the Iowa caucuses importantly shifted the direction of candidate coverage in what remained of the New Hampshire primary campaign. Table 3.11 (pp. 89-90) shows a marked reduction of candidate issue mentions in all three cosmopolitan papers after Iowa. This was particularly true of Cranston, Glenn, Hollings, and Mondale coverage. Before Iowa, 30 percent of all *Globe* items about Glenn had mentioned his policy views; after Iowa, only 8 percent of all Glenn items in the *Globe* mentioned issue stands. The *Times* said nothing at all about policy views in its coverage of six candidates after Iowa.

Table 3.11 shows no such dropoff in coverage of candidate policy views in the two local newspapers after Iowa. In contrast, the *Monitor* and *Union Leader* began to mention candidate scenarios and standings in the race much more often. Glenn's coverage in the *Monitor* illustrates the point: Before Iowa, 37 percent of all items about the Ohioan indicated his standing in the race; the post-Iowa figure was 62 percent. Much the same thing happened in the *Union Leader*.

After Iowa, the three cosmopolitan papers generally increased their coverage of candidate scenarios and, in some instances at least, of standings in the race. But, as noted above, they had stressed some aspects of the horse race earlier.

TABLE 3.11

PERCENTAGE OF NEWS ITEMS ABOUT EACH CANDIDATE'S
ISSUE STANDS AND HORSE-RACE ASPECTS OF CAMPAIGN
AFTER IOWA CAUCUSES

	Post	Times	Globe	Monitor	Union Leader	Differences Significant?
Askew						
Scenario	14	31	21	38	17	no
Endorsements	5	8	0	3	0	no[a]
Standing in race	52	61	54	41	48	no
Momentum	0	15	17	14	0	no[a]
Money problems	19	8	12	10	0	no[a]
Issue stand(s)	14	0	17	28	17	no[a]
(N of items)	(21)	(13)	(24)	(29)	(23)	
Cranston						
Scenario	29	35	38	31	17	no
Endorsements	0	0	11	8	4	no[a]
Standing in race	46	47	54	47	42	no
Momentum	17	0	15	14	0	no[a]
Able campaign	4	6	4	8	0	no[a]
Money problems	21	6	11	6	0	no[a]
Issue stand(s)	21	0	15	28	8	no[a]
(N of items)	(24)	(17)	(26)	(36)	(24)	
Glenn						
Scenario	33	67	31	42	29	yes[b]
Endorsements	6	4	3	2	3	no[a]
Standing in race	61	46	33	62	57	no
Momentum	42	50	36	31	20	no
Campaign problems	3	17	8	15	6	no[a]
Money problems	9	4	5	2	3	no[a]
Issue stand(s)	6	0	8	17	6	no
(N of items)	(33)	(24)	(39)	(48)	(35)	
Hart						
Scenario	27	48	26	47	21	yes[b]
Endorsements	7	6	4	9	8	no[a]
Standing in race	50	51	32	58	50	no
Momentum	45	39	46	28	10	yes[c]
Campaign problems	7	3	8	6	0	no[a]
Able campaign	12	9	12	6	3	no[a]
Money problems	12	9	10	6	0	no[a]
Issue stand(s)	12	9	10	21	13	no
(N of items)	(40)	(33)	(50)	(53)	(38)	

TABLE 3.11 *(continued)*

	Post	Times	Globe	Monitor	Union Leader	Differences Significant?
Hollings						
Scenario	12	11	23	36	29	no
Endorsements	0	0	4	5	0	no[a]
Standing in race	40	39	50	36	39	no
Momentum	4	0	11	8	0	no[a]
Money problems	8	0	11	3	0	no[a]
Issue stand(s)	8	0	27	26	18	no[a]
(N of items)	(25)	(18)	(26)	(39)	(57)	
Jackson						
Scenario	33	29	32	22	11	no
Endorsements	17	5	11	2	8	no[a]
Standing in race	33	33	29	27	30	no
Momentum	17	24	18	5	0	no[a]
Campaign problems	3	0	0	2	0	no[a]
Money problems	7	0	7	2	0	no[a]
Issue stand(s)	3	0	18	19	16	no
(N of items)	(30)	(22)	(28)	(41)	(37)	
McGovern						
Scenario	32	40	30	27	17	no
Endorsements	0	0	7	11	3	no[a]
Standing in race	36	30	40	40	43	no
Momentum	14	10	15	8	0	no[a]
Campaign problems	4	0	4	5	3	no[a]
Money problems	7	10	7	11	7	no[a]
Issue stand(s)	11	0	11	27	17	no[a]
(N of items)	(28)	(20)	(27)	(37)	(30)	
Mondale						
Scenario	37	29	23	47	20	yes[c]
Endorsements	35	40	32	27	24	no
Standing in race	65	60	45	53	56	no
Momentum	30	20	18	18	6	yes[b]
Campaign problems	5	3	3	1	0	no[a]
Able campaign	16	20	11	14	4	no
Issue stand(s)	9	6	11	21	13	no
(N of items)	(43)	(35)	(62)	(66)	(54)	

NOTE: None of the five newspapers mentioned problems in the Askew campaign organization or characterized his effort as effective or able; none mentioned problems in the Cranston organization or characterized the Glenn campaign as effective or able; none mentioned problems in the Hol-ings organization or characterized it as effective; and none characterized the McGovern campaign as able or effective.

a. "No" cells too small for valid test; b. p is less than .05; c. p is less than .01.

To sum up, Iowa fired the starting gun, and insofar as these newspapers were concerned, the horse race had begun.

What were the issues on which Democratic candidates expressed their views, at least as reported in the newspapers? A conservative count appears in table 3.12, based on open-ended coding of up to two issues per item.[68] The most often mentioned policy questions were arms control, economic issues related to federal spending, and defense. Specific foreign policy events figured less often than might have been expected given developments in Grenada, Lebanon, and Central America during the campaign. Social services and public schooling got remarkably little coverage in these newspapers despite their fre-

TABLE 3.12

PERCENTAGE OF ISSUES MENTIONED IN NEW HAMPSHIRE PRIMARY
COVERAGE, 1 OCTOBER 1983 THROUGH 2 MARCH 1984

Issue	Post	Times	Globe	Monitor	Union Leader	All Five Papers
Arms control	11	9	7	18	9	12
Federal deficit and Reaganomics	11	10	10	11	6	9
Defense	3	3	4	14	2	6
Women and minorities	3	2	3	8	4	5
Grenada, Central American policy	3	3	4	6	5	5
Environmental concerns	3	7	4	6	3	5
Middle East	2	2	2	5	6	4
Social programs	1	1	1	4	3	3
Other foreign policy	2	1	2	3	2	2
Educational policy	0	1	*	4	1	2
Other domestic policy	2	1	1	1	2	1
(N of items)	(51)	(53)	(93)	(302)	(151)	(650)

NOTES: "Arms control" included candidate statements about the nuclear freeze, horrors of nuclear war, availability of plutonium, and production of nerve gas. "Federal deficit and Reaganomics" encompassed various issues regarding the budget including a freeze on most spending, criticisms of the deficit, and tax reform. "Defense" took in military reform, reinstating conscription, the MX missile and B1 bomber, and Pentagon budgets. "Women and minorities" included the ERA, affirmative action, abortion, and rights of women, blacks, and gays. Among the "Environmental concerns" were acid rain, toxic waste dumps, nuclear power, and various proposals regarding energy. "Middle East" references were mostly to Lebanon. "Social programs" took in social security, Medicare, unemployment, hunger, poverty, veterans, vocational retraining, and children's care. "Other foreign policy" issues were foreign trade, UNESCO, Angola, Cambodia, and South Africa. "Other domestic policy" issues were new Supreme Court appointments, PAC funding of presidential candidates, gun control, farm policy, domestic content, and local taxes.

* p is less than 1 percent.

quent mention on the campaign trail. In any case, the *Monitor* stood out for its arms control and defense reporting.

Did all five newspapers see the horse race in the same way? The literature certainly favors an affirmative answer, and it is apparent in the summary scores provided by table 3.13 below. Derived from six of the seven horse-race indicators (all but scenarios) discussed above, these measures indicate the degree of positive or negative horse-race coverage given each candidate. Scores ranged from +100 (wholly positive) to −100 (wholly negative) with 0 (zero) as a midpoint when positive coverage was offset completely by negative horse-race information.[69] Although varying in degree, the five newspapers almost always were consistent in the direction of their coverage. Before Iowa, for example, they all assessed the directions taken by the Askew, Hart, Jackson, and Mondale campaigns in the same ways. Four out of five papers agreed on every candidate. All five agreed on seven of the eight campaigns after Iowa—a display consistent with the academic literature's emphasis on similarity in campaign journalism.

TABLE 3.13

DIRECTION OF CANDIDATES' HORSE-RACE COVERAGE

BEFORE AND AFTER IOWA CAUCUSES

	Before Caucuses				
Candidate	Post	Times	Globe	Monitor	Union Leader
Askew	−59	−71	−53	−21	−20
Cranston	−15	−18	−7	0	+7
Glenn	0	+19	+2	+36	+23
Hart	+40	+30	+62	+23	+78
Hollings	−46	−100	−30	−69	0
Jackson	+71	+71	+39	+9	+67
McGovern	+8	−78	−24	−69	−11
Mondale	+95	+89	+83	+77	+97
	After Caucuses				
Askew	−87	−67	−70	−50	−82
Cranston	−71	−80	−60	−43	−64
Glenn	−32	−59	−51	−78	−74
Hart	+70	+87	+68	+73	+100
Hollings	−85	−100	−80	−40	−64
Jackson	0	+8	+11	+25	+29
McGovern	−6	−20	−20	−21	−6
Mondale	+72	+68	+68	+55	+67

Table 3.13 also points up Iowa's impact on horse-race coverage. Note, for example, the sharp rise in Cranston's negative scores after his third-place scenario did not materialize. Glenn's coverage turned decidedly negative. Hart's positive coverage matched or exceeded Mondale's after Iowa. Jackson's coverage chilled notably after Iowa, in part no doubt because of the "Hymie" affair. Finally, McGovern got surprisingly little bounce out of doing much better than expected in Iowa. According to Robinson, network television news also deemphasized McGovern's Iowa showing.[70]

Sparse Coverage of Personal and Political Backgrounds

How much attention did these newspapers pay to the personal lives and political backgrounds of the Democratic candidates? The answer disclosed by table 3.14 (on page 94) is, Not much. The general tendency was to say little about political experience and less about personal history. Glenn's feats as a combat pilot and astronaut earned him the only personal coverage of any note. The *New York Times* said nothing at all about the formative experiences of six of his rivals in its New Hampshire primary coverage. Nevertheless, we should not forget the fairly extensive if infrequent candidate profiles published in each cosmopolitan paper (most of which were excluded from this analysis, since they were not specific to the New Hampshire primary).

As for political background, only McGovern's was mentioned in very many items by all five newspapers. The *Post* mentioned the careers of Glenn and Hart fairly frequently, and the *Monitor* paid similar attention to Hart and Mondale. In sum, newspaper coverage of the 1984 New Hampshire primary generally confirmed a lack of attention to candidate backgrounds.

The "Hymie" Crisis

How much play did these newspapers give the Hymie episode, and did the amount of coverage differ significantly? In the 11 days of post-Iowa coverage observed for this research, the five newspapers mentioned Hymie in 44 news items about Jackson. In other words, this controversy figured in 28 percent of their combined Jackson coverage after Iowa and was big news in each. Thirty percent of all *Post* news items mentioned Hymie, as did 29 percent of those in the *Times,* 43 percent in the *Globe,* 19 percent in the *Monitor,* and 24 percent in the *Union Leader.* These differences were not significant statistically and thus suggest another instance of highly similar campaign journalism. Blunders of the Hymie magnitude are news in local as well as cosmopolitan newspapers.

TABLE 3.14

PERCENTAGE OF COVERAGE OF PERSONAL LIFE AND
POLITICAL CAREER OF DEMOCRATIC CANDIDATES,
1 OCTOBER 1983 THROUGH 2 MARCH 1984

	Post	Times	Globe	Monitor	Union Leader
Askew					
Personal life	2	0	2	3	4
Political career	5	8	11	9	9
Cranston					
Personal life	5	0	2	2	2
Political career	6	4	2	8	1
Glenn					
Personal life	1	0	1	3	2
Astronaut/pilot	10	10	13	17	9
Political career	14	10	9	11	5
Hart					
Personal life	1	0	2	3	2
Political career	16	9	11	14	3
Hollings					
Personal life	0	0	2	2	2
Political career	6	2	3	13	7
Jackson					
Personal life	3	0	4	1	1
Political career	5	9	4	11	3
McGovern					
Personal life	2	2	2	2	4
Political career	29	28	21	31	20
Mondale					
Personal life	3	1	2	1	1
Political career	8	7	8	17	9

NOTE: Ns were large enough for valid chi-square tests only in comparing coverage of Mondale, Glenn, Hart, and McGovern political careers, as well as Glenn's background as a Marine pilot and astronaut. None was significant at p less than .05.

FINAL COMPARISONS

Three stories suffice to conclude this analysis. The first involved matters of national as well as local importance and was extensively reported by all five newspapers. The second was left almost entirely to the *Monitor* and *Union Leader* and illustrates their predictable concern to report news of interest to local readers. The third represented an attempt by the *Union Leader* to create as well as report the news.

A question of no small concern to candidates, state officials, party leaders, and New Hampshire voters in 1984 was the actual date of their primary. This lengthy dispute began in 1981 when it appeared that the Hunt Commission might try to force early state presidential nominating events inside the Democratic "window." The late Governor Hugh Gallen, a Democrat, worked out an agreement by which New Hampshire's primary would still be first but barely outside the window in 1984. The deal thus called for rescheduling the primary to 6 March. Gallen's death and a ruling by state officials against the new date forced New Hampshire Democrats to choose between state interests and national party rules. When they embraced the former, national party officials moved to force compliance with the Gallen agreement. A cloud thus hung over the primary with no firm assurance that candidates winning delegates in New Hampshire could get them seated at the San Francisco convention. This dispute remained unresolved until May 1984.

Since the dispute over dates involved not only New Hampshire Democrats but the national and other state party organizations as well, it got substantial coverage in cosmopolitan and local newspapers alike. Of the 1209 news items analyzed for this study, 129, or 11 percent, mentioned the date dispute. The *Monitor* did no more with the story than the *Post, Times,* or *Globe.* It got much more play in the *Union Leader,* which mentioned the dispute in 16 percent of all news items about the New Hampshire primary. Indeed, the difference was enough to make the *Union Leader*'s coverage of this story significantly greater than the other papers'.

A New Hampshire primary angle virtually ignored by the cosmopolitans but substantially reported by the locals was the "minor candidate." Nine such candidates appeared on the same ballot with Askew, Cranston, Glenn, Hart, Hollings, Jackson, McGovern, and Mondale. Of 53 news items about these bit players, 34 appeared in the *Union Leader,* 16 in the *Monitor.* Thus fully 10 percent of the *Union Leader*'s news items mentioned minor candidates, a news judgment further attesting to the uniqueness of this newspaper.

The final story raises questions about *Union Leader* journalism examined at greater length in David Moore's chapter in this book. Exactly two weeks before primary election day, the *Union Leader* disclosed that several disgruntled state Democrats had urged write-in votes for President Reagan in the Democratic primary. The actual write-in procedure was fairly complicated, and as primary election day approached, *Union Leader* editors spared no effort to educate the public on the technique and virtue of a Reagan write-in vote. The first of eight news stories in the final week appeared on 22 February under a banner headline, *Democratic Reagan Write-In Urged.* The next day's coverage of this effort included a page-one editorial, a news story, and a photograph showing "how to do it write [sic]." On the primary's eve, the *Union Leader* again explained how voters should write *Reagan's* name on the ballot. Four cartoons painstakingly illustrated each step in the process from "depress p.c. release lever" to "turn down voter handle on left of machine." Altogether, the *Union Leader* published 14 news items, 7 editorials, 2 editorial cartoons, 1 photograph, and 4 drawings in a 15-day period! Its final editorial lashed out against the national press for ignoring the write-in story. (Reagan got 5 percent of the Democatic primary vote, more than Askew, Cranston, or Hollings.) It indeed received little notice elsewhere, an opposing editorial and two items in the *Monitor* and seven brief notes in the cosmopolitan papers.

To summarize, all five newspapers agreed that the date dispute story was important and covered it accordingly. Only the two local papers viewed minor candidates as newsworthy, and the *Union Leader* was much more inclined to this perspective than the *Monitor*. And attesting to the *Union Leader's* uniqueness in this study, only that newspaper saw the write-in as a major event. In the process the paper unabashedly blended news reporting and editorial advocacy and soon made the write-in a cause.

Conclusions

Three general findings emerged from this research. First, local and cosmopolitan newspapers differed importantly in at least some aspects of their New Hampshire primary coverage. Hart's previously quoted contention that small newspapers covered his 1984 campaign differently from the national media was at least partly borne out. Second, the two local newspapers in this study often covered the primary in remarkably different fashion. Generalizations are risky from so small a sample, but one proposition for future research is that local newspapers vary more in their campaign coverage than national or regionally dominant ones do. And, third, the fact that Iowa has stolen some of New Hampshire's thunder can be seen in much greater horse-race coverage after the nation's first caucuses. The horse race begins in Iowa, not in New Hampshire, and candidate coverage in what remains of the New Hampshire primary campaign after Iowa reflects this.

Local-cosmopolitan differences were most evident in the findings for head-lines, news items mentioning candidates, exclusive coverage of candidates, and attention to minor candidates. The *Post, Times,* and *Globe* generally gave front-runners an enormous publicity advantage in their headlines and items men-tioning candidates. *Monitor* and *Union Leader* coverage in these respects was generally more even handed, though front-runners still fared better than long shots.

In contrast, the three cosmopolitans evidently followed a policy of rarely featuring any candidate on an exclusive basis. Even their candidate profiles specific to the New Hampshire primary seldom failed to mention rivals. This was not the case in the *Monitor* and *Union Leader,* where the exclusive can-didate item was fairly routine. The *Union Leader's* extensive use of brief notes doubtless inflated this finding, but the generalization still appears valid: Local newspapers are much more likely to feature candidates exclusively than cosmo-politan papers as a standard part of their primary coverage. And, noted above, local newspapers in this connection are as likely to single out dark horses as front-runners.

Evidently operating on different understandings of what constituted news, the two local papers occasionally made note of minor and truly hopeless can-didates ignored by the cosmpolitans. Nevertheless, there were several instances in which *Monitor* and *Union Leader* coverage varied greatly. Setting aside its editorial on the subject, for example, the *Monitor* paid scarcely more atten-tion to the *Union Leader's* write-in project than did the *Post, Times,* and *Globe.* And, as noted earlier, the *Union Leader* stood out for news items about the primary that took no notice of the major candidates.

Despite all this variability, New Hampshire primary coverage was in cer-tain respects remarkably uniform. All five newspapers paid more attention to the horse race than policy pronouncements before the Iowa caucuses, and once the Iowa returns were in, they shifted even more to horse-race coverage. With the few exceptions noted, local and cosmopolitan papers alike generally did not supply information about the personal lives of candidates. All five did fre-quently mention McGovern's 1972 loss to Nixon. Finally, all five extensively reported the "Hymie" affair.

In sum, media uniformity has been exaggerated in the academic litera-ture. Generalizations in this vein are derived almost entirely from the national media. Despite all the pressures for news convergence, local and cosmopolitan coverage of presidential nominating contests differs in important respects.

Notes

1. Doris R. Graber, *Mass Media and American Politics,* 2d ed. (Washington, D.C.: Congressional Quarterly Press, 1984), 199. See also Donald R. Matthews's discussion of "the great New Hampshire overkill" in *Race for the President,* ed. James D. Barber (Englewood Cliffs, N.J.: Prentice-Hall, 1968), 64-66.

2. See "Presidential Vote Summary," *Congressional Quarterly Weekly Report* 42 (16 June 1984): 1443.

3. Delegation size data came from *Final Call for the 1984 Democratic National Convention* (Washington, D.C.: Democratic National Committee, 1983), 2-3.

4. In this vein, see L. Sandy Maisel, "Should Mice That Roar Decide the Nomination?" *New York Times,* 7 March 1984, A23.

5. Michael J. Robinson and Karen A. McPherson, "Television News Coverage Before the 1976 New Hampshire Primary: The Focus of Network Journalism," *Journal of Broadcasting* 21 (Spring 1977): 177-86.

6. Michael J. Robinson and Margaret A. Sheehan, *Over the Wire and on TV: CBS and UPI in Campaign '80* (New York: Russell Sage Foundation, 1983), 176-77.

7. These data were tabulated from *Television News Index and Abstracts* published by the Vanderbilt Television News Archive, October 1983 through June 1984. Brief capsule descriptions allowed determination of which caucuses or primaries were covered in a given story and computation of each story's time precisely in news seconds. Timing of segments about different contests in a story about more than one event could not be computed without actually viewing the programs, and so data for stories combining multiple contest reports have been reported here. This procedure doubtless overestimated New Hampshire's total airtime, but only somewhat, and, in any case, the general point of gargantuan television coverage is no less valid. In comparison, all three networks combined set aside 14,815 news seconds for Super Tuesday contests, including stories linking Super Tuesday events to later ones. Total coverage by the three networks combined of the final round of primaries in New Jersey, California, West Virginia, New Mexico, and South Dakota came to 7070 news seconds—fewer than the 7155 the networks allocated to the Iowa caucuses.

8. For an interesting account of network television news preoccupation with the New Hampshire primary and details of 1984 coverage, see Martin Schram, *The Great American Video Game* (New York: Morrow, 1987).

9. The author collected every item in each newspaper about the 1984 Democratic race, including all columns, editorials, op/ed essays, and news items. Only news items specifically about one or more state primaries or caucuses were included in the present analysis.

10. The Glenn, Hart, and Mondale campaigns kindly provided complete lists of respective candidate visits to New Hampshire. Askew's campaign frequently claimed their candidate had spent 70 days in the state. The Hollings estimate was derived from conversations with his New Hampshire campaign officials.

11. Elizabeth Drew, *Campaign Journal: The Political Events of 1983-1984* (New York: Macmillan, 1985), 310.

12. For an account of Connally's unorthodox decision to contest South Carolina rather than New Hampshire, see Jack Germond and Jules Witcover, *Blue Smoke and Mirrors: How Reagan Won and Why Carter Lost the Election of 1980* (New York: Viking Press, 1981), 121.

13. Jules Witcover, *Marathon: The Pursuit of the Presidency, 1972-1976* (New York: Viking Press, 1977), 223.

14. James M. Perry, *Us and Them: How the Press Covered the 1972 Election* (New York: Clarkson N. Potter, 1973), 83.

15. Theodore H. White, *America in Search of Itself: The Making of the President, 1956-1980* (New York: Harper & Row, 1982), 30.

16. Michael Robinson, "Where's the Beef? Media and Media Elites in 1984," in *The American Elections of 1984*, ed. Austin Ranney (Durham: Duke University Press, 1985), 191.

17. See Graber, *Mass Media and American Politics*, 77-79.

18. Thomas R. Marshall, "The News Verdict and Public Opinion during the Primaries," in *Television Coverage of the 1980 Presidential Campaign*, ed. William C. Adams (Norwood, N.J.: Ablex, 1983), 54.

19. *Mass Media and American Politics*, 190.

20. *Over the Wire and on TV*, 9.

21. Herbert Gans, *Deciding What's News* (New York: Random House, 1980), 183. Some authors dispute these points and argue that reporting cannot be objective in any respect. In this vein, see W. Lance Bennett, *News: The Politics of Illusion* (New York: Longman, 1983), 75-97; and Michael Parenti, *Inventing Reality* (New York: St. Martin's, 1986). For a good overview of disputes about objective journalism, see Michael Schudson, *Discovering the News* (New York: Basic Books, 1978), 176-94.

22. *Over the Wire and on TV*, 34.

23. Timothy Crouse, *The Boys on the Bus* (New York: Ballantine, 1972), 15.

24. Nelson W. Polsby, *Consequences of Party Reform* (New York: Oxford University Press, 1983), 142-46.

25. *The Boys on the Bus*, 9-10.

26. See *Over the Wire and on TV*, 76-82.

27. Quoted in ibid., 116.

28. "Media Coverage of Campaign '84: A Preliminary Report," in *The Mass Media in Campaign '84*, ed. Michael J. Robinson and Austin Ranney (Washington, D.C.: American Enterprise Institute, 1985), 10-14.

29. See George Gallup, Jr., *The Gallup Poll: Public Opinion 1983* (Wilmington, Del.: Scholarly Resources, 1984), and, by the same author and publisher in 1985, *The Gallup Poll: Public Opinion 1984*. This discussion is based on 11 polls taken between 10-13 December 1982 and 10-13 February 1984.

30. In December 1982, 73 percent of the Democrats and 79 percent of the Independents polled nationwide by Gallup said they had heard of McGovern. Glenn's recognition at this point was 69 percent among Democrats and 50 percent among Independents. Only Mondale enjoyed more recognition than McGovern, at 86 percent of all Democrats and 88 percent of the Independents. McGovern remained the second-most-known candidate in the Democratic race in Gallup's March 1983 and October 1983 surveys. See *The Gallup Poll: Public Opinion 1983*, 7-8, 67, 250.

31. Had Jackson not been such a novelty candidate, it is hard to credit that the news media would have given his campaign anything like the lavish publicity it received. For example, support for Jackson's nomination in the Gallup poll ranged from 7 to 13 percent among Democrats and from 3 to 9 percent among Independents prior to the Iowa caucuses. Even so, the networks gave him more time on their evening news

programs just for thinking about running than they used to report news of all other long-shot candidates combined. But this was nothing compared to coverage of his "Syrian primary," or winning the release of Lt. Goodman from Syria in January 1984. From 25 December 1983 through 6 January 1984, Jackson's exposure on the three network evening news programs (each lasting 30 minutes) was as follows:

	ABC	CBS	NBC	All 3 Networks
Total stories	9	11	15	35
Total news seconds	1714	1884	1658	5266
Stories featuring only Jackson	8	9	13	30
Jackson news seconds	1342	1044	1528	3914
Percentage of all news seconds about Jackson only	78	55	92	74

SOURCE: *Television News Index and Abstracts,* December 1983 and January 1984.

Michael Robinson ("Where's the Beef?" 180) concluded that this was the most prolonged and favorable television news coverage ever given a third-place candidate. The *Washington Post, New York Times,* and *Boston Globe* published a total of 40 news articles and 22 columns and editorials about the Syrian affair from 25 December 1983 through 17 January 1984. Again, nearly all of this coverage focused exclusively on Jackson. After New Hampshire, of course, the field eventually narrowed to Mondale, Hart, and Jackson. Twice in danger of losing his matching federal funds, seldom able to win more than 5 percent of the white vote in big primary states, and winner of the preference vote in only two primaries—Louisiana and the District of Columbia—Jackson still continued to receive time on the evening news out of all proportion to the chances of his nomination. Jackson got 2750 news seconds of exclusive coverage on all three networks from 29 February to 5 June 1984—more than double the exclusive time given Mondale and Hart combined.

32. George McGovern, "The Target Talks Back," *Columbia Journalism Review* 22 (July/August 1984): 27.

33. Jonathan Moore, ed., *Campaign for President: The Managers Look at '84* (Dover, Mass.: Auburn House, 1986), 51.

34. *Over the Wire and on TV,* 78.

35. "The Target Talks Back," 27.

36. See William Keyserling, "Longshot Democrats Never Had a Chance in the Media," *Washington Post,* 25 December 1983, 84.

37. Susan Berry Casey, *Hart and Soul: Gary Hart's New Hampshire Odyssey and Beyond* (Concord, N.H.: NHI Press, 1986), 291.

38. Richard Joslyn, *Mass Media and Elections* (Reading, Mass.: Addison-Wesley, 1984), 133.

39. "The Target Talks Back," 28.

40. Thomas Patterson, *The Mass Media Election* (New York: Praeger, 1980), 168.

41. F. Christopher Arterton, *Media Politics* (Lexington, Mass.: Heath, 1984), 46.

42. *Over the Wire and on TV,* 162.

43. Henry E. Brady and Richard Johnston, "What's the Primary Message: Horse Race or Issue Journalism?" See chapter 5 in this volume.

44. See Arterton, *Media Politics,* for an extended discussion of horse-race coverage broken down into benchmarks, standards, and scenarios.

45. *Mass Media and American Politics,* 206.

46. *Over the Wire and on TV,* 155.

47. "Where's the Beef?" 191.

48. Jack W. Germond and Jules Witcover, *Wake Us When It's Over* (New York: Macmillan, 1985), 194.

49. See *Hart and Soul,* especially 269-93.

50. See *Campaign for President,* 53-54, for an estimate of "Hymie" damage by Jackson advisers.

51. David L. Paletz and Robert M. Entman take an especially dim view of such stories and maintain that reporters seize the opportunity to inject personal opinions of candidates otherwise suppressed under the rules of objective journalism. See their account in *Media Power Politics* (New York: Free Press, 1981), 50.

52. See Walter Robinson, "Media Ignoring the Pack?" *Boston Globe,* 1 January 1984, 55. See also Martin Schram, "Early Leaders of the Presidential Pack Lure the News Hounds," *Washington Post,* 18 January 1984, A3.

53. T.R. Reid, "Exorcising the Ghost of 1972," *Washington Post,* 14 January 1984, A6.

54. On Bush, see Jeff Greenfield, *The Real Campaign: How the Media Missed the Story of the 1980 Campaign* (New York: Summit, 1982), 34-53.

55. Drew, *Campaign Journal,* 189.

56. *Mass Media in American Politics,* 202-3.

57. See Thomas E. Patterson and Richard Davis, "The Media Campaign: Struggle for the Agenda," in *The Elections of 1984,* ed. Michael Nelson (Washington, D.C.: Congressional Quarterly Press, 1985), 112-28. A problem with their conclusion about Hart is that Patterson and Davis looked at invisible primary coverage only, and the press did not really focus on his "new ideas" until after Iowa and New Hampshire.

58. *Boys on the Bus,* 369.

59. *Mass Media Elections,* 113.

60. Hart quoted by William A. Henry, III, *Visions of America: How We Saw the 1984 Election* (Boston: Atlantic Monthly Press, 1985), 100.

61. Author's observations of the press, including a brief stint on the Glenn press bus, during the 1984 primary.

62. For a good general discussion on this point, see Roger H. Davidson and Walter J. Oleszek, *Congress and Its Members,* 2d ed. (Washington, D.C.: Congressional Quarterly Press, 1986), 151-58. See also Michael J. Robinson, "Three Faces of Congressional Media," in *The New Congress,* ed. Thomas E. Mann and Norman J. Ornstein (Washington, D.C.: American Enterprise Institute, 1981), 55-96.

63. Two relatively recent books about the *Union Leader* are Eric Veblen, *The Manchester Union Leader in New Hampshire Elections* (Hanover, N.H.: University Press of New England, 1975), and a highly critical biography of its late publisher by Kevin Cash, *Who the Hell Is William Loeb?* (Manchester, N.H.: Amoskeag Press, 1975). For a critical discussion of the *Union Leader's* coverage of the 1972 Democratic presidential primary, see Jules Witcover, "William Loeb and the New Hampshire primary: A Question of Ethics," *Columbia Journalism Review* 11 (May/June 1972): 14-25.

64. Audit Bureau of Circulation figures obtained by telephone inquiries; thanks to Dennis Roddy of the *Pittsburgh Press* for assistance in this regard.

65. Joseph Kraus, Scott Andrick, Hillary Pettigrew, Ben Powell, and David Schreyack helped in measuring column inches and coding at various stages of this research. Additional coding information can be obtained from the author. Thanks to the Denison University Research Foundation (DURF) for funds to employ these students.

66. Items focusing on more than one state contest were judged to be about New Hampshire *(a)* if the primary was prominently mentioned three or more times and *(b)* linked to at least one of the other events in the story. Some items pertained only to the New Hampshire primary, others to Iowa and New Hampshire, and still others to New Hampshire and subsequent contests.

67. Identical for each candidate, the actual horse-race questions were:

A. Does this item indicate where X expects to do well, whose support he expects to get, or where he plans to campaign?
1 = Yes.   0 = No.   9 = Inappropriate.   X not mentioned in item.

B. Does this item mention groups or prominent individuals who have endorsed X?
1 = Yes.   0 = No.   9 = Inappropriate.

C. Does this item say how well X is doing compared to others?

1 = X apparent front-runner.	5 = X generally doing well.
2 = X probably second.	6 = X not doing well generally.
3 = X third of fourth.	0 = Item does not say how X is doing.
4 = X among bottom four.	9 = Inappropriate.

D. Does this item say whether X is moving ahead, holding steady, or slipping relative to his Democratic rivals?

1 = X increasing lead over rivals.	7 = Other.
2 = X holding steady.	0 = Item does not indicate X momentum.
3 = X slipping.	9 = Inappropriate.

E. Does this item report that the X campaign is experiencing problems such as conflict between top aides, high turnover, poor coordination in the field, or similar difficulites?
1 = Yes.   0 = No.   9 = Inappropriate.

F. Does this item report that the X organization is highly effective, ably run, or otherwise is waging an effective campaign?
1 = Yes.   0 = No.   9 = Inappropriate.

G. Does this item report campaign finance problems for X, such as debts, deficits, unpaid staff, tight budgets, or similar constraints?
1 = Yes.   0 = No.   9 = Inappropriate.

68. A few items mentioned three or more issues, so the count is underenumerated somewhat. Small numbers precluded a before- and after-Iowa breakdown. The N in table 3.12 refers to items noting issue stands by one or more candidates.

69. The scores in table 3.13 were computed with the equation $(P - N/T \times 100)$ where P = all positive indications, N = all negative ones, and T = all indications as derived from combining variables B-G in note 67 above. B and F were not changed, so an affirmative answer to either gave the candidate +1. E and G were recoded so

affirmative answers yielded −1 in each instance. In Mondale's case, C was recoded so that 1 or 5 were combined as +1 and 2, 4, and 6 were collapsed into a single −1 category. For Glenn, 1, 2, and 5 were collapsed into +1, while 3, 4, and 6 were combined into a single −1 category. In all other cases, 1, 2, 3, and 5 were collapsed into +1 and 4 and 6 into −1. Of course, 0 categories made no difference and all 9s were treated as missing data. The Hart score of +100 in the *Union Leader* after Iowa in table 3.13 should be understood as follows: All of the news items mentioning one or more aspects of Hart's horse-race performance were favorable.

    70. "Where's the Beef?" 189.

4

The *Manchester Union Leader* in the New Hampshire Primary

DAVID W. MOORE

That the *Manchester Union Leader* exerts a profound influence on state politics is an acknowledged, if not completely accepted, fact of political life in New Hampshire. What is not so often recognized is the actual and potential influence of the *Union Leader* on the New Hampshire presidential primaries. Yet, in 1980, this newspaper may very well have saved the stumbling candidacy of Ronald Reagan, whose advanced age and low energy levels were already being questioned by the national press when he unexpectedly lost to George Bush in the Iowa caucuses. Public opinion polls in New Hampshire showed Bush had jumped to the lead among New Hampshire voters after his victory in Iowa, despite his trailing far behind Reagan before Iowa.

In 1980, however, there was a full month between the Iowa caucuses and the New Hampshire primary, which gave Reagan time to recover from his loss. Though it may not have been especially evident at the time, the *Union Leader* was an essential ingredient in that recovery. Its role was overshadowed by Reagan's surprisingly decisive victory, immediately preceded by the famous Nashua debate, when Bush's petulant insistence that the other Republican candidates not be allowed to participate (as already arranged with Reagan) contrasted sharply with the apparently more generous Reagan, who at that point seemed to side with the other candidates. Reagan's advisers had so desperately wanted that one-on-one debate with the front-runner Bush that the arrangements had been paid for by the Reagan campaign. Thus, when the moderator attempted to proceed with the debate, Reagan asserted himself with the now famous words: "I am paying for this microphone, Mr. Breen!"

The *Union Leader* was certainly not responsible for Bush's self-destructive actions, nor for the instinctively masterful response by Reagan, which showed him as a decisive leader and propelled him to his overwhelming victory in the New Hampshire primary. But the data presented in this chapter—based on three statewide public opinion surveys and a systematic content analysis of the *Union Leader*'s news coverage during the two months before the primary— suggest that the advocacy role played by that newspaper was nevertheless crucial in setting the stage for Reagan's recovery. Without the *Union Leader*'s active participation, Reagan's fall in popularity after Iowa would have been more dramatic, Bush almost certainly would not have felt pressured to participate in this second debate in New Hampshire (a debate with all the candidates had been held just a few days earlier in Manchester), and the likely victor in New Hampshire would have been the upset winner in Iowa, George Bush.

Had Bush actually won the New Hampshire primary, at the very least, the Republican nomination process probably would have been more spirited, and more divisive than it was, with potential consequences for the general election against Carter. It is also possible that two losses in a row, for a man who many already thought was too old to be President, would have completely derailed the Reagan candidacy.

Apart from what happened in 1980, the potential for the *Union Leader* to influence the 1988 New Hampshire primary cannot be ignored. Some have argued that with the death in 1981 of William Loeb, the publisher of the paper and the author of most front-page editorials, the *Union Leader* has declined in influence. If so, that loss is marginal at most. The front-page editorials, written now mostly by Nackey Loeb, William Loeb's widow and the current owner and publisher, are not nearly as abrasive these days, but the structure of the paper and its philosophy remain unchanged. And its circulation has increased.

Background

To many reporters who visit New Hampshire for the first time, the most startling fact about this state's politics is the biased reporting of the *Manchester Union Leader*. With its screaming headlines, signed editorials on the front page, biased choice of lead stories, and tendentious writing, the state's leading-circulation newspaper is often derided (in private conversations, not in print) as so blatantly partisan that citizens must surely see through the misinformation the newspaper foists on its readers.

The reporters are even more incredulous when they come to realize that the general consensus among politicians and political analysts in the state, as well as the more experienced from out of state, is that the *Union Leader* exerts a profound influence on politics in New Hampshire. Candidates for state office often plan their campaigns around the anticipated reaction of the paper to their candidacies; indeed, they may even decide *not* to run, depending on the paper's attitude toward them.[1] Further, even though it is difficult to demonstrate conclusively the paper's electoral influence, the *Union Leader* is widely believed to have exerted decisive influence in many electoral contests at various levels within the state.[2] Once elected, state legislators and the governor all pay attention to the paper's positions; few in Concord doubt the paper's ability to step into a controversy and completely transform the debate to its own grounds, even if the final outcome is not always in accord with the paper's editorial preferences.[3]

While the evidence is strong that the *Union Leader* is influential in state politics, it is not as obvious that the paper has been especially influential in the presidential primaries held in New Hampshire. A cursory review of primary contests since 1952 shows few instances when the paper can be said to have exerted a crucial or even major role in the outcome. Either the candidates it supported lost in the primary or they were so strong that they did not need the support of the *Union Leader*.

In the category of those who lost are such candidates as Barry Goldwater, who was surprisingly upset by Henry Cabot Lodge in the Republican primary in 1964; Sam Yorty, who did very poorly in the Democratic primary in 1972; and Ronald Reagan, the favorite, who lost to Gerald Ford by two percentage points in 1976.

In the category of those who were so strong that they did not need the newspaper's support are such candidates as Richard Nixon, who won the Republican primaries in 1960, 1968, and 1972; and Ronald Reagan in 1984. As vice-president in 1960 and President in 1972, Nixon certainly needed no help from the *Union Leader*. Nor did incumbent President Reagan in 1984. In 1968, Nixon's major opponent initially was George Romney, who bowed out of the contest after his comments about being "brainwashed" by the military in Vietnam undercut his credibility. The national press coverage of these comments, not the *Union Leader*, appeared crucial to Romney's decision.

The most frequently cited occasion when the *Union Leader* may have influenced the outcome of a presidential primary occurred in 1972. The effect of *Union Leader* support was apparently not to gain voters for its own candidate (Yorty) but to dissuade voters from supporting the front-runner (Muskie). Asher analyzes the newspaper's role:

> Compounding the atypicality of New Hampshire was the presence of the now deceased William Loeb and his influential newspaper. Loeb did his best to hurt the Muskie candidacy and apparently was successful in holding down Muskie's margin in Manchester, where the circulation of his paper was greatest.[4]

The newspaper's influence in that election, however, may have been more indirect than direct. Just a few days before the election, Muskie attacked the paper for comments it had printed that were critical of his wife. He did so while standing on the front steps of the *Union Leader* building, apparently crying. That unflattering event received extensive coverage in the state, and his performance on election day was worse than expected. He received 46 percent support compared to McGovern's 37 percent, lower than the "minimum 50 percent" that his advisers had predicted and much closer to McGovern than anyone had anticipated. The subsequent media portrayal of these results as a "victory" for McGovern wounded Muskie's candidacy among Democratic voters nationwide, and it never recovered. Strangely enough, the "victory" did not help McGovern; instead, in the short run, it helped Hubert Humphrey.[5]

It seems doubtful that the *Union Leader*'s attacks on Walter Mondale in 1984 and Kennedy in 1980 were similarly influential in the respective candidates' losses. The newspaper was as critical of Jimmy Carter (the "wimp") and Jerry Brown (the "flake") as it was of Kennedy in 1980, and described all the Democrats in 1984 (including the moderate-to-conservative John Glenn) as a pack of "turkeys." Since the *Union Leader* singled out no Democratic candidate for special attention, either negative or positive, its influence in the Democratic primary was nil.

Given this quick review, it is tempting to think that whatever the influence of the *Union Leader* on state politics, it does not extend to presidential primaries, except in the most unusual circumstances (e.g., Muskie). But the point of this chapter is to demonstrate that the newspaper probably did exert significant influence in 1980, when it may very well have saved the Reagan candidacy, and that in 1988, with an open field in both the Democratic and Republican parties, the newspaper could once again play a significant, if not decisive, role.

Characteristics of the Union Leader

The *Union Leader* is an unabashedly conservative newspaper. William Loeb used the newspaper to support his conservative agenda, much in the way that newspapers typically operated in the early part of the nineteenth century. In those days of the "partisan press," newspapers were mostly oriented toward political parties; indeed, they were frequently owned by one or another political party or faction. Partisan newspapers were an integral part of the growth of political parties during the last century. The news they presented was interpreted through the conceptual lens of the party and structured to support the party's agenda and positions.[6]

The move in American journalism toward the "objective" standards it espouses today was largely motivated by economic considerations. The success of the penny press in the 1830s was the result not only of the reduced price of the paper but of the mass market the paper could attract. And it attracted that mass market by presenting a paper that was decidedly nonpartisan (a major departure from the practices of the day) so that people of all political persuasions would feel comfortable reading it. Nonpartisan news, sold in large quantities, was the economic basis of the penny press's success, as well as the success of the wire services and the larger newspaper organizations that succeeded the penny press.

It is not surprising that a general press philosophy supporting objective journalism emerged from the newspaper experiences of the nineteenth century. The philosophy does not point to the crass commercial advantages of objective news, however, but to the important role of the press in the democratic process. According to this philosophy, the press's role is to provide citizens with the unadorned truth and let them draw their own partisan conclusions about those events.

This notion of an "objective" participant (the press) in the political process is alien to the philosophy reflected in the other structures of American government. In those structures, the prevailing philosophy is that factions compete with one another, and the resulting compromise is the best we can achieve for the general welfare. That was the theme of Madison's *Federalist No. 10*, and it was reflected in the decentralized form of government established in the U.S. Constitution.

But the philosophy of objectivity that prevails in American journalism presumes the existence of a truth that everyone can agree upon and everybody should report. Interpretations of the right and left should be reserved for the editorial page, put inside the newspaper so as to preserve the objectivity of the news. While those ideals were challenged by the "new journalism" of the 1960s and 1970s, objectivity remains an important standard of journalistic quality today.

The *Union Leader*, however, sees truth on the right, not in the center, and in that sense follows in the tradition of the partisan press, a tradition mostly rejected in the United States, but one that remains as the dominant characteristic in the West European press. (Partisan journalism should not, of course, be equated with "yellow journalism," a term used in the latter part of the nineteenth century that came to signify the deliberate distortion of news, even the reporting of events that did not happen.)

The publisher and editors of the *Union Leader* do not agree that their paper is partisan; they steadfastly maintain that they retain the distinction between editorials and news, and that the latter is presented objectively. In a 6 February 1980, front-page editorial, entitled "The Hypocritical *New York Times*," Loeb attacked that newspaper for its biased coverage in favor of Bush ("The *New York Times'* favorite candidate"), compared to the *Union Leader*'s objective coverage. That charge came as a surprise to those who were reading both newspapers, but the editorial illustrates the widespread acceptance, even by the *Union Leader,* of the norm of objectivity.

At issue was the selection of delegates to the Republican National Convention made on Saturday, 2 February 1980. Reagan had received 6, Baker 4, and Bush only 1. The item was covered on the front page of the *New Hampshire Sunday News* (the Sunday edition of the *Union Leader*), but was buried in the last section of the *New York Times,* next to the obituary section, 3 February 1980.

In the editorial, Loeb lambasted the *Times* for being "dishonest, while at the same time, being holier-than-thou." He expressed skepticism that editorials were especially influential, but asserted that the way in which newspapers present the news about candidates could influence voters. Loeb's comments are enlightening for what they reveal about his view of the power of the press, as well as the framework through which he, and for the most part his newspaper, viewed the world:

> The New York Times' burying of the news of the Reagan victory is a perfect example of the type of influence by the news media. It is dishonest, it is entirely wrong, but THAT is the way the leftist-controlled communications media in the United States plays the game. They favor Bush; he gets all the news play, and Reagan's victories are buried on the obituary page.
>
> A newspaper has a right, as this newspaper does, to have a very strong editorial opinion, with no "ifs, ands, or buts." We make no apologies for our strong editorial stands.
>
> HOWEVER, THE TYPE OF NEWS SLANTING AND MANIPULATION DEMONSTRATED BY THE NEW YORK TIMES IS A DISGRACE. ANY EDITOR WHO WOULD ENGAGE IN THIS TYPE OF ACTIVITY AT THE UNION LEADER OR NEW HAMPSHIRE SUNDAY NEWS WOULD BE FIRED IMMEDIATELY!
>
> We make no pretense of being angelic or holier-than-thou, but we do promise you that news is news, and we publish it as it happens, whether we *like* what we have to publish or not. We pledge never to engage in the kind of dishonest journalism demonstrated by the *New York Times* on Monday![7]

This charge of bias against the *Times,* no doubt unpersuasive to those few readers of both the *Union Leader* and the *New York Times* during that 1980 primary campaign, nevertheless illustrates the problem with defining *objectivity.* Indeed, in one sense the *Times* is biased, often presenting news from an antiparty, middle-of-the-road perspective (which also means from a leftist perspective for conservatives, and a rightist perspective for liberals). The *Washington Post, Wall Street Journal,* and other nationally respected news organizations have their own particular biases. And news judgments about which items to include in the paper, and what emphasis to give each item, will differ between newspapers with one bias from those with another, even though it will not always be clear to those who make the judgments that a bias is operating.

In that light, it is important to note that by almost any standards of analysis, the *Union Leader* has a decidedly conservative bias, Loeb's claims of objectivity notwithstanding. In the 1980 primary campaign, its bias was evident not only in the editorials, as Loeb would admit, but in the news stories it selected, the emphasis it gave them in the paper, and the headlines that called attention to them.

The Layout of the Union Leader

The format of the *Union Leader* is different in many respects from other newspapers in the state and contributes significantly to the newspaper's influence. It is easy for a reader, even a casual reader, to know what the *Union Leader* is about, what its views are on the current issues, even what issues are really most important from the paper's perspective—largely because of the way the news and opinions are presented in the paper.

In 1980, an editorial appeared daily on the front page, outlined in black and spread across two columns. It was usually signed by William Loeb, although occasionally it was signed by the editor.[8] Sometimes the space was reserved for a guest editorial.

When written by Loeb, the editorial often called attention to another, longer editorial on the same subject, usually on the back page at the top, written by a guest writer. In most cases, the headlines were pungent: *Let's Not Be Sucker Bait; Only a Bush Leaguer; George Bush Says: "Go — Yourself"; Is Everybody Lying but George?*

At the top of the front page was often a commentary article, headlines extending across most of the paper. The day before the election, for example, the newspaper carried a piece by the Senate president, Robert Monier, entitled "George Bush Is a Liberal." Former New Hampshire Governor Wesley Powell wrote such top-of-the paper articles as "Bush Shouldn't Take Us, Either—He Got Texas Oil, But Not Texas" and "We Need More Than Wallpaper." A statement by Reagan on the three hundredth birthday of New Hampshire's government was published with the headline *Ronald Reagan Lauds N.H. on Tricentennial—Cites State History in Opposing Excessive Taxation.*

Typically, articles not completed on the first page carry over to the back page of the first section, which makes it possible to continue the articles without opening the paper. The front page of either the second or third section is the main editorial page, containing the editor's comments plus syndicated and special columns. All of the nationally known columnists published in this section are conservative (e.g., William Buckley, Ralph De Toledano, Jeffrey Hart, Phyllis Schlafly). There is no effort to ensure a cross-section of ideological opinion.

The back page of the back section of the paper is laid out like a front page, with the paper's banner at the top and headlines of major stories not covered on the front page. Here again, there may be commentary pieces at the top of the page, such as the one by Lucille Lagasse, a Republican activist, whose headline read *God Has Chosen Reagan to Lead This Country.* In the article, Reagan was compared to Moses.

The net result of this structure of the paper is that it is easy for the reader to discover the major stories of the day and read them from the beginning to end (because of the ease of continuing the front-page story on the back page of that section). Further, the "second" front page (the very last page) gives the editors an added opportunity to highlight their major stories.

It is also easy for the reader to absorb the opinions of the editors. The front-page, oversized editorials by Loeb are difficult to miss, and their frequent references to other commentary—also prominently displayed, either on the front page or the "second" front page—give added opportunity for the paper to emphasize its views. Moreover, the frequent top-of-the-page commentary, whether mentioned in the Loeb editorial or not, emphasizes the paper's views.

Although the daily front-page editorial is labeled as such, as is the editorial page, the net result of the paper's layout is a general blending of "news" and opinion. Columns by guest writers are not always labeled "commentary," and even when they are, it is unlikely that readers take much time to note the distinction between regular news stories and commentary. This is the same problem, of course, faced by any newspaper, such as the *New York Times,* which publishes "analytical" articles on the front page even when labeled as such. But this problem of blending news and opinion is much more pronounced in the *Union Leader* because it includes the overt opinion articles published on the front page as well as the regular front-page editorials.

In addition, when the publisher and editor of the paper give speeches to local audiences, these events are sometimes covered as first-page stories, which allows the opinions of the editor and the publisher to be printed as news stories rather than editorials. The careful use of headlines and selection of news stories to be covered are additional ways by which news sections are often made to reflect the editor's and publisher's conservative views.

The Content of the Union Leader
During the Primary Campaign

To assess the stories presented during the New Hampshire primary, a systematic analysis was made of *Union Leader* coverage between 1 January and 25 February 1980, the day before the primary election. Two people were trained to classify and record the information about each story and picture dealing with the candidates and their campaigns. The coders also rated the items as positive, negative, or neutral.

Positive stories presented the candidate in a favorable light, which might attract readers to vote for him. Negative stories had the opposite effect. Neutral stories contained both positive and negative elements or were neither positive nor negative throughout. All stories dealing with the "horse-race" aspects of the campaign, such as factual reports about how well the candidates did in Iowa and who was leading in the latest scientific polls, were considered neutral.

The coders worked independently of one another and obtained agreement on the ratings for 92 percent of the items; where a disagreement occurred, the item was ultimately classified as neutral.

Almost two-thirds of the 630 items in the *Union Leader* about all presidential candidates included mention of at least one Republican. Of the 415 items about Republicans, over half were about Reagan and/or Bush, and almost 90 percent included at least Reagan or Bush, either alone or with other candidates. As table 4.1 shows, there were twice as many stories exclusively about Reagan as there were about Bush. Further, Reagan was included in over 60 percent of all items, compared to 45 percent for Bush.

More significant than the amount of coverage is the type of coverage received by the candidates. Overall, 46 percent of the stories about Reagan were

TABLE 4.1

REAGAN-BUSH TOTAL COVERAGE IN UNION LEADER,

1 JANUARY-25 FEBRUARY 1980

	Percent
Reagan alone	24
Bush alone	12
Reagan and Bush only	18
Reagan and others (but not Bush)	19
Bush and others (but not Reagan)	15
Other Republicans (but not Reagan or Bush)	12
Total	100
(N of items)	(415)

TABLE 4.2
REAGAN-BUSH POSITIVE AND NEGATIVE COVERAGE IN UNION LEADER,
1 JANUARY-25 FEBRUARY 1980

Coverage in Percentage of Stories

	Overall		Front Page		Back Page		Editorial		Other	
	Bush	Reagan	Bush	Reagan	Bush	Reagan	Bush	Reagan	Bush	Reagan
Positive	5	46	0	51	7	27	0	79	12	47
Neutral	47	52	30	47	83	70	5	21	50	51
Negative	48	2	70	1	11	3	95	0	38	1
Total	100	100	100	99	101	100	100	100	100	99

Coverage in Number of Stories

	Overall		Front Page		Back Page		Editorial		Other	
	Bush	Reagan	Bush	Reagan	Bush	Reagan	Bush	Reagan	Bush	Reagan
Positive	9	113	0	35	3	20	0	23	7	35
Neutral	85	127	17	32	38	52	1	6	29	38
Negative	87	5	40	1	5	2	19	0	22	1
Total	181	245	57	68	46	74	20	29	58	74

NOTE: Some percentages do not add to 100 because of rounding.

positive, compared to only 5 percent for Bush. On the front page, the figures were even worse for Bush: There were no positive stories, while over half the stories about Reagan were positive.

Similarly, negative stories about the two candidates show a decided advantage for Reagan. Overall, only 2 percent of the stories about Reagan were negative, compared to 48 percent of the stories about Bush. On the front page, the only negative story about Reagan was his failure to campaign in Iowa, whereas there were 40 negative stories about Bush (70 percent of his front-page coverage).

Union Leader *Before the Primary Campaign*

Although a comprehensive content analysis was not conducted for other months, the general pattern of positive coverage for Reagan is clearly evident. From 1 January to 15 February 1979, for example, just a year before the pri-

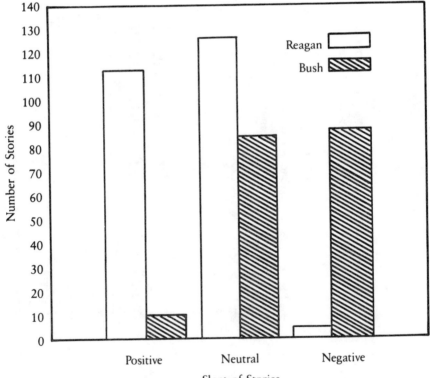

FIGURE 4.1

NUMBER OF STORIES IN UNION LEADER ABOUT REAGAN AND BUSH

mary, Reagan contributed 5 guest columns and was the subject of 11 stories or editorials; 7 of these were clearly positive, the rest neutral. A couple of negative articles each for Bush and Philip Crane and a more general one on Republican candidates were also included.

In September 1979, about six months before the primary, there were 18 articles about Reagan; 11 clearly favored him, the rest were neutral. Reagan also contributed 6 guest columns. During this same period, there was no focus on any one candidate (Bush had not yet emerged as the principal challenger), but earlier the *Union Leader* had carried a series of scathing articles on Crane's personal and professional life, and in September included a front-page story about his daughter's alleged harassment of two loons on Squam Lake. Howard Baker was termed the "political chameleon" and John Connally "Oily John: the Arab Candidate" and a "Born-Again Wheeler Dealer." Baker and Bush were "Bakerbush" (liberals not moderates); later, Bush was "the candidate of all the 'clean fingernail' Republicans, the sales-taxers and income-taxers."

In sum, the figures measuring the number of positive and negative stories about Bush and Reagan reveal one of the most lopsided "campaigns" ever conducted by the *Union Leader* for one of its candidates. Some people may disagree with the classification of one story or another as positive, negative, or neutral, but even the casual reader of the *Union Leader* in 1980, or in the year leading up to the primary, would have to conclude that the newspaper presented a strong case to vote for Reagan and against Bush.

Major Themes of the Union Leader *during the Campaign*

For many years, the *Union Leader* had been a staunch supporter of Ronald Reagan, and in the 1980 campaign it went after any candidate who posed a challenge to him. As noted, the newspaper ran a series of scathing attacks on Crane, who was a young, very conservative candidate, often viewed as the "young" Ronald Reagan. Crane's candidacy never got off the ground, and the paper's attention focused more on other possible challengers, such as Howard Baker and George Bush ("Bakerbush"). After the Iowa caucuses, Bush became the lightning rod for the paper's attacks.

A number of major themes were developed against Bush. Above all, he was portrayed as a liberal pretending to be a conservative. He was also portrayed as a "silk-stocking" Republican, an elitist appointed to several positions in government (director of the Central Intelligence Agency, ambassador to the United Nations, etc.) as a result of his connections, not his talent. His membership in the Trilateral Commission was raised as a "terrifying" prospect for

America: like Jimmy Carter, also a member of the Trilateral Commission, Bush would be under the commission's control.[9]

Bush's losses in campaigns in Texas for the U.S. House of Representatives and the Senate were cited as examples of his being a "loser." He was disdained as a "Bush-Leaguer" for the way he handled the Nashua debate, and as a hypocrite (for many reasons). He was attacked for being "soft" on his views of the Soviet Union. And he was attacked repeatedly for his supposed connection with the Nixon slush fund, revealed during the Watergate investigations.

The Union Leader's *Influence on Voters*

A number of theories of mass persuasion suggest that the ability of the media to influence people's opinions is limited. People bring to any message they read or hear their own predispositions and knowledge, and thus the "hypodermic needle" effect suggested by early theories of mass persuasion (implying that the media can inject their views directly into readers/viewers) is generally discounted.[10] Nevertheless, a key ingredient in forming opinions about current issues and candidates is the kind and amount of information people have about such matters. Any persistent news source providing information to people about an activity can thus have a profound influence on the opinions formed.

In the presidential primaries in New Hampshire, people generally receive little information about the candidates from national television. Most of their information comes from the local print and visual media, which give more extensive coverage at that point in the campaign than do the national networks. Newspapers are especially effective in providing information because they have more of a "newshole" in which to cover the subject matter than do radio or television news programs.

In the 1980 primary campaign, the *Union Leader* provided an immense amount of information about the candidates, especially a great deal of negative information about one candidate and positive information about the other. If ever a news source can influence voters' opinions, the *Union Leader* should have influenced voters during that campaign.

And it did.

Three public opinion polls, conducted as part of student projects for the University of New Hampshire poll, provide the data used to measure the influence of the *Union Leader* on the Republican electorate. The first survey was conducted in the first part of October 1979 and included 305 potential Republican voters (registered Republicans or registered Independents who leaned toward the Republican party), randomly distributed across the state. The survey in February 1980 included 585 potential Republican voters and was conducted two weeks before the primary. The third survey, conducted the week after the primary election, included 208 people who said they had voted in the Republican primary the week before.

While no election results can measure the accuracy of the first two polls, the postelection poll (using the same method of random sampling and the same student interviewers employed in the first two polls) can be compared with the actual vote outcome. Reagan won the primary with 49.9 percent of the vote; Bush received 22.9 percent. The postelection poll results, based on 208 Republican voters, show Reagan with 49 percent of the vote and Bush with 20.7 percent of the vote, results that are very close to the election figures and obviously well within the approximately 8 percent margin of error for a sample of this size.

The results of the three University of New Hampshire polls reveal two very different electorates in 1984: those who read the *Union Leader,* and those who did not. In October 1979, when Bush was still one of the "pack" of challengers, along with Baker, Anderson, Dole, and others, he received only 4 percent of the vote among *Union Leader* readers, but a respectable 16 percent among nonreaders. Reagan's support was overwhelming among the paper's readers, with 54 percent, but much lower among nonreaders, with 30 percent. Thus the net "effect" of the newspaper appears to have decreased Bush's support by 12 points and increased Reagan's support by 24 points.

TABLE 4.3

VOTER PREFERENCES AMONG READERS AND NONREADERS
OF THE MANCHESTER UNION LEADER

Read *Union Leader?*	October 1979		February 1980		March 1980	
	Yes	No	Yes	No	Yes	No
Voter preference:						
Bush	4%	16%	22%	49%	14%	26%
Reagan	54	30	53	17	68	32
Others/unsure	42	54	15	34	18	42
Total	100%	100%	100%	100%	100%	100%
(N)	(141)	(164)	(264)	(316)	(97)	(111)

Percentage Difference between Readers and Nonreaders of *Union Leader*

	October 1979	February 1980	March 1980
Bush	−12[a]	−27	−12
Reagan	+24[a]	+36	+36

a. The −12% means that Bush did 12 points *worse* among readers than nonreaders; the +24 points means that Reagan did 24 points *better* among readers than nonreaders.

In February, after Bush's surprising victory in the Iowa caucuses, Reagan's support among those who did not read the *Union Leader* had plummeted to 17 percent, while it held steady among readers at 53 percent, just a point lower than the poll in October. Bush's support, in contrast, had surged among both *Union Leader* readers and nonreaders: up by 18 percent among readers and by 33 percent among nonreaders. Here the net "effect" of the *Union Leader* appears to have increased Reagan's support by 36 points and decreased Bush's support by 27 points.

Indeed, the influence of the *Union Leader* in staving off disaster for Ronald Reagan after Iowa appears most evident here. Among the newspaper's readers, *Reagan still led Bush by 31 points, 53* percent to 22 percent. Among nonreaders, it was a mirror image, *with Bush leading Reagan by 32 points,* 49 percent to 17 percent.

The Nashua debate apparently disillusioned many about Bush, for his support among the group of voters that did not read the *Union Leader* dropped 23 points, whereas Reagan's support jumped by 15 points. The net result was that even among nonreaders, Reagan beat Bush by 32 percent to 26 percent (with the other 44 percent of the vote distributed among the rest of the candidates). For hard-core supporters of Bush, who had witnessed the pounding of their candidate by the *Union Leader* on one issue after another for months,

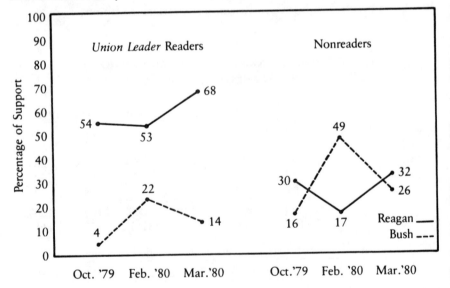

FIGURE 4.2

VOTER SUPPORT FOR REAGAN AND BUSH
COMPARED AMONG READERS AND NONREADERS

the spectacle of the Nashua debate was only moderately influential: Among that group, Bush lost just 8 points. Reagan's support among *Union Leader* readers, however, increased by almost the same margin (13 points) as it did among nonreaders. Thus, among the paper's readers, Reagan beat Bush by 68 percent to 14 percent

Figure 4.2 demonstrates clearly the existence of the two different electorates in New Hampshire. The dynamics of the campaign, from before the Iowa caucuses to that period between the Iowa and New Hampshire contests and to the actual election, are considerably different depending on whether voters were or were not following the campaign through the eyes of the *Union Leader.* Among voters who did *not* read the *Union Leader,* the dramatic surge of support for Bush by February 1980 (after the Iowa caucuses), compared with his support in October 1979 (before the Iowa caucuses), parallels the dramatic surge in support Gary Hart was to receive from his second-place showing in the Iowa caucuses four years later.[11] But among voters who read the *Union Leader,* the Iowa caucuses had only a limited impact. Reagan supporters who read the newspaper, bolstered by the barrage of positive information in the paper about their candidate and negative information about the challenger, held fast after the Iowa caucuses, although supporters of other candidates tended to rally around Bush. It is difficult to avoid the conclusion that the *Union Leader*'s biased coverage exerted a profound effect on its readers.

Since readers of the *Union Leader* tend to be more conservative than nonreaders anyway, one might argue that the apparent influence of the *Union Leader* is somewhat illusory. Perhaps it is just a matter of self-selection that accounts for this apparent influence: People read the *Union Leader* because they agree with its political orientation, including support for Reagan. Thus, readers are not influenced by the newspaper to support Reagan but are merely reinforced in the views they already have.

There are many reasons why people do *not* read a newspaper. One reason, for example, is that the newspaper is not local. Conservatives who want a local paper, but who do not live in Manchester, will usually read only their local paper; similarly, liberals in Manchester may read the *Union Leader,* even though it disagrees with their political views, because they want a local paper or because they want to keep informed about state news (the *Union Leader* is still without peer in the thorough coverage it gives to New Hampshire state government in Concord). In any case, readers do not choose a paper only on ideological grounds; some liberals read the *Union Leader,* and some conservatives do not.

It is thus possible to test the hypothesis that differences between *Union Leader* readers and nonreaders reflect the greater number of conservatives (over liberals) who read the paper, by comparing the views of conservatives who do read the paper with those who do not. Similarly, we can examine the views of liberals who do and do not read the *Union Leader*.

The results of such an examination show that while it is true the readers of the *Union Leader* are more conservative than nonreaders, it is not conservatism that explains the large differences between the newspaper's readers and nonreaders. As shown in figure 4.3, among voters in our February poll who considered themselves "strong conservatives," there was a 57-point gap between *Union Leader* readers and nonreaders in their support for Reagan! Some 84 percent of the "strong conservative" *readers* support Reagan, whereas only 27 percent of the "strong conservative" nonreaders support Reagan.

Similar differences between readers and nonreaders of the *Union Leader* can be found all along the ideological spectrum. Among "moderate conservatives," Reagan receives 49 percent support from readers and just 14 percent support from nonreaders, a difference of 35 points. Similarly, among "lean conservatives," Reagan's support is 39 points higher among readers than nonreaders; among those whose philosophy is "in-between" liberal and conservative, Reagan does 32 points better among readers than nonreaders; and among liberals (the

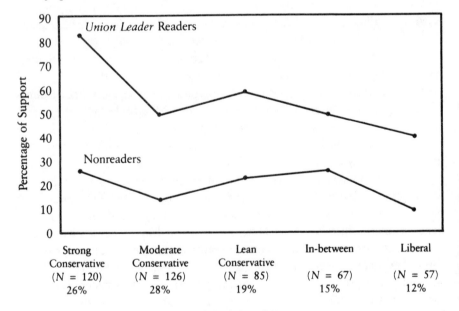

Political Philosophy of Voters

FIGURE 4.3

VOTER SUPPORT FOR REAGAN, FEBRUARY 1980

"lean," "moderate," and "strong" liberals are all grouped together here because of their small number among Republicans), readers give Reagan 32 points more support than do nonreaders. Political philosophy may indeed correlate with vote choice, but it does not explain away the large gaps between *Union Leader* readers and nonreaders.

Political philosophy is not the only factor that might explain differences between *Union Leader* readers and nonreaders. To examine the potential of other factors, a multiple regression analysis was run using the February poll data and the results are reported in table 4.4. Vote choice was the dependent variable and was recoded into two categories, Reagan and all others; 18 issue questions were included as independent variables, along with age, gender, education, and income of respondent. Both political philosophy and readership of the *Union Leader* were included as well. Several runs were made, with the last run retaining only those independent variables that enjoy a statistically significant correlation with the dependent variable, controlling for the other independent variables.

By far the most important factor, controlling for all other factors, was the *Union Leader,* with a beta[12] of .40 (see table 4.4). The second-most-important factor, again controlling for all other factors, was political philosophy, with a beta of .15. That means the newspaper had over *two and a half times* as much impact on voting choice as did political philosophy.

Although many issue variables are correlated with voter choice, once their effect is controlled for by the *Union Leader* variable and political philosophy, only one retains a statistically significant relationship with the dependent vari-

TABLE 4.4

FACTORS INFLUENCING VOTERS' CHOICE FOR REAGAN,

FEBRUARY 1980 POLL

	Regression Analysis					
	Overall (N = 379)		Union Leader Readers (N = 170)		Union Leader Nonreaders (N = 209)	
Multiple R	.486		.424		.183	
Adjusted R²	.228		.165		.019	
Factors	Beta	Signif.	Beta	Signif.	Beta	Signif.
Union Leader	.40	.000	—	—	—	—
Political philosophy	.15	.002	.26	.000	.15	.034
U.S. too weak	.15	.001	.21	.004	.08	.274
Income	−.09	.051	−.28	.000	.07	.317

able. That issue was a measure of voters' responses (*agree* or *disagree*) to the statement that the United States is too weak to defend the Middle East. (The question was asked during the period of the Iranian hostage crisis, when U.S. military strength was a campaign issue.) The results indicate that *in addition* to the effect of the *Union Leader* and political philosophy, attitudes about U.S. military strength affected voters' choices between Reagan and the other candidates. The more critical the voters were of U.S. military strength, the more likely they were to vote for Reagan.

Finally, income appears to have some effect on voter choice, with the lower-income Republican primary voters more likely to choose Reagan than higher-income voters.

The regression was repeated for *Union Leader* readers and again for non-readers. Note in table 4.4 the difference in the factors that influence readers from those influencing nonreaders. The *Union Leader*'s emphasis on Reagan being a conservative and Bush a "liberal" is reflected in the high correlation among readers between conservative philosophy and choice for Reagan. With a beta of .26, political philosophy is a large and statistically significant influence on the readers' choice for President; but for nonreaders, political philosophy is only weakly related to voter choice (beta = .15).

Note also that, for *Union Leader* readers, attitudes about U.S. strength correlate strongly (beta = .21) with choice for Reagan (those who agree the United States is too weak are more likely to vote for Reagan than those who disagree). For nonreaders, however, the relationship between U.S. strength and vote choice is not statistically significant (beta = .07). The *Union Leader* frequently emphasized Reagan's commitment to a strong America, accusing Bush, among other things, of being "soft" on Soviet goals.

Similarly, note that among readers of the *Union Leader,* low income is strongly associated with choosing Reagan (with a beta of .28), but income is insignificant among nonreaders. This difference probably reflects one of the *Union Leader*'s major themes about Bush, that he is of the "clean fingernail," rich eastern establishment Republicans, in contrast to Reagan, who is one of the common folk.

Summary and Conclusion

Two facts stand out about the New Hampshire Republican primary in 1980:

1. The *Union Leader* "campaigned" against George Bush and for Ronald Reagan in unmistakable terms, in editorials, news stories, and commentaries.

2. The *Union Leader* seemed very effective in influencing its readers' views of the two candidates. On average, readers of the *Union Leader* were more likely than nonreaders to support Ronald Reagan by a margin of 35 to 40 points, a pattern that held true whatever a voter's ideological predisposition (from strong conservative to liberal). Indeed, a simultaneous comparison of numerous factors demonstrates that the *Union Leader* was overwhelmingly the most important influence on the choice Republicans made in the primary election.

Thus a reasonable case can be made that the *Union Leader* played a major role in helping "save" Ronald Reagan in New Hampshire and, perhaps, save Ronald Reagan's candidacy for President as well. Such an argument does not deny the responsibility that George Bush must take for his own actions, especially in the Nashua debate, but it points to the role of the *Union Leader* in shaping the campaign in New Hampshire that eventually led to that debate.

George Bush came out of Iowa with a surprise victory over a candidate who was almost universally expected to win. We know now, from Gary Hart's experience in 1984, that public opinion can be volatile in New Hampshire and that even a poor *second-place* showing in Iowa can propel a relatively unknown candidate into first place in New Hampshire over a well-known political figure. The analogy with Bush's campaign is striking, except that Bush emerged with a *first-place* finish. Certainly, in retrospect, we might expect such a first-place finish to have immense positive consequences for Bush's standing in the electorate.

And it did, but in only *one* of the two electorates: those who did *not* read the *Union Leader.* Among these nonreaders, Bush went from a 14-point deficit to a 32-point lead, a net difference of 46 points! The loser of the Iowa caucuses, Ronald Reagan, lost 13 points in New Hampshire, while the winner, George Bush, gained 33 points.

Among the *other* electorate, however—those who obtained their information from the *Union Leader*—the loser in the Iowa caucuses (Reagan) lost virtually no support. The winner of the caucuses (Bush) did pick up support in New Hampshire from this electorate, but to a much smaller extent than in the other electorate (18 points as opposed to 33), and apparently all of the support from voters who had previously supported "also-rans" in Iowa. Bush's net gain in this second electorate was just 19 points, compared to 46 points in the first electorate.

The result of these two different electorates was that the contest in New Hampshire appeared quite close during the month after the Iowa caucuses, leading Bush finally to agree to the one-on-one debate sought by the Reagan campaign. All the candidates had debated in Manchester the Wednesday before the election, and Bush certainly would not have felt pressured to debate Reagan one-on-one had he been further ahead in the polls—as he no doubt would have been, except for the *Union Leader.* Without the Nashua debate, and even *with* the *Union Leader's* attacks, Bush might well have won. Without either the debate or the *Union Leader,* it is difficult to see how Bush could have lost.

This argument should not be taken as a note of gratitude to the *Union Leader* for having saved the country or a criticism of its style of journalism. A case can easily be made that a partisan press is a more "responsible" press than an "objective" press, responsible at least to its vision of the truth.[13] In fact, one well-known analyst of the media points out that "social responsibility journalism is popular with a sizable proportion of the news profession" and cites statistics showing that less than 35 percent of the journalists in North America today believe in "neutral" reporting.[14]

A "socially responsible" press is another way of saying a press that attempts to influence its readers toward a particular view, which in the minds of the editors is the correct view. Clearly, the *Union Leader* fits this model. And, just as clearly, it can be effective in its efforts.

As for 1988, the *Union Leader* has not yet[15] indicated its preference among Republican candidates. It has already lambasted Bush, in an editorial entitled *Bushgate,* for not admitting that the Reagan administration made a mistake in trying to sell arms to Iran in exchange for hostages. But now that Reagan has admitted it was a mistake, and Bush has said the same, there appears to be no burning desire to pursue an anti-Bush campaign.

On the Democratic side, the *Union Leader* has chosen a neutral role in the past few elections because of its antipathy for all the Democrats who have trooped across the state. In 1988, however, it may well focus its scorn on Michael Dukakis, the Massachusetts governor who has played a major role in opposing the New Hampshire nuclear power plant at Seabrook. Before a nuclear power plant can be authorized to go on-line, all towns within a ten-mile radius must have emergency evacuation plans approved by the Nuclear Regulatory Commission. By refusing to submit the emergency evacuation plans of nearby Massachusetts towns, Dukakis has held up the licensing process, incurring the wrath of both the New Hampshire governor, John Sununu, and the *Union Leader,* among others. Dukakis has also endeared himself to a sizable group opposed to the power plant.

Besides his opposition to the Seabrook nuclear power plant, Dukakis symbolizes what the *Union Leader* finds most objectionable in liberal Democrats: support for human service programs and a willingness to raise taxes to pay for them.

It is too early to say which candidates the *Union Leader* might help or hurt in 1988, but its potential influence in the presidential primary is underscored by a former congressman from California, Paul McCloskey, who wrote in 1980 that the newspaper was "a major campaign document worth tens of thousands of dollars to the lucky beneficiary."[16] In fact, for Ronald Reagan it may well have been worth much more: the Presidency itself.

Notes

1. See Eric Veblen, *The Manchester Union Leader in New Hampshire Elections* (Hanover, N.H.: University Press of New England, 1974).

2. In ibid., Veblen analyzes aggregate voting data and *Union Leader* circulation figures, from which he concludes that the newspaper had a significant influence on certain statewide elections. For a recent study using survey data, which concludes that the paper probably made the crucial difference in the gubernatorial election of 1982, see David W. Moore, "The Legacy of William Loeb," *Public Opinion*, December/January 1983.

3. Although Veblen's study, which includes numerous interviews with political leaders attesting to the *Union Leader*'s influence on state issues, has not been systematically updated, that influence is still noted by political analysts. A 17 February 1987 article in the *Boston Globe* presents interviews with selected analysts who support this point.

4. Herbert B. Asher, *Presidential Elections and American Politics: Voters, Candidates and Campaigns Since 1952*, 3d ed. (Homewood, Ill.: Dorsey, 1984), 210.

5. C. Richard Hofstetter and David W. Moore, "Television News Coverage of Presidential Primaries," *Journalism Quarterly* 59, no. 4 (Winter 1982).

6. Richard L. Rubin, *Press, Party and Presidency* (New York: Norton, 1981).

7. The bold print and capitalization are part of Loeb's style and were in the original editorial.

8. The tradition of the front-page editorial continues, but Nackey Loeb writes editorials much less frequently than her husband did.

9. The *New Hampshire Sunday News* (the Sunday edition of the *Union Leader*), 3 February 1980, p. 1.

10. Doris Graber, *Mass Media and American Politics*, 2d ed. (Washington, D.C.: Congressional Quarterly Press, 1984).

11. It should be noted that the surveys in this study were not conducted right before and after the Iowa caucuses, so one cannot conclusively say—based on these surveys—that Bush's greater support in February 1980, compared to October 1979, was due to the Iowa caucuses. Nevertheless, it is difficult to attribute any factor other than the Iowa caucuses to Bush's increased support in February 1980, and the Hart phenomenon in 1984 indirectly supports that interpretation. One also cannot conclusively say that Bush's loss of support in the election was due to the Nashua debate, since the survey in this study was not conducted just before the debate took place. Nevertheless, the February University of New Hampshire poll was completed just ten days before the election and just one week before that debate. The timing is close and leads at least

to reasonable speculation that the debate was the crucial factor in Bush's unexpectedly poor showing.

12. *Beta* is a measure of association between the independent and dependent variables, controlling for all other independent variables. It can range between -1 and $+1$, with 0 meaning no association, and $+1$ (or -1) meaning a perfect one-to-one association. The positive sign means the greater the value of one variable, the greater the value of the other. A negative sign means the variables are inversely related.

13. For a discussion of various models of press behavior, see Fred Siebert, Theodore Peterson, and Wilbur Schramm, *Four Theories of the Press* (Urbana: University of Illinois Press, 1963).

14. Graber, *Mass Media and American Politics*, 23.

15. As of May 1987.

16. Letter to the Honorable George Bush, 14 March 1980; copy provided by Representative McCloskey.

5
What's the Primary Message: Horse Race or Issue Journalism?

HENRY E. BRADY AND RICHARD JOHNSTON

1. Introduction

The lessons of the preceding chapters seem clear: Iowa and New Hampshire are unique media and political events, and their uniqueness systematically distorts the presidential nominating process. The claim that Iowa and New Hampshire are unique seems incontrovertible, but the claim that they distort the nominating process is highly contestable without some standards for judging the nominating process. For in politics as in art, one person's notion of distortion is another person's notion of representativeness. This chapter tackles the problem of providing an overall perspective for judging the way the primary system, by emphasizing the outcomes in Iowa and New Hampshire, distorts the American nominating process.[1]

The basic question for political scientists studying presidential nominations is the degree to which the mass electorate should be involved in the nominating process. On the one side are "reformers" who favor having the mass electorate narrow the field of candidates through a succession of primaries; on the other side are "traditionalists" who prefer old-style conventions where party elites made these choices.[2]

Until 1968, presidential nominees were chosen by bargaining among political elites in the often exciting and always colorful atmosphere of political conventions. Since 1968, presidential campaigns have shifted from the circus of conventions to the traveling road show of presidential primaries and media events. This change from bargaining to voting has, unsurprisingly, provoked comment, concern, and even alarm among traditionalists who believe that the new process has had unfavorable consequences for the future of government in America.[3]

Yet it is premature to make a summary evaluation of this change. We lack both standards for judging the nominating process and facts about how the old and new systems operate. These problems emerge clearly in discussions of "momentum" in primaries. The preoccupation of politicians with getting and keeping momentum has produced some of the more charming and pungent anecdotes about presidential candidates, but it has produced little enlightenment about the concept. Only a few scholars have investigated momentum in any detail,[4] and there is still a great deal of mystery about whether it really exists and whether it is good or bad. This is partly because an emphasis on momentum neglects the basic issue: How do primaries work?

The American nomination process is dominated by a weekly succession of caucuses and primaries that begin, as journalists are fond of noting, in the snows of Iowa and New Hampshire and end in the sun of California. Commentators on presidential primaries all agree that during this 15-week period the media bombard citizens with an astonishing amount of information that fixes national attention on the nominating process. They disagree on the kind of information generated, the media's role in disseminating it, the way that it is used by citizens who receive it, and its implications for the nominating process.

Reformers have argued that presidential primaries provide the public with an opportunity to learn about the personal characteristics, policy positions, and electability of candidates, and to make an informed choice based on this information. Sometimes this argument rests on a naive belief in populist democracy, but in its more sophisticated version it rests on the notion that primaries provide citizens with a chance to learn about the candidates and to choose the best of the lot. An even stronger notion is Steven Hess's belief[5] that primaries provide "tests" of those qualities needed in a President and that those who can work the pinball machine of the modern primary system are more suited for the job. From this perspective, momentum, if and when it exists, simply reflects the public's considered judgment that one candidate is clearly superior to all the others.

Opposed to this perspective is the belief, vigorously argued by Nelson W. Polsby,[6] that primaries are essentially lotteries driven by media expectations and candidate name recognition that do little to provide a political education. Polsby ruefully notes that the task of a presidential hopeful "is not to win a majority but rather to survive"[7] by advertising and promoting name recognition, and that "an overall nomination process dominated by primary elections and their electorates tends to force an early definitive choice on the party."[8]

Others have argued that the information produced, and acted upon, about candidates during the primary season consists primarily of impressions about who is winning and who is losing. In its extreme form, this view of the process transforms voting into a kind of betting with news reports as little more than the daily racing form.[9] These critics are somewhat vague about the exact mechanisms which produce these results, but they are convinced that momentum occurs and that it is mostly harmful.

Are primaries public instruction and moral uplift or poorly designed lotteries? Do primaries inform voters about issues, or do they involve them in betting on a horse race? These are difficult questions to answer. One difficulty is the small number and idiosyncratic character of the examples. Another difficulty is the lack of compelling theories of leadership selection and media behavior. Although political theorists from Plato through Machiavelli have had something to say about what makes a good leader, they have had surprisingly little to say about the best mechanisms for identifying leaders. Even democratic theorists have not had much to say about how to formulate the list of candidates presented to the electorate. The Founding Fathers, faced with little guidance on this matter, developed the unwieldy and quickly amended procedures of the electoral college. Even after amendment, this method was soon replaced by the congressional caucus and then a succession of other institutional mechanisms—the national convention and presidential primaries. Similarly, while political theorists from Aristotle to Habermas have discussed political rhetoric and communication, they have had little to say about what an ideal process of political communication—much less an ideal role for the mass media in elections—might look like.

What does one do when both standards and data are lacking? Rather than ask whether the outcomes of conventions are better than those produced by the primary system, we follow the lead of administrative court judges who examine the process of decision rather than its substance. By asking about the decision-making process of the voters and the media in the primaries, we are rescued from the conundrum of describing good or bad candidates. We intend, then, to describe the process of decision making, and to ask whether it satisfies the requirements for a good decision-making process.

2. Criteria for a Good Decision-Making Process

Luckily, once we focus on the decision-making process, there are some natural and plentiful subjects for study. For primaries, the locus of decision making is the voters. If their calculations are flawed, then it seems likely that the outcomes of primaries are also flawed. For the 1984 Democratic nomination, we are lucky to have some remarkably useful data about the American electorate. In 1984, the National Election Studies (NES) designed a weekly "rolling cross-section" that interviewed a random sample of about 65 Americans every week from 11 January to 30 November 1984. During this time, many questions about the characteristics of candidates and the characteristics of the individual respondents were repeated from week to week. With these data we can study, for the first time, the evolution of the beliefs and attitudes of the American electorate as the primary season progressed. These data, however, do have one significant limitation: They are samples of the national electorate and not the state electorates that actually voted in the the primaries.

What should we look for in the survey data? What criteria distinguish a good from a bad decision-making process? Our introductory discussion mentioned some of the concerns of both supporters and critics of the primary system. A more systematic discussion of the criteria for a nomination process appears in James Ceasar's two books[10] and in a paper by Henry Brady.[11] Our discussion draws on Ceasar's work, although we have rearranged his categories to suit our own tastes.

JUDGING CHARACTER

A good nomination process should judge the character of a candidate. We rightly ask whether leaders are persons of competence, empathy, and integrity. Quite apart from the managerial contributions such characteristics make, they also play an exemplary role. Politics is not just the delivery of goods but also something of a morality play. Even if personal characteristics as perceived are themselves the product of calculation, deference is still being paid to ideals of virtue.

The National Election Studies ask about 12 traits for each candidate. Nine of the traits seem to us to be personal characteristics; the other 3 are about the capacity to govern. The personal characteristics cover the three dimensions mentioned above: competence, empathy, and integrity. Competence is assessed by ratings on the adjectives *hardworking, intelligent,* and *knowledgeable.* Empathy is covered by *compassionate, kind,* and *really cares.* Integrity is represented by *decent, moral,* and *good example.* Respondents are asked whether the adjective "fits your impression" of the candidate "a great deal," "somewhat," "a little," or "not at all." These will constitute our measures of personal abilities. As we are judging process and not outcome, we do not want to assume that certain traits must be considered for a nominating process to be judged a good one, but we believe that at least some traits must be considered, and the NES provides enough different traits so that almost anyone's taste should be satisfied.

ASSESSING PURPOSE

Admirable personal qualities, as Jimmy Carter and Herbert Hoover attest, are not enough. A nominating process must also consider the policy goals put forth by candidates, and it should probably guard against candidates who are mere ciphers with no notions of their own. The NES data include many measures of the policy positions of the candidates and the positions of decision makers who support one or another of the candidates. As with traits, we believe that the range of policy positions is broad enough so that one can argue that at least some of them should be considered.

FOSTERING ELECTABILITY AND LEGITIMACY

Still more is required. Character and purpose are necessary qualifications for a political executive, but hardly sufficient. A politician must also have some external resources to be able to get things done, and the American Presidency, for example, comes equipped with remarkably few intrinsic resources. Power is required, and it must be stored up in the process of obtaining a popular mandate. As a first step, a nominating process must consider a candidate's electability. More broadly, a nominating process must ensure that a candidate is perceived as a legitimate wielder of the power of the executive. If the process by which a candidate is nominated is not deemed legitimate, then it is unlikely that support will be found even within his or her own party. Some argue, for example, that the 1968 Democratic nomination process suffered from a crisis of legitimacy that caused widespread dissatisfaction with the nominee of the party, Hubert H. Humphrey. Character and electability, then, represent competencies or potentials—one personal and the other political. Just as character ensures that a person has the ability to be an executive, electability (and, more broadly, legitimacy) provides the political and social potential for action.

A successful nomination process should ensure that the electability of its nominee is considered. Electability may sometimes be rejected as a lesser goal, as when policy goals are deemed paramount, but it certainly should be considered, and it cannot always be ignored unless a party wishes to remain in impotent opposition. For the American data, we can measure perceptions of electability with a 100-point "chances of being elected" scale that was asked throughout the 1984 survey.

CREATING THE CAPACITY TO GOVERN AND TO LEAD

Character must be guided by purpose; lacking it, an executive is aimless. Similarly, electability must be complemented by a capacity to govern—often in the form of a political coalition—that can utilize power to achieve a set of goals. Without such a coalition, election to office is a pyrrhic victory. Nelson Polsby, for example, contends that the modern primary system causes candidates to woo factions for the purpose of securing the nomination and the election, but it does not impel them to create true coalitions for getting things done once elected. Polsby's contention requires further empirical analysis, but his argument certainly emphasizes the need for a nominating process that fosters the capacity to govern.

How can a nomination process ensure that its candidate will be capable of governing once elected? Must it create a network of alliances, attachments, and agreements for a candidate? Or should it strive to avoid such entanglements, leaving the candidate free to mobilize public opinion against the entrenched networks of power and influence? One's theory of government has much to do with one's answers to these questions. We shall not advance any theories here, but we shall propose that one aspect of the capacity to govern — the leadership ability of the candidate — can be imperfectly measured by the three NES traits of *commands respect, inspiring,* and *strong leader.* We shall usually analyze these three traits in conjunction with the nine traits described above.

DEALING WITH VIABILITY

We also have a measure of a fifth characteristic of a nominating process — the degree to which it is preoccupied with the relative chances of candidates winning the nomination itself. In the NES data there is a measure of the perceived viability of candidates that is similar to the electability measure described above. In journalistic accounts, a preoccupation with viability takes the form of a fascination with "momentum" — who has it, and who does not. At the root of the debate between traditionalists and reformers is a disagreement about the role of viability and momentum. To the traditionalists, viability is an overwhelming concern of the media and consequently of the primary process. This concern, say the traditionalists, makes primary coverage more like the sports reports on the last week of a pennant race than debates over the character, goals, electability, and governing capacity of the candidates. Reformers doubt whether a concern for viability really dominates the media's coverage in this way, and they consider momentum the wholesome result of citizens learning about the candidates and exercising rational and strategic preferences.

In another paper,[12] we have compared mathematical models where voters learn about the character, policy positions, electability, and leadership skills of the candidates with models where voters learn about the viability of candidates. In the first model, the growth of recognition and knowledge about the candidates has the normatively appealing dynamic of education leading to broadly self-interested and rational behavior, whereas the second model, with its emphasis on viability, resembles a lottery whose odds are fixed by the judgments of the news media. Viability, it seems, can swamp consideration of the "issues" and replace this concern with "momentum" that is self-generated and virtually unrelated to other, arguably more important, considerations.

Which model, then, fits the facts? To what extent do voters learn about the characteristics of candidates—their abilities, their goals, and their electability—and take them into account in their voting decisions? And to what extent does viability overwhelm any other considerations in the calculus of individual voters? We attack these questions in the following sections.

3. Preconditions for a Good Decision-Making Process

A good nominating process must nurture candidates of character and purpose, and it must ensure that they are girded with legitimacy and a capacity to govern. A succession of primaries can achieve these results only if the voters are aware of these criteria and if they take them into account in their voting decisions. Moreover, the voters cannot be expected to be aware of them unless the mass media provide information about them. A minimal requirement, then, for the success of primaries is the availability of information about the character, purposes, electability, and leadership abilities of candidates.

For this reason, we have supplemented the NES data with a complementary set: a content analysis of every UPI story on one of the eight Democratic candidates from 1 January to 31 July 1984. These data allow us to analyze the media's coverage of viability and its role in fostering candidate momentum. In our content analysis, each story was broken up into story parts which involved a unified discussion of a *candidate,* on a particular *subject,* drawing from a particular *base* of information. Table 5.1 summarizes the number of lines for each subject by each type of basis. Six major subjects, characterizing the content of the parts, were included in the study. These were chosen so as to answer the basic questions that might occur to a journalist or a newspaper reader. The major subjects and their subtopics along with the question motivating each category are listed below:

1. *Is the candidate winning?* "The potential or actual success of the candidate" including viability, electability, campaign organization, and fund-raising abilities
2. *Who supports the candidate?* "Sources of support or opposition" including individuals (e.g., Thomas P. ("Tip") O'Neill), organized groups (AFL-CIO, Sierra Club), and unorganized groups (Hispanics, environmentalists)

3. *What is the candidate like?* "Candidate issues" including experience (record of public service, previous offices held), leadership ability (intelligence, knowledge, strength, decisiveness, self-confidence), personal qualities (honesty, sincerity, integrity, likability, appearance, health), and human interest (news about the candidate's wife, children, parents, childhood, or background)

4. *What does the candidate stand for?* "Issues of government policy" including social, economic, defense, government operations, and all other policy areas

5. *What does the candidate say about his opponents?* "Comments about other candidates" including Ronald Reagan, the eight Democrats, the Republican party generally, or general comments about the other Democratic candidates

6. *What other events have involved the candidate?* "Other events" including debates, campaign appearances, social events, noncampaign public events, noncampaign private events

The bottom row of table 5.1 indicates that coverage was spread relatively evenly over the six major categories with a low of 8.6 percent for stories about support or opposition and a high of 22.9 percent for stories about candidate issues. Through design, many of these categories can be directly related to the NES data described above—for example, "leadership ability" in the content analysis is a combination of "leadership" and "competence" from the traits battery; "personal qualities" from the content analysis data is a combination of "integrity and empathy" from the traits; and viability, electability, and some policy issues are directly comparable. The NES data, however, do not have any questions on support for the candidates, what they say about their opponents, or on other campaign events (categories 3, 5, and 6 in the content analysis data). Indeed, it is hard to think of appropriate questions for these last two categories (except possibly about debates among primary candidates).

The base of information, or "basis" for short, identifies the source for the story. Three major sources were considered: facts, attributed views, and unattributed views. The "description of facts" includes actual results of an election, caucus, or convention; the result of a scientific opinion poll; and other undisputed information. "Attributed views" include the views of those supporting the candidate (the candidate himself and members of his staff or someone else clearly identified in the story as a supporter); the views of those opposing the candidate (other candidates and members of their staff or someone else clearly identified in the story as an opponent); and views of nonpartisan observers. "Unattributed views" include those views that the reporter reputes to be widely held, commonly believed, or agreed upon by most observers and those views that were speculation by the reporter. The right-hand column of table 5.1 indicates that more than 29 percent of the coverage used the candidate himself as the source of information about the candidate, and 14 percent of the coverage used a candidate as a source about another candidate—for a total of almost half the coverage (44 percent) being based on the candidates. The remainder of the coverage was based on undisputed information (24 percent), nonpartisan sources (12 percent), partisan supporters or opponents of the candidates (9 percent), actual results or polls (5 percent), or unattributed views (5 percent).

Finally, for each story (with one exception), we asked our coders to judge on a five-point scale "the overall impression of the candidate conveyed by the discussion in this part of the story." This was probably the most difficult judgment our coders had to make (although some felt that determining the basis was even harder), but it is very important for much of the following analysis. When making these judgments, we asked our coders to think like an average newspaper reader. Through repeated discussion sessions, we felt that we reached some consensus on how to do this. The one exception occurred when the story was about one candidate commenting about another. In that case, we asked the coders to tell us what the candidate's evaluation was of the subject of his comments.

We are interested in whether primary voters could conceivably learn what they must learn to make reasonable voting choices. This leads us naturally to the following questions, which we regard as increasingly stringent tests of whether a primary electorate engages in a deliberative decision process rather than a lottery:

1. Do the media inform citizens about the character, purpose, electability, and leadership ability of candidates? Do they say much about viability, and if they do, what do they say about it?
2. If the media do inform the citizenry, do voters know about the most important characteristics of the candidates?
3. Or do voters learn about the most important characteristics of the candidates? What do they learn about viability?
4. If they do know or learn about the candidates, do voters make choices with these characteristics in mind? To what extent do they base their choices on viability?

It is hardly believable that a decision process could be a good one if the media do not inform citizens about the candidates, if the voters who make

TABLE 5.1

EVIDENTIARY BASIS BY MAJOR SUBJECT

	Potential Success	Sources of Support	Candidate Issues	Policy Positions	Candidate Comments	Other Events	Total
Facts	1633 (32.37)	594 (28.65)	1496 (27.00)	454 (11.51)	0 (0)	2825 (58.37)	7,002 (29.00)
Actual results	441 (8.74)	4 (.19)	4 (.07)	0 (0)	0 (0)	0 (0)	449 (1.86)
Opinion polls	584 (11.58)	77 (3.71)	86 (1.55)	0 (0)	0 (0)	3 (.06)	750 (3.11)
Undisputed information	608 (12.05)	513 (24.75)	1406 (25.38)	454 (11.51)	0 (0)	2822 (58.31)	5,803 (24.03)
Attributed views	2911 (57.72)	1371 (66.13)	3712 (66.99)	3439 (87.15)	2705 (100)	1783 (36.84)	15,921 (53.95)
Candidate	1657 (32.85)	136 (6.56)	1353 (24.42)	2801 (70.98)	0 (0)	1158 (23.93)	7,105 (29.42)
Supporter	358 (7.10)	594 (28.65)	425 (7.67)	120 (3.04)	0 (0)	52 (1.07)	1,549 (6.41)

Opposing candidate	224	69	270	73	2705	149	3,490
	(4.44)	(3.33)	(4.87)	(1.85)	(100)	(3.08)	(14.45)
Other opponent	132	231	317	137	0	70	887
	(2.62)	(11.14)	(5.72)	(3.47)	(0)	(1.45)	(3.67)
Nonpartisan observer	540	341	1347	308	0	354	2,890
	(10.71)	(16.45)	(24.31)	(7.81)	(0)	(7.31)	(11.97)
Unattributed views	500	108	332	53	0	232	1,225
	(9.92)	(5.21)	(6.00)	(1.34)	(0)	(4.80)	(5.07)
"Common belief"	249	33	151	10	0	163	606
	(4.94)	(1.59)	(2.73)	(.25)	(0)	(3.37)	(2.51)
Speculation	251	75	181	43	0	69	619
	(4.98)	(3.62)	(3.27)	(1.09)	(0)	(1.43)	(2.56)
Total	5044	2073	5540	3946	2705	4840	21,443
	(20.9)	(8.6)	(22.9)	(16.3)	(11.2)	(20.0)	

NOTE: Upper entry is number of lines; entry in parentheses (except bottom marginals) is column percentage.

choices are initially ignorant of the candidates, do not learn about them, or do not base their choices on this information. These four questions, then, provide hurdles that the primary process must cross before we can even begin to judge it favorably.

4. UPI and the 1984
Democratic Nomination

STANDARDS FOR JUDGING MEDIA COVERAGE

It is not obvious what is news is and what is not. The news media confront a world much like the unscored baseball game described by Walter Lippmann where "the more you try to imagine the logic of so absurd a predicament, the more clear it becomes that for the purposes of newsgathering (let alone the purposes of playing the game) it is impossible to do much without an apparatus and rules for naming, scoring, recording."[13] Reporters must often attempt to construct news from an unscored game, and those who wish to audit the reporters' performance must first score the game at several removes. The task seems virtually impossible, and certainly thankless.

Nevertheless, a tradition of media criticism based upon content analysis has developed and prospered. One recent book, by Michael Robinson and Margaret Sheehan,[14] has done an especially good job of providing a scoring system for the game. Robinson and Sheehan analyzed the coverage of CBS television news and the United Press International (UPI) wire during the 1980 campaign, and their results provide us with both a framework for analysis and some findings comparable to our own. We shall rely heavily on their conceptual framework.

Robinson and Sheehan propose five criteria for judging the job done by the media: objectivity, access, fairness, seriousness, and comprehensiveness. We shall employ the first four in the following pages. "Objectivity includes, above all, a considerable reluctance to go beyond what was actually observed by the journalist, and an even greater reluctance to draw any explicit conclusions or inferences about the events being covered, unless the conclusion or inference comes from another legitimate source, not the journalist him/herself."[15] Objectivity, then, is a bedrock requirement for balanced coverage that is closely related to the basis for a story. It requires that stories be reported without editorial content. Of course, coverage may be objective while completely ignoring some candidates or while choosing to quote only negative opinions of some and only positive opinions of others. For example, it seems likely that many articles on the 1984 presidential campaign in the *New Republic* or

National Review meet this standard of objectivity while failing the following tests.

Access and fairness require more. *Access* demands that "similar" candidates receive "equal amounts" of coverage, although it says nothing about the tone of this coverage. We shall judge access by looking at the amount of coverage each candidate received in each subject area (potential success, support, candidate issues, policy positions, comments, and events). *Fairness* stresses tone rather than amount of coverage. It requires that "similar" candidates be evaluated similarly. Our judgment of fairness will use our evaluation of each story as well as its other characteristics.

Justice may be served if similar candidates receive similar coverage and similar tone, but wisdom may not be. If the media cover only human interest stories or the "horse race," there will be no way for the electorate to learn about the characters, purposes, electability, and leadership abilities of the candidates. *Seriousness* requires that the news media take these things seriously. We shall judge seriousness by examining the stories that UPI covered in 1984.

Objectivity. Table 5.1, on pp. 136-37, demonstrates that coverage was basically objective. Ninety-five percent of the lines of the UPI stories were either factual (29 percent) or attributed to various sources (66 percent). The remaining 5 percent were split evenly between "views that the reporter reputes, implicitly or explicitly, to be widely held, commonly believed, or agreed upon by most observers" and "speculation by the reporter." Although we used a somewhat different coding procedure than Robinson and Sheehan, these results are consistent with theirs.

In the aggregate, reporting appears to be objective. Is it also objective with respect to specific candidates and subjects? The percentage of lines based on unattributed information ranges from 1 percent for Cranston and McGovern to around 5 percent apiece for Hart, Hollings, Jackson, and Mondale to over 11 percent for Askew, Glenn, and Ferraro. Four of these candidates, Cranston, McGovern, Hollings, and Askew, received so little coverage (fewer than 628 lines) that it seems unlikely that these differences are truly significant, but statistical significance appears to be an especially recondite concept when considering data from a content analysis of UPI stories, and it seems useful to stop and discuss its meaning before proceeding.

As is well known, statistics is based on the idea of sampling from some population, and the starting place for most statistical work is making some assumptions about the underlying population that makes the problem tractable. For the content analysis data, all UPI primary stories for 1984 are in the data, so it cannot be considered a typical sample from a population that could be, at least in principle, enumerated. One can, however, employ the usual fiction that the data at hand are a sample from a larger population of stories that might have been written. This leads to a second difficulty: The usual statistical formulas assume that each observation is a random draw from the same population distribution. As a result, each observation, as a random variable, is independently and identically distributed. In what sense is this true of the content analysis data? Specifically, can we use the well-known formulas for standard errors that divide the standard deviation by the square root of the sample size? What, exactly, is the sample size for these data? Is it the number of stories (about 1600), the number of story parts (5475), or the number of lines (24,152)?

We suspect that the story is the best unit to use for calculating standard errors because each story is probably written by one person at a specific time and place. For most of the things we will be studying, it seems best to conceive of the reporter as choosing the story form according to some internalized journalistic rules and the logic of external events. Where the logic of events is similar across candidates, our purpose is to discover the probabilistic rules of choice. The pattern of these rules probably varies across reporters so that one might argue for the more conservative practice of using the smaller number of reporters who wrote the UPI stories, but the variation across reporters (and hence the correlation among stories written by the same reporter) is probably relatively small. Indeed, one could also argue that reporters actually make many specific decisions about a story at the level of a story part (or even at the level of a line) so that these larger numbers should be used. The number of stories, however, seems like a reasonable compromise between using the number of reporters or the number of story parts.[16]

Unfortunately, there is a practical problem with using the number of stories. Because we are analyzing story parts of differing lengths, it would be very difficult to obtain the number of stories in each category of one of our typical tables. As a rule of thumb, we have usually computed standard errors by setting the "effective" number of units for analysis as the number of lines divided by 15. This factor is obtained by dividing the total number of lines by the total number of stories.

Using this rule of thumb along with a .05 level of statistical significance, it appears as if Cranston and McGovern received less unattributed coverage than the overall average, and Glenn and Ferraro received more. For Glenn, most of these story parts concerned his viability, and they appeared around the time when he dropped out of the race. For Ferraro, the story parts were about her family and her husband's financial situation. All in all, our judgment is that these differences are not large enough for us to complain about the different standards of objectivity for different candidates.

Although there do not appear to be any major biases across the candidates, there does seem to be a different pattern of coverage for some candidates than others. Thus, there is a greater use of polls (about 6 percent of the total lines) for Glenn, Hart, and Mondale than for the rest of the candidates (about 1 percent), and there is a greater reporting of actual results for Hart and Mondale (5 percent and 3 percent) than for the other candidates (around 1 percent). Finally, there are many more stories (about 4 percent) based upon opposing candidates for Hart, Jackson, and Mondale than for the other candidates (less than 1 percent). None of this is surprising, and it can easily be attributed to the special roles played by these candidates during the campaign. In terms of our earlier discussion about statistical issues, reporters made different choices because of the logic of the situation rather than their reportorial biases. Of course, it is worth knowing more about what distinguishes one candidate's situation from that of another.

The standard of objectivity may be the same across candidates, but table 5.2 shows that there are certainly different standards for different subjects. The

TABLE 5.2

SUBJECT BY UNATTRIBUTED COVERAGE

	Percent "Common Belief"	Percent Speculation	Total Lines	Total Percent
Potential success				
Viability	7.25	6.56	2883	13.81
Electability	.82	2.85	736	3.67
Campaign organization	3.96	4.19	1291	8.15
Sources of support				
Individual support	1.26	.87	1030	2.13
Group support	1.20	4.97	584	6.17
Unorganized group support	2.83	8.06	459	10.89
Candidate issues				
Personal qualities	3.87	5.86	853	9.73
Other issues	2.52	2.79	4687	5.31
Policy positions, all categories	.25	1.09	3946	1.34
Other events, all categories	3.37	.43	4840	4.80

NOTE: Percentages are expressed as percent of total coverage.

greatest amount of unattributed coverage is for viability, 14 percent, while the lowest is in the reporting of policy positions, at 1 percent. This disparity is very large and highly significant. Fourteen percent is only one-seventh of the total coverage of viability, but the disparity in the sources for coverage of viability versus that for policy positions suggests that the coverage of the horse race may allow reporters more license than other sorts of stories. Table 5.2 also shows that the tendency for reporters to speculate about candidate support increases as the basis of the support becomes more diffuse. This result is based on relatively small numbers of lines, but it is suggestive. Finally, a candidate's personal qualities appear to offer more room for unattributed views than other characteristics of the candidate.

    Access. Access demands that "similar" candidates receive "equal amounts" of coverage. Candidates for the Democratic nomination are probably most equal before any caucuses or primaries have been held. In 1984, this means before the Iowa caucus. Table 5.3 summarizes the number of lines on each subject for each candidate from 1 January through 21 February, the day after the Iowa caucus (the results are virtually identical for coverage through 14 February). The most striking feature of this chart is the extraordinary amount of coverage received by Jesse Jackson. Jackson received half the coverage accorded all eight candidates! A plot of the total number of lines for Glenn, Hart, Jackson, and Mondale by week shows that much of Jackson's coverage was in the first two weeks of the year when he was involved in obtaining the release of an American naval lieutenant, Robert Goodman, from Syria. Yet, whatever initially motivated this coverage, it had the effect of spawning stories on Jackson's viability, his base of support, his personal characteristics, and his policy positions. Jackson, without a doubt, was the major media star of the first part of the campaign.

    Although he received only about one-third of the coverage accorded Jackson, Walter Mondale still received about three times as much coverage as any other candidate, and between the third week of the campaign and before Iowa, Jackson and Mondale received about equal amounts of coverage. Furthermore, Mondale received more of what can be broadly called horse-race coverage—stories on his potential success—than did Jackson. This suggests that Mondale was the clear front-runner at this stage of the campaign.

    The remaining six candidates together received slightly more coverage (1632 lines) than Mondale, and they can be broken up into three groups based on the amounts of this residual coverage they received. Reubin Askew and Alan Cranston were treated as "hopeless" cases. A "fair" share of the residual coverage allocated to these six candidates would be 16.7 percent apiece, but Askew received only 4.3 percent, and Cranston received just 9.7 percent. Moreover, the UPI stories said virtually nothing about Askew's or Cranston's potential for success, their sources of support, what they were saying about the other candidates, or what the other candidates were saying about them. They were not treated as part of the horse race.

The next two candidates were treated as "probably hopeless, but interesting" candidates. Ernest Hollings was a quotable southerner with an engaging demeanor, while George McGovern used his prestige as a former Democratic presidential nominee to run an admittedly quixotic "policy-oriented" campaign. The final two candidates, Glenn and Hart, were "plausibles"[17] who each received more than 25 percent of the residual coverage, although only Glenn seems to have been considered part of the horse race. There was virtually no coverage of Hart's potential for success or his sources of support, and there were no comments about him. Whether or not Hart was a "plausible" candidate in the eyes of the press, the overwhelming conclusion is that all of the candidates other than Jackson and Mondale received very little coverage from the UPI.

The UPI coverage between Iowa and the last primary in California on 5 June is summarized in table 5.4 (pp. 146-47). For this period, Hart, Jackson, and Mondale dominated the coverage, with Hart receiving 30 percent, Jackson 21 percent, and Mondale 29 percent. Of the remaining candidates, only Glenn received more than 3 percent of the coverage, and he received only 8 percent — most of it between Iowa and the time he dropped out in the tenth week. From Iowa to California, there was also a distinctive pattern of coverage for Glenn, Hart, and Mondale. Figure 5.1 (p. 148) displays the coverage for Hart in the six major subject areas. When the percentage of coverage in these subjects is correlated across Glenn, Hart, and Mondale, the correlations run from .85 to .96. The same chart for Jesse Jackson is displayed in figure 5.2 (p. 148). This profile is slightly negatively correlated (around −.15) with those for Glenn, Hart, and Mondale. While about one-third of the total coverage for these three candidates was potential for success and another one-third covered candidate issues and policy positions, only about 10 percent of the coverage for Jesse Jackson dealt with potential for success, while more than 40 percent of it dealt with his character and policy positions. The media covered Glenn, Hart, and Mondale as part of a horse race; Jesse Jackson provided personality and issues — his trip to Syria, his comments about "Hymie town," his involvement with Louis Farrakhan, and his decision to go to Cuba.

In addition to these differences in the content of the coverage for Jackson versus the other candidates, there were some important temporal variations in coverage. Jackson's ups and downs will engage our attention later on; for the moment, we wish to focus on the rise of Gary Hart. In the Iowa caucuses during the eighth week of the year, Mondale took a decisive 45 percent of the

TABLE 5.3

SUBJECT COVERAGE BY LINES OF COVERAGE IN THE EARLY CAMPAIGN

(BEFORE IOWA)

	Askew	Cranston	Glenn	Hart	Hollings	Jackson	McGovern	Mondale	Total
Potential success	13	19	182	41	56	284	43	372	1010
Viability	12	8	84	18	31	145	19	210	527
Electability	0	0	8	0	0	23	17	45	93
Campaign organization	0	8	68	18	23	55	4	56	232
Fund-raising	1	3	22	5	2	61	3	61	158
Sources of support	0	1	21	1	0	188	2	297	510
Individuals	0	1	11	1	0	128	0	96	237
Organized groups	0	0	10	0	0	38	2	191	241
Unorganized groups	0	0	0	0	0	22	0	10	32
Candidate issues	6	31	8	52	9	1229	54	179	1568
Experience	0	0	2	8	3	36	0	4	53
Leadership	0	20	0	9	0	839	0	14	882
Personal qualities	0	0	1	23	0	86	6	26	146
Human interest	6	11	5	12	6	268	48	135	491

									Total
Policy positions	11	43	41	164	116	409	64	150	998
Social	8	0	0	12	0	53	0	15	88
Economic	0	7	18	49	15	31	0	18	138
Defense	3	28	20	81	38	228	46	99	543
Government operations	0	8	3	22	12	90	18	18	171
Other	0	0	0	0	51	7	0	0	58
Comments about other candidates	0	10	130	91	47	95	40	189	602
Hart	0	0	0	—	0	0	0	0	0
Jackson	0	0	12	0	14	—	0	28	54
Mondale	0	0	75	31	0	48	0	—	154
Reagan	0	10	37	58	33	44	37	138	357
Democrats	0	0	6	2	0	3	3	5	19
Ferraro/Glenn/McGovern	0	0	0	0	0	0	0	18	18
Other events	40	54	74	71	44	1502	53	96	1934
Debates	1	1	6	2	1	1	1	8	21
Campaign appearances	38	50	65	67	41	371	28	85	745
Public appearances	1	2	2	2	2	972	2	3	987
Private appearances	0	1	1	0	0	158	22	0	181
Totals	70	158	456	420	272	3707	256	1283	6622

TABLE 5.4
SUBJECT COVERAGE BY LINES OF COVERAGE IN MID-CAMPAIGN
(IOWA TO CALIFORNIA)

	Askew	Cranston	Glenn	Hart	Hollings	Jackson	McGovern	Mondale	Total
Potential success	77	77	373	1139	63	247	57	928	2961
Viability	63	30	333	779	48	208	47	679	2187
Electability	1	0	9	134	3	17	2	100	266
Campaign organization	0	0	3	157	5	17	0	110	298
Fund-raising	13	47	28	69	7	5	8	39	216
Sources of support	9	5	52	286	7	257	7	391	1014
Individuals	4	0	30	178	2	89	0	184	487
Organized groups	3	5	4	44	4	66	4	134	264
Unorganized groups	2	0	18	64	1	102	3	73	263
Candidate issues	2	14	80	522	20	520	8	561	1727
Experience	0	0	12	17	0	3	0	29	61
Leadership	2	0	11	76	2	81	0	40	212
Personal qualities	0	9	11	87	0	201	0	46	354
Human interest	0	5	46	342	18	235	8	446	1100

									Total
Policy positions	1	189	122	475	68	394	90	331	1670
Social	1	0	18	42	1	66	0	46	174
Economic	0	32	36	106	65	66	9	87	401
Defense	0	143	59	273	0	139	61	160	835
Government operations	0	1	0	34	0	129	0	38	202
Other	0	13	9	20	2	4	20	0	68
Comments about other candidates	0	17	25	245	37	174	38	351	887
Hart	0	0	12	—	21	14	1	269	317
Jackson	0	0	0	10	0	—	17	1	28
Mondale	0	0	10	159	0	67	1	—	237
Reagan	0	17	0	74	0	42	19	81	229
Democrats	0	0	3	2	5	41	0	0	51
Ferraro/Glenn/McGovern	0	0	0	0	11	10	0	0	21
Other events	8	17	93	242	11	443	27	218	1069
Debates	0	0	3	30	0	22	0	27	82
Campaign appearances	8	10	77	206	9	310	11	170	801
Public appearances	0	6	10	1	2	69	8	16	112
Private appearances	0	1	3	5	0	42	8	5	64
Totals	97	319	745	2909	206	2035	227	2780	9328

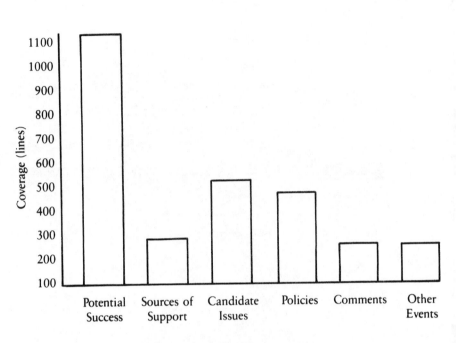

FIGURE 5.1

HART COVERAGE BY SUBJECT, IOWA TO CALIFORNIA

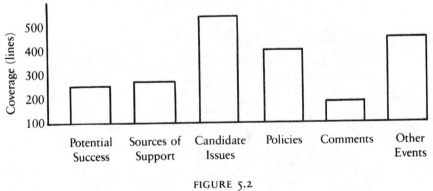

FIGURE 5.2

JACKSON COVERAGE BY SUBJECT, IOWA TO CALIFORNIA

preference votes. Hart was a relatively weak second (15 percent), beating out George McGovern (13 percent). Glenn received only 5 percent of the preference votes. In the week before the Iowa caucuses, the coverage for Hart and Glenn was approximately equal (138 and 117 lines, respectively), although each received only half the coverage afforded Walter Mondale (256 lines). In the next (ninth) week, however, Hart received more than three times the coverage obtained by John Glenn (208 to 59 lines), and he received more coverage than Walter Mondale (129 lines), even though Mondale had won the Iowa caucuses. At the end of this week, Hart unexpectedly won the New Hampshire primary with 37 percent of the vote. Mondale was second with 28 percent of the vote, Glenn received 12 percent, and Jackson got 5 percent. Two weeks later, on Super Tuesday, Hart won primaries in Massachusetts and Florida, and Mondale won primaries in Alabama and Georgia. Mondale was still ahead in delegates, but during these weeks, Mondale's coverage dropped precipitously while Hart's rose to 564 lines in the week after Super Tuesday compared to 307 lines for Mondale. During this period, John Glenn's coverage first faded and then revived as reporters debated whether or not he would continue in the race. At the beginning of the tenth week, he dropped out of the race.

Does all of this add up to equal access? It is hard to argue that it does. Before Iowa, Jackson and Mondale received much more coverage than any of the remaining candidates. This pattern of coverage poses some especially difficult questions: If the news media should focus on the front-runner (which Mondale surely was at that point), then why did Jackson get so much coverage? If they should not focus on the front-runner, then why was Jackson singled out? One of the reasons, of course, is that Jackson's trip to Syria was the kind of event that the news media find compelling. It involved individuals—a black American serviceman and a black American politician—and it involved an area that has been the focus of media attention during the last two decades. All of this made the event newsworthy; but it did not ensure equal access for the Democratic candidates.

If one forgets about Askew, Cranston, Hollings, and McGovern, and if one just looks at the aggregate coverage for Glenn, Hart, Jackson, and Mondale (especially the last three), then UPI's coverage after Iowa seems to have provided equal access. But what about Askew, Cranston, Hollings, and McGovern? Should they have been so quickly consigned to the also-rans? And what about the details of the coverage of Glenn, Hart, Jackson, and Mondale? Why the distinctive coverage for Jackson and the burst of coverage for Hart after Iowa? The distinctive coverage for Jackson may have been dictated by events. As the first black man to make a serious run for a major-party nomination,

Jackson, it could be argued, was different from the other candidates. He could not just be dropped from coverage like the other candidates, even though there was not much to be said about his progress in his quest for the nomination. Consequently, the news media had to find other stories to tell about him, and he obliged by (sometimes) skillfully finding newsworthy events. This argument explains why journalists were fascinated by Jesse Jackson and why he received a different kind of coverage, but it is not very compelling if our fundamental concern is the operation of the primary process, for it suggests that public learning through this process can be easily affected by those candidates who find ways to make themselves newsworthy, even though their newsworthiness may have little to do with their qualifications for the nomination. The burst of media attention received by Gary Hart is less explicable. It seems hard to doubt that he received much more attention than his performance in Iowa merited.

Fairness. For Robinson and Sheehan, "Tone involves the overall (and admittedly subjective) assessment we made about each story: whether the story was, for the major candidates, 'good press,' 'bad press,' or something in between. 'Fairness' as we define it, involves the sum total of a candidate's press tone; how far from neutrality the candidate's press score lies."[18] This is one of two closely related definitions of the "tone" of a story. This notion emphasizes the journalist's search for a "balanced" story by presenting all relevant perspectives. By this definition, events per se have no place in good press or bad press. Robinson and Sheehan, for example, argue:

> When, in late April, CBS and UPI reported that Carter's commandos failed to free the hostages and that eight of the commandos died in the attempt, that story was not necessarily considered bad press. We considered it bad press only if the source said something critical or presented critical comments about the mission in an unbalanced (one-sided) way. We are, after all, evaluating press, not Carter's foreign policy. In our research, good press/bad press did not include hard news events, unless the journalist drew or implied a conclusion from those events.[19]

Another definition emphasizes the candidate's search for good press whether or not it is balanced. Because our ultimate goal was to relate assessments of UPI stories to public opinion as measured by the the the rolling cross-section, we utilized this second notion when we asked our coders to rate, on a five-point scale, the "overall impression of the candidate conveyed by the discussion in the story part." Our definition of fairness, then, considers hard news events, and it leads to positive or negative evaluations of some stories that Robinson and Sheehan would consider neutral.

There is good reason to believe that the evaluative tone of a political story will depend upon its sources, especially "attributed sources." Table 5.5 shows

TABLE 5-5
EVALUATIONS BY BASIS

Basis	Number of Lines	Average Evaluation	Percentage of Lines with Zero Evaluation
Supporter	1,549	.844	16.9
"Common belief"	606	.586	22.1
Actual results	449	.523	9.6
Candidate himself	7,105	.402	54.2
Undisputed information	5,803	.294	54.1
Speculation	619	.246	27.8
Nonpartisan observer	2,894	.136	25.7
Opinion polls	750	.087	9.2
Opposing candidate	785	−.468	27.8
Other opponent	887	−.715	16.0
Candidate comments	2,705	−.928	15.7
Totals	24,152	.148	38.0

that this is true by listing bases from the most positive to the most negative. (These are the same categories as in table 5.1, but they have been rearranged.) The average evaluation for a particular basis varies from .844 (on the five-point evaluation scale that runs from −2 to +2) for supporters of a candidate to −.928 for candidate comments about other candidates. This is not surprising, and there is a quite reasonable ordering of the evaluative tone of story parts according to their "attributed sources." Supporters say the most positive things about their chosen candidate. Candidates (probably due to modesty, real or feigned) say fewer positive things about themselves, and they tend to make many neutral statements (as indicated in the last column of the table). Nonpartisan observers are essentially neutral. Opposing candidates (when quoted in a story part about another candidate) are somewhat negative, and candidates commenting about other candidates are quite negative. None of this seems surprising, and it demonstrates what is already well known. A reporter who wants to convey a particular tone can achieve it by choosing the right sources.

What is somewhat surprising is the degree to which some "factual" and "unattributed" story parts are highly evaluative. This is especially true of parts identified as "commonly believed" and "actual results." Evaluation is not confined to the selection of attributed sources. It also seeps into these two other areas, and it may be most disquieting to see the degree to which unattributed views are charged with evaluative content.

Evaluative tone also depends on what is being evaluated. Table 5.6 presents three measures of the strength of evaluation: the average evaluation for the subject, the percentage of lines with zero evaluation (small percentages indicate an evaluatively charged category), and the percentage of lines with extreme evaluations of −2 or +2. By these measures, story parts about "leadership," "candidate comments," "viability," and "sources of support" are the most evaluative. For all these categories, the absolute value of the mean evaluation is more than twice the overall average evaluation (see the bottom line of the table), the percentage of lines with zero evaluation is less than half the average percentage of such lines, and the percentage of lines with extreme evaluations is above 17 percent. The least evaluative are story parts about "policy positions," "human interest," and "other events." (This last category has a fairly high average evaluation, but over 57 percent of the lines are evaluated at zero and only 5 percent are evaluated at −2 or +2.)

These results suggest that the real evaluative punch in UPI stories comes from two kinds of stories: (1) horse-race stories (Who is viable and who is not? Who supports whom? Who is commenting on whom?); and (2) leadership stories. Policy positions, human interest stories, and other events provide only a low level of evaluation. This is intriguing, but we wish to be cautious. We

TABLE 5.6

EVALUATIONS BY SUBJECT

	Number of Lines	Average Evaluation	Percentage of Lines with Zero Evaluation	Percentage of Extreme Evaluations
Potential success	5,044	.187	19.5	21.0
Viability	3,017	.324	16.8	25.2
Electability	736	-.132	20.7	16.4
Campaign organization	914	.079	39.3	9.0
Funding	377	-.103	9.3	25.7
Sources of support	2,073	.500	13.4	17.8
Candidate issues	5,540	.319	36.2	15.1
Experience	185	.032	29.2	22.2
Leadership	1,784	.715	8.9	33.6
Personal qualities	853	-.101	23.3	19.0
Human interest	2,718	.211	58.7	1.2
Policy positions	3,946	.127	67.4	3.9
Candidate comments	2,705	-.928	15.7	31.7
About Jackson	381	.108	17.1	21.8
About others	2,324	-1.099	15.4	32.5
Other events	4,840	.388	57.5	5.4
Campaign appearances	2,000	.283	68.2	2.8
Public events	2,159	.536	41.2	9.4
All other	681	.225	77.5	0
Totals	24,148	.148	38.1	14.6

can think of two reasons why our coding produced these results. One reason is that stories on the horse race and leadership probably did contain more evaluative phrases ("strong leader," "impressive showing," "decisive move"). If this is all, then our result is an important one. Another reason is that it is harder to be sure about "impression conveyed about a candiate" from a policy story because this impression may depend a great deal on how one feels about the policy. We considered this when we were coding the stories, and it may explain the weak evaluation of policy positions. Yet, one could argue that stories about sources of support also present such difficulties, and our coders had much less trouble with them. We suspect that this is because the standard story about political support is written in a positive and upbeat fashion—the reader is given the impression that an endorsement indicates the growing strength of the candidate. Policy stories are not written in this way. Reporters do not tend to emphasize how a policy position will increase the strength of a candidate.

Before leaving table 5.6, it is worth noting one other interesting point. Under "candidate comments," we separated comments about Jackson from comments about any other candidate because comments about him were so distinctive. For the five other candidates with at least 30 lines of coverage (Glenn, Ferraro, Hart, Mondale, and Reagan), the comments were, as we expected, highly negative. The highest evaluation was −.53 (for Ferraro), and all the other evaluations were below −.90. But for some reason (we can guess why), candidates did not want to criticize Jesse Jackson.

Was coverage fair? Following Robinson and Sheehan, we have evaluated the fairness of coverage by excluding, as much as possible, overtly partisan information and information about winning or losing.[20] Thus we excluded two subject-matter areas (viability and candidate comments), and we excluded six basis categories (actual results, polls, and the views of candidates themselves, their supporters, opposing candidates, and other opponents). After doing this, what remained of the three major basis categories were factual story parts that did not discuss winning or losing, nonpartisan comments, and unattributed views—a total of 9059 lines.

With the data at hand, there are many ways to assess the variations in media coverage. Three measures of the monthly media verdicts on each candidate are displayed in each box of table 5.7. On the first line of each box is the sum of all the lines weighted by their evaluation for that candidate in that month. This is the "net evaluation" of the candidate in that month. On the third line is the total number of lines, and on the second line is the ratio of these two numbers, which we shall call the intensity of positive (or negative) coverage. A candidate can be said to have unambiguously "good press" if his or her net evaluation, intensity, and amount of coverage are all large and positive. For example, Jesse Jackson in January 1984 certainly had good press, and Walter Mondale in May 1984 had bad press. It is not always so easy to identify good and bad press. One problem is that the candidate with the most positive (or most negative) intensity may not have the largest (or smallest) net evaluations. This is often simply a matter of sample size. When there is a small number of lines about a candidate, then the estimate of the intensity tends to be very unstable. If one is careful about small sample sizes, then intensity and net evaluation are very highly correlated so that intensity serves as an excellent measure of good and bad press.

Table 5.7 tells a fascinating story, but it is best studied in conjunction with table 5.8, which presents information about net evaluation, intensity, and total coverage for story parts about viability. Viability is one of the most important categories omitted by Robinson and Sheehan in their measure of fairness, and as noted above, it is the most problematic for students of the primary process. There is one other set of measures that might be useful: We could look at the overall evaluation (only excluding candidate comments) of each candidate for each month. We shall cite some of these overall evaluations in the following paragraphs, but we have not included a table for them because they tend to be an average of the results in tables 5.7 and 5.8.

Dealing with so many measures at once can be confusing. Hence when we use the word *fairness* or when we speak of *good* or *bad* press, we shall be referring to Robinson and Sheehan's narrow measure of fairness. When we talk about *viability*, we shall just be referring to viability, and when we talk about *overall evaluations* or *intensities*, we shall mean the results from using all the stories (excluding candidate comments).

Consider what tables 5.7 and 5.8 tell us about the lineup of candidates in January before any caucuses or primaries. There was very little viability coverage for Askew, Cranston, Hollings, and McGovern, and what there was tended to be negative. (McGovern had some positive coverage, but the number of lines is very small.) In addition, none of these candidates received very good press. The highest intensity score for these four in January in table 5.7 was .098 for Askew, and the remainder were all negative. These four candidates were not given very much coverage, they had bad press, and they were not considered viable. By February, Askew, Cranston, Hollings, and McGovern were all receiving zero or negative viability coverage, and with the exception of Cranston, they were receiving bad press. This pattern was repeated in March (except that Cranston received bad press and Hollings received a small amount of good press), and by April these candidates had fallen from view.

The situation for John Glenn and Gary Hart is quite different. Their overall evaluation was similar in January (an intensity of .438 for Glenn and .381 for

TABLE 5-7
GOOD AND BAD PRESS FOR CANDIDATES, BY MONTH

	January	February	March	April	May	June	July	Total
Askew	4	-2	6	—	—	—	—	8
	.098	-.083	1.000					.108
	41	24	6					74
Cranston	-3	9	-38	—	—	—	—	-32
	-.051	.321	-.481					-.170
	59	28	79					188
Glenn	9	-9	-28	—	—	—	—	-20
	.102	-.129	-.171					-.053
	88	70	164					374
Hart	23	15	150	-24	129	-1	11	303
	.295	.144	.299	-.185	.594	-.025	.088	.254
	78	104	501	130	217	40	125	1195
Hollings	-3	2	9	—	—	—	—	4
	-.044	.059	.281					.026
	68	34	32					151

Jackson	1149	90	18	44	92	403	52	1848
	.661	.262	.115	.195	.289	.345	.174	.435
	1737	344	156	226	318	1167	299	4247
McGovern	−18	−17	−1	0	0	−3	−41	−80
	−.439	−.198	−.056	0	0	−.750	−.586	−.336
	41	86	18	14	5	4	70	238
Mondale	17	81	151	79	−94	13	0	247
	.093	.286	.456	.497	−.393	.074	0	.124
	183	283	331	159	239	176	615	1986
Ferraro	—	—	—	—	3	2	194	199
					1.00	.500	.324	.328
					3	4	599	606
Total	1178	169	267	96	130	418	219	2477
	.513	.174	.208	.175	.162	.292	.127	.273
	2295	973	1287	549	801	1432	1722	9059

NOTE: First entry in each cell is net evaluation; second is ratio of first and third entries; third is total lines for that candidate. A dash indicates a number of lines too small to enter. Consequently totals sometimes exceed the sum of individual entries.

TABLE 5.8
VIABILITY COVERAGE FOR CANDIDATES, BY MONTH

	January	February	March	April	May	June	July	Total
Askew	-4	-10	-31	—	—	—	—	-45
	-.364	-.217	-1.72					-.600
	11	46	18					75
Cranston	-2	-13	-17	—	—	—	—	-32
	-.667	-.542	-1.55					-.842
	3	24	11					38
Glenn	45	-47	-136	—	—	—	—	-148
	.763	-.758	-.467					-.355
	59	62	291					417
Hart	-2	49	413	39	40	14	12	565
	-.667	.628	.843	.375	.408	.424	.188	.649
	3	78	490	104	98	33	64	870

Hollings	−28 −.933 30	0 0 12	−63 −1.91 33	—	—	—	—	−94 −1.21 78
Jackson	19 .176 108	−24 −.649 37	−29 −.363 80	21 .292 72	44 .830 53	0 — 0	−6 −1.50 4	25 .071 354
McGovern	9 .643 14	−8 −.500 16	−24 −.727 33	—	—	—	—	−29 −.439 66
Mondale	166 1.66 100	148 .813 182	65 .180 361	93 1.00 93	109 .768 142	63 .969 65	28 .700 40	672 .684 983
Total	203 .619 328	95 .208 457	178 .135 1317	149 .550 271	178 .589 302	77 .786 98	34 .309 110	914 .317 2883
Percentage of all lines	11.4	15.9	45.7	9.4	10.5	3.4	3.8	

NOTE: First entry in each cell is net evaluation; second is ratio of first and third entries; third is total lines for that candidate. A dash indicates a number of lines too small to enter. Consequently totals sometimes exceed the sum of individual entries.

Hart), but Glenn received a great deal of positive viability coverage and much less positive press while Hart received virtually no viability coverage and a significant amount of positive press. Jackson and Mondale, at a much higher level of total coverage, present a similar picture. They had about equal positive intensities of overall coverage, but Mondale, like Glenn, was viable (with an extraordinary 1.66 intensity), although he did not receive very good press (an intensity near zero). Jackson, however, was not considered very viable (although he received a lot of coverage on this topic), but he did receive the most favorable press of the entire campaign.

By February, with Iowa and New Hampshire, Glenn and Hart had reversed their positions. Glenn's viability intensity went from .763 in January to −.758 in February, while Hart's went from −.667 to .628. In addition, Glenn started to receive negative press coverage, and Hart's press coverage became less positive. Glenn obtained the same kind of coverage in March until his withdrawal from the race. After his defeat in New Hampshire, Mondale's viability went down, but his press coverage became more positive so that it reached the level of Jesse Jackson's coverage. Jackson, throughout the rest of the campaign, would always have positive press coverage.

From March until July, the major changes are the ups and downs of Hart and Mondale. Hart received an enormous amount of positive viability coverage in March, as well as a significant amount of good press. But after his success on 27 March in Connecticut, Hart began to suffer a number of setbacks in New York, Pennsylvannia, and other states. As a result, he began to receive, for the first time, some bad press, and his viability coverage became less positive. Indeed, Mondale received his best press of the season in April, and his viability intensity rebounded to 1.00. In May, there was another reversal; Mondale received his worst press of the year, and Hart received his best. Mondale's viability intensity sank (although it remained above Hart's) and Hart's rose. In June, after the New Jersey primary, which virtually clinched the nomination for Mondale, Mondale's viability increased, but both Hart and Mondale received essentially neutral press. Press neutrality continued through July for both Hart and Mondale, but Jesse Jackson received excellent press in June and good press in July.

In summary, the four "hopeless" candidates (Askew, Cranston, Hollings, and McGovern) were never treated as anything but hopeless. Glenn never received very good press, even though he had a very positive viability rating in January. Once he started to do badly in the official events of the campaign, his fate was certain. Hart started out with a positive press and a negative assessment of his viability. By taking second place in Iowa, he was in a good position to capitalize on his positive press image. He suffered somewhat in

April as a result of his series of defeats at the polls, and, one suspects, as a result of Mondale's highly successful query, "Where's the beef?" His successes in May led to a rebound that was cut short by the New Jersey primary. Mondale did not begin with a very good press image, but it improved after his tough campaigning in response to Hart's ascendancy in March. Mondale suffered as a result of Hart's successes in May, but he managed to survive and obtain the nomination. Jackson, despite a series of major difficulties, still received the best coverage of the campaign.

Good press and bad press are not equally divided among candidates or across time periods. One might argue that this is the result of different degrees of success in the primaries, but good press and bad press are not very highly correlated with viability coverage. Jesse Jackson received very good press despite his continued failure to gain a significant number of delegates. Walter Mondale and John Glenn did not receive very good press when they were most viable, and Mondale received some of his best press coverage when his nomination seemed precarious. One can develop reasons and explanations for UPI's behavior throughout the 1984 primary season. Hart ran a different kind of campaign that was newsworthy; Jackson was the first black man to run for a major-party presidential nomination; Glenn had started with a big buildup that never seemed to get anywhere. All these things, and many other things, are undoubtedly true. We do not want to attribute the results we have found to a calculated maliciousness or manipulativeness on the part of the press. At this point, we wish only to claim that there are enormous swings in the quantity and tone of the press coverage of presidential candidates, and it seems likely that these swings have a significant impact on the citizens who vote in presidential primaries.

Seriousness. Defining *seriousness* is even harder than defining *fairness.* Some stories, like those about Santa Claus or the Easter bunny, are clearly frivolous, although, like the judge in the movie *Miracle on 34th Street* who finds it impossible to rule that Santa Claus does not exist, we would not want to ban such stories from the news. Beyond such frivolous stories, it is even harder to judge what is serious and what is not. Some commentators would like to see the media focus on "policy issues," but are not "candidate issues" equally important? Shouldn't we know whether a candidate is trustworthy, competent, and empathetic? Shouldn't we also know whether a candidate is a good campaigner who has a chance of winning the general election? Indeed, our introduction to this chapter provided an argument as to why citizens should know about the character, policy positions, electability, and leadership abilities of the candidates. We shall assume that serious coverage must pay some attention to these subjects.

TABLE 5.9

COVERAGE OF SUBJECTS

	Lines	Percentage of Subtotal	Percentage of Total
Potential success	5044	100	20.89
Viability	3017	59.82	12.49
Electability	736	14.59	3.05
Campaign organization	914	18.12	3.78
Fund-raising	377	7.47	1.56
Sources of support	2073	100	8.58
Individuals	1030	49.69	4.27
Organized groups	584	28.17	2.42
Unorganized groups	459	22.14	1.90
Candidate issues	5540	100	22.94
Experience	185	3.34	0.77
Leadership	1784	32.30	7.39
Personal qualities	853	15.40	3.53
Human interest	2718	49.06	11.26
Policy positions	3946	100	16.43
Social	501	12.70	2.07
Economic	699	17.71	2.90
Defense and foreign	1935	49.04	8.01
Government operations	592	15.00	2.45
Others	219	5.55	0.91
Comments about other candidates	2705	100	11.20
Hart	410	15.16	1.70
Jackson	381	14.09	1.58
Mondale	683	25.25	2.83
Reagan	897	33.16	3.72
Democratic opponents	212	7.84	0.88
Ferraro/Glenn/McGovern	122	4.51	0.51
Other events	4840	100	20.04
Debates	150	3.10	0.62
Campaign appearances	2000	41.32	8.28
Public appearances	2159	44.61	8.94
Private appearances	531	10.97	2.20

Table 5.9 summarizes the coverage by each of the subject areas. The amount of "serious" coverage, using our initial definition (electability, experience, leadership, personal qualities, and policy positions), is 31 percent of the total. Sixteen percent of the total coverage is on policy positions, 7 percent is on leadership, over 4 percent is on character, and 3 percent is on electability. Despite the propensity of critics to fault the amount of policy coverage by the news media, we are rather impressed that one-sixth of the coverage is on the policy positions of the candidates. We are less pleased with the meager attention paid to character, electability, and leadership. (The last category, by the way, contains an extraordinary amount of coverage, 1385 lines, of Jackson's leadership abilities.) To some extent, this may be the result of our accounting system. If we add stories about campaign organization and fund-raising activities, arguably measures of the ability to get elected, to those about electability, then the coverage of electability is a more respectable 8 percent. The coverage of character and leadership can be inflated in a similar fashion.

Instead of focusing on stories that seem serious and uplifting, we can also try to identify stories that may be less informative to the primary voter. Human interest stories may fit into this category, as may stories about public and private appearances. Together these account for 22 percent of the total coverage. This is hardly an overwhelming amount of frivolous coverage, and we are not even sure that all of it is even remotely frivolous. Finally, we can look at those stories that do not seem to fit easily into the frivolous or serious categories. These include stories about support, candidate comments about one another, and campaign appearances. Stories about support for a candidate do not directly deal with the character, policy positions, electability, and leadership abilities of candidates, but they usually send indirect messages to the voters about these things. Candidate comments provide a chance for candidates to confront and question one another through the news media. They do not seem like frivolous or unimportant stories. Stories about campaign appearances may be the least important of this trio because they deal with the ephemera of American politics: kissing babies, eating pizza, and shaking hands.

Campaign coverage, then, does not appear to be frivolous; instead, it seems to be remarkably serious in many ways. Still, there is a significant component devoted to the horse race. At least 12 percent of the total coverage is about viability, and many other stories focus on topics related to the horse-race: What is the status of the campaign organization and fund-raising? Who supports whom? What are the candidates saying about one another? Moreover, these stories provide a disproportionate share of extreme evaluations. For example, 14 percent of the viability stories are unattributed versus only 1 percent of those regarding policy positions (see table 5.2 on p. 141), and viability stories have a high average evaluation, a small percentage of lines with zero evaluations, and a large percentage of lines with extreme evaluations, whereas policy stories have the opposite characteristics (see table 5.6 on p. 153). Finally, these highly evaluative stories occur at the beginning of the primary season (73 percent from January to March and 46 percent in March alone) when they constitute over one-third of the total coverage (see the bottom of table 5.8 on pp. 158-59).

The average voter, then, is presented with substantial amounts of information on the character, purpose, and leadership abilities of candidates (less on their electability) during the primary season. The media (at least the UPI) provide voters with a chance to learn about the candidates. At the same time, the voter is also presented with a substantial amount of highly evaluative horse-race information during the early parts of the season. We now turn to an analysis of the effects of this pattern of coverage.

5. Knowledge and Interest during the Primary Season

KNOWLEDGE OF THE CANDIDATES

Do knowledge about the candidates and interest in the campaign increase during a primary season? Such an increase in knowledge and interest seems to be a

TABLE 5.10

KNOWLEDGE OF CANDIDATES' NAMES AND TRAITS BY TIME PERIODS

(FRACTION OF NES RESPONDENTS WITH KNOWLEDGE)

	1	2	3	4	5	6	7
Name recognition							
Know all names	.83	.87	.89	.91	.91	.91	.91
Know Reagan	1.00	1.00	.99	1.00	1.00	1.00	1.00
Know Mondale	.96	.98	.99	.99	.99	.99	1.00
Know Jackson	.97	.98	.97	.98	.99	.99	.99
Know Hart	.43	.58	.88	.95	.96	.98	.98
Know Askew	.43	.49	.64	.63	.61	.58	.58
Know Hollings	.31	.38	.51	.52	.42	.41	.46
Knowledge of traits							
Reagan traits	.97	.98	.99	.99	.96	.99	.99
Mondale traits	.92	.91	.94	.96	.96	.98	.95
Jackson traits	.95	.93	.97	.98	.98	.99	.97
Hart traits	—	—	.95	.97	.97	.97	.97
Glenn traits	.93	.91	.94	.96	—	—	—
(Approximate N)	(196)	(292)	(166)	(302)	(310)	(305)	(154)

TABLE 5.11

KNOWLEDGE OF CANDIDATES' POLICY POSITIONS

BY TIME PERIODS

(FRACTION OF NES RESPONDENTS WITH KNOWLEDGE)

Knowledge of Policies and Ideological Position	1	2	3	4	5	6	7
Reagan policies	.97	.98	.99	.99	.97	.98	.98
Reagan lib.-con.	.93	.92	.90	.95	.96	.92	.94
Mondale policies	.90	.93	.91	.97	.92	.91	.92
Mondale lib.-con.	.88	.89	.91	.94	.93	.91	.94
Glenn policies	.83	.85	.90	.89	—	—	—
Glenn lib.-con.	.85	.86	.86	.87	—	—	—
Hart policies	—	—	.84	.92	.90	.87	.91
Hart lib.-con.	—	—	.82	.88	.89	.91	.92
Jackson lib.-con.	.87	.85	.87	.93	.91	.91	.92
(Approximate N)	(175)	(265)	(145)	(270)	(300)	(295)	(150)

minimal requirement for a rational nominating process, and with the amounts of press coverage described in the preceding sections, the public certainly has an opportunity to become knowledgeable. In the following paragraphs we ask whether the public learns anything during the course of the primary season. In subsequent sections, we ask about the character and quality of what they learn.

Tables 5.10 and 5.11 summarize a variety of measures of knowledge over the primary season from the beginning of the rolling cross-section on 11 January until 19 June 1985.

The seven periods are as follows:

1. "January": 11 January to 31 January (3 weeks).
2. "February": 1 February until the New Hampshire primary on 28 February (4 weeks)
3. "First half of March": after New Hampshire and before Super Tuesday on 13 March (2 weeks)
4. "Second Half of March": after Super Tuesday and before the Pennsylvania primary on 10 April (4 weeks)
5. "April": after Pennsylvannia and before Indiana and Ohio on 8 May (4 weeks)
6. "May": after Indiana and Ohio and before California and New Jersey on 6 June (4 weeks)
7. "June": after California and New Jersey until 19 June (2 weeks)[21]

Overall knowledge certainly increased during the primary season. Name recognition for 11 different political figures (Ronald Reagan, George Bush, Ted Kennedy, and the 8 candidates for the Democratic nomination) was virtually complete (an average of 10 out of 11 names) by 10 April, although it was surprisingly high during the first polling period (more than 9 out of 11). Over 95 percent of the respondents knew Walter Mondale's name in the first period, and the proportion recognizing Gary Hart rose from 43 percent (among the 8 Democratic candidates only Hollings had a lower level of name recognition at this point) in the first period to 58 percent by the second, 88 percent in the third, and 95 percent by the fourth.

There can be no doubt that primaries alert the public to the names of the candidates. At the same time, they do this somewhat selectively. For example, knowledge about Ernest Hollings and Reubin Askew rose about 20 percent from the first to the third period and then slumped once it became clear, after Super Tuesday, that they did not have a chance of winning the nomination. This decline of about 5 to 10 percent is statistically significant and substantively interesting because it suggests that for at least some members of the public, their knowledge of these two candidates was fleeting and ephemeral. Even at their zenith, only about one-half to two-thirds of the public knew of Hollings and Askew, and even their knowledge was probably very limited. This is not surprising given the amount of press coverage the two men received.

Indeed, what did the public know about these candidates? The second part of table 5.10 indicates the average number of 12 traits for which respondents who recognized a candidate's name were willing to provide a rating. Knowledge of Mondale's traits reached a plateau by the third period (94 percent for those people who recognized Mondale's name), although it was already at 92 percent in the first period. We lack data for Hart for the first two periods, but by the third period, Hart had matched Mondale. This is not surprising given the barrage of coverage enjoyed by Hart after Iowa. If the preceding sections had not tallied the coverage that Jesse Jackson received in the first month of January, it might be surprising to find that the level of knowledge about him was as high as that for Walter Mondale. As with name recognition, it is clear that a willingness to rate candidates' traits grows during the primary season, but as before, the willingness to rank traits is remarkably high to begin with. If a citizen recognizes a name, then he or she seems remarkably willing to describe the person's traits.

Table 5.11 on p. 165 shows that people are less willing to place candidates on policy issues and a liberal-conservative scale. This is very striking for Gary Hart where the difference between the fraction of traits supplied and the probability of providing an issue placement or liberal-conservative placement varies between 5 percent and 10 percent. One might be tempted to argue that this demonstrates that Hart was, as his critics claimed, the most ambiguous of the candidates, but the data for John Glenn reveal a similar pattern. Moreover, the average gap between traits and policies is less than 1 percent for Reagan and only 2 percent for Mondale, whereas it is 7 percent for Glenn and Hart, and this gap does not narrow as the primary season progresses. These results suggest that it is harder for citizens to become conversant with the policy positions of the candidates, and that there may be some candidates whose positions are less clear-cut than others. Of course, as with name recognition and traits, it is well to remember that usually over 90 percent of people who recognize a candidate can also place the candidate on an issue scale.

These data suggest that our respondents knew a great deal about some of the candidates even before the primary season officially began, and they quickly learned the names and then some characteristics of dark-horse candidates, such as Gary Hart. The media's intensive coverage of Hart was not lost on the electorate. Nevertheless, knowledge about the candidates did not increase so rapidly as to make it impossible for lack of knowledge and voter risk aversion to play a significant role in the early primaries.[22] This is especially true for candidates, such as Ernest Hollings and Reubin Askew, treated as hopeless by the news media. For them, the lack of name recognition was probably one of the reasons for eventually dropping out of the race.

INTEREST IN THE CAMPAIGN

A campaign, like a good seminar, should probably do more than teach those involved a lot of facts about the candidates; it should try to get them interested in the subject. The first two measures in table 5.12 indicate that the respondents' interest in public affairs or the campaign was at best constant over the course of the campaign. Yet the next two measures show that attention to the campaign on television or the newspapers peaked during the fourth period (right after Super Tuesday) with a slight upturn at the very end, after the California

TABLE 5.12
INTEREST AND INVOLVEMENT IN CAMPAIGN BY TIME PERIODS

	1 + 2	3	4	5	6	7
Proportion interested in public affairs	.44	.34	.42	.46	.40	.42
Proportion interested in campaign	.46	.37	.50	.44	.48	.48
Followed campaign on television	.28	.37	.49	.39	.37	.41
Followed campaign in newspaper	.17	.21	.34	.24	.19	.25
Proportion attempting to persuade others	.14	.19	.29	.28	.26	.28

and New Jersey primaries. Finally, the last measure shows that there was a significant increase in the proportion of people who attempted to persuade others during the first four periods of the campaign, but this figure then remained stable for the last three periods.

These results suggest that the nominating process provides the rudiments of a civic education for the mass public, but except for occasional periods of excitement, this education is neither very compelling nor interesting to the average citizen.

6. Learning about Traits, Policies, and Electability

IMPRESSIONS OF CANDIDATE TRAITS

What impressions do citizens form of the candidates? Do they have distinct images of them? Table 5.13 organizes the 12 traits into four categories (competence, leadership, integrity, and empathy) suggested by Donald Kinder,[23] and it presents each candidate's average trait ratings. Each trait was measured on a 1-5 scale with 1 indicating that the trait described the candidate "a great deal" and 5 indicating that it was "not at all" appropriate. Jesse Jackson is rated lowest (numerically highest) on all four major categories, while Gary Hart and John Glenn are rated very high. Walter Mondale and Ronald Reagan, however, are generally rated somewhere in the middle, with Reagan perceived as having slightly more integrity and a great deal more leadership capacity and Mondale perceived as having slightly more competence and a lot more empathy. These results suggest that the traits measure an overall judgment of the candidates—Jackson is disliked; whereas Hart and Glenn are liked—and some specific judgments about their individual characteristics—Reagan is a leader; but Mondale is empathetic.

To separate the general from the specific, the numbers in parentheses control for the overall judgment by adjusting the traits downward (or upward) by the amount by which a candidate's average rating on the traits exceeds (falls short of) the grand mean of all the traits over all the candidates. The adjusted scores are what we would obtain if each candidate's average rating across all traits were the same as every other candidate's rating across all the traits so they control for the degree to which one candidate is generally liked or disliked. These numbers reveal the patterns described above even more clearly—Reagan far outstrips all other candidates on the leadership dimension and falls far behind all the others on empathy. This adjustment also allows us to compare the ranges of the adjusted summary traits to see which one varies the most across the candidates. This range is listed at the far right of the table, and it

TABLE 5.13

SUMMARY OF TRAITS

(AVERAGE TRAIT RATINGS)

Characteristic	Glenn	Hart	Jackson	Mondale	Reagan	Range
Competence	1.78	1.64	2.02	1.79	1.85	
(adjusted)	(1.89)	(1.76)	(1.85)	(1.74)	(1.84)	.15
Hardworking	1.84	1.57	1.83	1.85	1.97	
Intelligent	1.64	1.60	1.96	1.71	1.68	
Knowledgable	1.86	1.76	2.26	1.82	1.89	
Leadership	2.12	2.08	2.36	2.41	2.03	
(adjusted)	(2.23)	(2.20)	(2.20)	(2.35)	(2.02)	.33
Commands respect	1.82	1.92	2.21	2.13	1.77	
Inspiring	2.18	2.14	2.32	2.64	2.37	
Strong leader	2.37	2.17	2.55	2.46	1.96	
Integrity	1.65	1.80	2.06	1.89	1.81	
(adjusted)	(1.75)	(1.92)	(1.90)	(1.84)	(1.80)	.15
Decent	1.53	1.66	1.91	1.77	1.68	
Moral	1.63	1.78	1.93	1.75	1.63	
Good example	1.78	1.95	2.34	2.16	2.12	
Empathy	1.98	1.95	2.16	2.08	2.31	
(adjusted)	(2.09)	(2.07)	(2.00)	(2.02)	(2.30)	.30
Compassionate	1.94	1.90	1.95	2.00	2.34	
Kind	1.78	1.79	1.93	1.85	1.89	
Really cares	2.23	2.17	2.61	2.39	2.69	
Range (4)	.47	.44	.34	.62	.50	
Range (12)	.84	.60	.88	.93	1.06	
Standard Deviation	.060	.041	.065	.089	.097	

NOTE: Higher numbers indicate less favorable ratings.

is much greater for leadership and empathy (.33 and .30) than for competence and integrity (.15), so that once we adjust for whether the candidate was on average disliked or liked, the respondents pretty much thought all the candidates were competent and men of integrity.

The respondents, however, had diverse images of these candidates' capacity for leadership and empathy. Indeed, Mondale and Reagan are mirror images of one another on these two traits, and although the differences are not as large, they are also mirror images on competence and integrity: Mondale is more competent and Reagan has more integrity. The images for Glenn, Hart, and Jackson are more homogenized than those of Mondale and Reagan once the adjustment is made, but Glenn is rated highest on integrity, Hart is viewed as most competent and Jackson as most empathetic, although Jackson's empathy is seen as relatively impersonal. He fares badly on the item that asks whether the candidate "really cares about people like you." Finally, the three are essentially tied on leadership.

Further work is needed to see how much these images agree with those projected through the media, but we are struck by how much they seem to accord with our own impressions of the news stories carried throughout the 1984 nominating season. Mondale was the candidate who cared, but Reagan could lead. Glenn was a man of integrity—though apparently little else. Hart was competent, and Jackson cared—at least he cared about his "rainbow coalition." At the same time, we are struck by the less positive assessments of Mondale and Reagan than of Glenn and Hart, and the somewhat sharper images they created. (Note that the range of traits reported at the bottom of table 5.13 was greatest for Reagan and Mondale and lowest for Glenn and Hart.) Are these facts related? Do images become sharper and more negative as a campaign progresses? If so, what does this imply for a nominating process that emphasizes the early results in Iowa and New Hampshire?

Changing Impression of Traits

At what point, if ever, do impressions become crystallized? Indeed, what is a "crystallized impression"? For us, a firm impression will generally have two characteristics: It will be relatively distinct or differentiated so that it will involve a recognition of some strengths and some weaknesses of the candidate. It will also be relatively stable so that the characteristics identified in one week will also be identified in a subsequent week.[24]

To measure distinctiness, we have taken the means of the traits for the 25 weeks from 11 January to 19 June and have examined how the standard deviation of the 12 trait averages changed from week to week. In this context, the standard deviation serves as a measure of how much the means for the same candidate vary across the different traits. For well-known candidates with distinct images, we expected that the standard deviation of the 12 traits would be relatively large; on average, our respondents would give quite different answers to questions about different traits. For less-well-known candidates, we expected the standard deviations to be small because, on average, most people would not give very different answers to questions about different traits. Finally, as time went on and more was learned about the candidate, we expected that the standard deviation would become larger.

To measure stability, we have analyzed how the correlation between one week's averages and the next week's have changed over time. For well-known

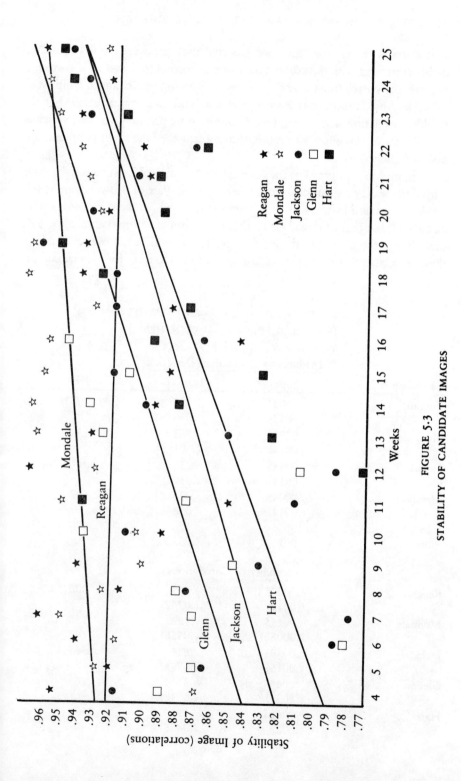

FIGURE 5.3
STABILITY OF CANDIDATE IMAGES

candidates with stable images, we expected that one week's traits would be highly correlated with those of the next week, whereas for less-well-known candidates, the correlations would be lower as their images changed from week to week. And as more was learned about a candidate, we expected that the weekly correlation would tend toward unity (more precisely, to .985, which is the theoretical maximum as a result of the noisiness of the small samples available for each week).

Figure 5.3 on p. 171 plots the correlations over time. Not surprisingly, these correlations vary a great deal from week to week. Part of this variation is undoubtedly caused by the very small samples from which the correlations were calculated, but part of it may also reflect the action of various campaign events that change the images of the candidates. To summarize the overall trends in these correlations, we have fitted some straight lines to them for each candidate.

TABLE 5.14

TRENDS IN DISTINCTNESS AND STABILITY

(STANDARD ERRORS IN PARENTHESES)

Candidate	Distinctness or Standard Deviations		
	Slope	Intercept	R^2
Reagan	.00031	.325	.0030
	(.0012)	.090)	
Mondale	.00243	.285	.132
	(.0014)	(.101)	
Jackson	.00159	.255	.0921
	(.0011)	(.0805)	
Glenn	.00449	.223	.447
	(.0014)	(.0385)	
Hart	.00554	.126	.476
	(.0016)	(.0322	
	Stability or Correlations		
Reagan	− .000054	.919	.000119
	(.0011)	(.0742)	
Mondale	.00155	.922	.150
	(.00083)	(.0558)	
Jackson	.00501	.824	.365
	(.0015)	(.0996)	
Glenn	.00646	.841	.263
	(.0033)	(.0748)	
Hart	.00625	.794	.286
	(.0028)	(.0486)	

The slopes and intercepts of these lines are reported in table 5.14. The slope indicates how much the measure of stability (i.e., the correlation) for the candidate changes from week to week. Note that the slope for the correlations is essentially zero for Ronald Reagan, indicating no change over time, slightly positive for Walter Mondale, and signficantly positive for Jackson, Hart, and Glenn, indicating substantial change over time. The intercept in each of these equations is the best estimate of the true correlation between the traits on 11 January and 18 January. Hence, they can be interpreted as the stability of each candidate's image at the beginning of the primary season. The intercepts reveal the same picture as the slopes: Mondale and Reagan presented very stable images from the beginning (an average correlation of about .92), whereas Hart, Jackson, and Glenn started out with relatively low correlations (between .79 for Hart and .84 for Glenn) and slowly increased the stability of their images to the level of Mondale and Reagan.

A figure for the standard deviations reveals a similar pattern, and the corresponding straight lines are also reported in table 5.14. Hart and Glenn seem to form one group with high slopes (.0055 and .0045) and small intercepts (.126 and .223), Mondale and Jackson seem to form another with moderate slopes (.0024 and .0016) and moderate intercepts (.285 and .255), and Reagan is in a separate class with a slope that is essentially zero and a larger intercept (.325). As expected, the images of Hart and Glenn were indistinct at first and became much more differentiated over the course of the primary season, whereas the images of Reagan and Mondale were distinct to begin with and did not change very much. The data for Jackson tell an interesting story. His image was fairly distinct from the beginning, undoubtedly as a consequence of the saturation coverage he received in the first few weeks of January, just before the rolling cross-section began, but it was not very stable. This instability mirrors the ups and downs of the UPI coverage of his traits (stories on his personal qualities and his leadership ability).

Table 5.15 (p. 174) summarizes the slopes and intercepts of straight lines fitted to graphs of the sum of the trait ratings of candidates versus time. The positive slopes indicate that the average trait ratings became larger, and less complimentary, over time, but the size of this effect is not very large for any candidate except Hart. The preceding paragraphs suggest that we should expect a small effect for Mondale and Reagan because people knew a lot about them, and their ratings remained very stable during the primary process. Jesse Jackson's position as a highly outspoken and noncentrist candidate might explain why there is no substantial change for him, but the story for Jackson is actually much more complicated than this. His trait ratings do go down substantially during the middle of the primary season, when he experienced diffi-

TABLE 5.15

TRENDS IN TRAIT RATINGS

(STANDARD ERRORS IN PARENTHESES)

Candidate	Slope	Intercept	R^2
Reagan	.0618	23.31	.107
	(.0389)	(2.87)	
Mondale	.0454	24.07	.0853
	(.0325)	(2.40)	
Jackson	.0554	25.16	.0582
	(.0486)	(3.59)	
Glenn	.0600	22.06	.135
	(.0438)	(1.17)	
Hart	.161	19.84	.414
	(.0592)	(1.06)	
Glenn (first 10 weeks)	.194	21.45	.712
	(.0436)	(.58)	

culties as a result of his comments about "Hymie" town and his association with Louis Farrakhan, but they rebound toward the end of the primary season, when his press coverage improved as a result of his planned trip to Cuba. A straight line does not adequately capture these nonlinear ups and downs. Notice that Jackson's ratings are the lowest of all candidates, even though his overall coverage was the best of anyone in the race (see table 5.7 on pp. 156-57).

This leaves Glenn and Hart. Glenn's ratings did go down substantially through the twelfth week of the year (the tenth week of the survey) when he dropped out of the race on 16 March, but then they rebounded upward for the remaining periods for which data were collected. This accounts for the small slope coefficient reported in table 5.15, and it does not seem unreasonable to suppose that this rebound in his ratings was the result of some feelings of sympathy for him that otherwise would not have developed. Consequently, a second slope and intercept are reported for Glenn for just the first 10 weeks, and the results are very similar to those for Gary Hart. For Hart, the slope indicates that the effect of 20 weeks of the primary season would be an increased score of about .27 on each of the traits. This is equal to about two-thirds of the unadjusted range of the four trait variables in table 5.13, and it is more than enough to make Gary Hart's average trait ratings as unfavorable as Jesse Jackson's.

People do learn about candidates during the primaries. But they probably learn much too late about some candidates, such as Glenn and McGovern, who dropped out by the tenth week of our surveys (in the first month of the primary season). Moreover, it seems as if the images of political newcomers become more distinct and stable over time. If one believes that distinctness and stability are good because they ensure that voters have a refined image of the candidates, then the primary process can be commended because it produces distinct and stable images. But it takes time to do this, and the preceding analysis can be used to determine how long it would take any of our candidates to reach a predetermined level of distinctness and stability.

Consider, for example, Gary Hart. Let us assume that the distinctness and stability of Walter Mondale's image during the first week of our survey (11-18 January) is a reasonable amount of image crystallization. Then the results reported in table 5.14 suggest a standard deviation of .285 (representing Mondale's distinctness) and a correlation of .922 (representing the stability of Mondale's image) as the target values. Some simple calculations, based on the results for Hart in table 5.14, indicate that it would take him almost 30 weeks to reach this level of distinctness (starting at .126 and proceeding at the rate of .0055 per week) and 20 weeks to reach this level of stability (starting at .794 and proceeding at the rate of .0063 per week). Since the primary season was completed by the twenty-first week of our survey, it appears as if the voters chose between Hart and Mondale before Hart had an image that was as distinct and stable as Mondale's during the middle of January.

Crystallization, it appears, takes too long. Yet there is another process at work as well. As a newcomer's image is crystallizing, his or her image is also becoming tarnished. If it truly takes 20 or 30 weeks for this to happen — a period longer than the primary season — then the newcomer, like Gary Hart or Jimmy Carter, has a conspicuous advantage over a well-known politician such as Walter Mondale or Henry Jackson, because it will probably take at least that long for the newcomer's image to become as tarnished as that of the old-timer. Of course, if the newcomer is intemperate and outspoken, like Jesse Jackson, or if the newcomer cannot overcome the obstacles of name recognition and viability (see below), like John Glenn, then this advantage may not be available. But, for a Gary Hart or a Jimmy Carter, this possibility seems to exist.

LEARNING ABOUT POLICIES

Do citizens know about the policy positions of the candidates? The first part of table 5.16 indicates that they have a good idea where candidates stand on the issues. (The numbers have been adjusted so that high numbers indicate conservative positions, and 3 is the center of the scale.) On every issue, Reagan is seen as a conservative — often as extremely conservative — and Mondale is seen as liberal, although not as extreme as Reagan except on the question about women helping themselves. Hart is perceived as less liberal than Mondale on every issue except the one on which he took an unequivocally liberal position:

TABLE 5.16

OVERALL POLICY IMPRESSIONS

(AVERAGES FOR RESPONDENTS WHO GAVE ANSWERS)

Placement of Candidates

	Government Spending	Defense	Central America	Women	Russia
Reagan	3.90	4.35	4.14	3.32	3.55
Mondale	2.50	2.24	2.45	2.45	2.54
Hart	2.83	2.28	2.41	2.54	2.72
Glenn	2.99	2.99			

Policy Positions of Supporters

First-Choice Candidate	Liberal-Conservative	Government Spending	Defense	Central America	Women	Russia
Reagan	5.19	3.35	3.15	2.64	3.37	3.29
Mondale	4.31	2.83	2.72	2.35	2.83	2.55
Hart	4.33	3.02	2.87	2.29	3.15	2.82

Central America. Glenn is viewed as basically centrist. As with the traits, these results accord with our own subjective notions of where the candidates stood on the issues. It appears as if the voters had a reasonably clear idea where the candidates stood on the issues.

This is confirmed by the second part of table 5.16, which presents the average position of Mondale supporters, Hart supporters, and Republicans (as a proxy for Reagan supporters) on six policy scales. On every issue except Central America, the Republicans are on the right, and to the right of both Mondale and Hart. Hart supporters are once again to the right of Mondale supporters on every issue except Central America, and there are conspicuous differences on government spending, aid to minorities, aid to women, and getting tough with Russia. This table also shows that candidate choices are correlated with

TABLE 5.17

TRENDS IN ELECTABILITY

(AVERAGES ON 100-POINT SCALE)

	1	2	3	4	5	6	7
Reagan	75.46	78.39	75.51	76.90	76.44	78.48	81.23
Mondale	53.71	55.95	51.30	55.61	56.79	53.33	51.09
Jackson	35.30	27.79	19.59	22.06	23.87	21.60	22.05
Glenn	45.76	41.85	32.60	26.19	–	–	–
Hart	–	–	59.27	56.62	51.87	49.03	52.76

the fit between a voter's own position and the perceived position of the candidates.

Unfortunately, there are too few issues to repeat the kinds of analysis undertaken in the preceding section. Nevertheless, our inspection of the data does not reveal any obvious trends over the course of the primary season.

ELECTABILITY

Table 5.17 summarizes the changes in electability from period to period. Reagan's perceived electability is certainly stunning, especially when it is compared with the figures for the Democrats. While Reagan never dips below a 75 percent chance of winning the general election, no Democrat ever exceeds 60 percent. Still, this is not really surprising given the strong economy and relatively unblemished foreign policy of Ronald Reagan.

There are some less obvious facts to be gleaned from table 5.17. It is not surprising to see the electability of Glenn and Jackson decline over time (with Jackson reaching a low point during his difficult period after New Hampshire and then rebounding slightly to a steady-state value of about 22 percent). It is also not surprising that Mondale's electability fell after New Hampshire— voters must have begun to wonder how a candidate who could not even beat an unknown in New Hampshire could win the general election—but it is intriguing to see it rising in periods 4 and 5 and then falling toward the end of the primary season in periods 6 and 7, just as Ronald Reagan's electability began to increase significantly. It is also interesting that Hart's electability declined so little (indeed, it turned upward in the last period), despite the increasing certainty that he would not win the nomination. This suggests that Mondale was perceived as a relatively weak nominee.

TABLE 5.18

TRENDS IN VIABILITY

(AVERAGES ON 100-POINT SCALE)

	1	2	3	4	5	6	7
Mondale	65.51	71.72	59.76	68.69	74.77	75.98	80.36
Jackson	37.41	30.44	17.41	23.39	25.86	24.09	23.61
Glenn	49.93	44.13	28.71	18.01	—	—	—
Hart	—	—	65.93	61.57	54.04	54.52	52.30

VIABILITY AND MEDIA COVERAGE

Table 5.18 summarizes changes in viability during the primaries. The ups and downs in these data are, as we would expect, much greater than with electability, and they mirror the progress of the candidates during the primaries. Glenn quickly nose-dived, with his biggest decline right after his poor showing in New Hampshire and with another big decline in the fourth period when he officially dropped out of the race at the beginning of this period. Jackson exhibited the same low-point in period 3 that we have seen in all other data. Finally, it is not surprising that the viabilities for Mondale and Hart in the NES surveys were negatively correlated (at −.98 if just the 7 periods are used) because their viability coverage in our content analyses were also negatively correlated (at −.28 if all 32 periods of coverage are used). It is also not surprising that Mondale's viability dropped significantly after New Hampshire and then slowly increased, with only a very small gain in the sixth period (essentially May), as a result of Hart's resurgence, to a high point in the last period. This is the same trend that occurs in the UPI data displayed in table 5.8 (pp. 158-59). Moreover, although correlating media coverage with the rolling cross-section presents some especially difficult problems, we have obtained a raw correlation of the intensity of viability coverage in the UPI data with the average of the viability scale from the NES surveys of .19 for Glenn, .24 for Jackson, .42 for Hart, and .15 for Mondale. These numbers suggest that a carefully developed model and powerful estimation techniques might be able to find some very strong relationships between these two time series.[25]

Viability is certainly the most volatile factor we have examined. None of the other measures examined changes so much so fast, and goes both up and down from week to week. Yet it, and all the other factors we have examined, will not ultimately be important unless they affect the voters' choice in the primary elections. We now turn to an examination of that choice.

7. Voters' Decision Process

How Voters Make a Decision

We have shown that respondents in a nationwide sample of citizens learn about the traits, policies, and electability of candidates during the course of the nomination process. We have also suggested that they learn slowly about what might be considered important factors (e.g., traits), whereas they learn very quickly about factors like viability, which we do not believe are as important. But do these factors affect choices?

Figure 5.4 presents a model of how we think knowledge, policies, traits, and electability should affect choice. At the center of this model, determining choice, are viability and utilities. Some detailed explanations and tests of the model are contained in another paper,[26] but for our purposes here, it should suffice to say that we believe that voters take into account both their preference

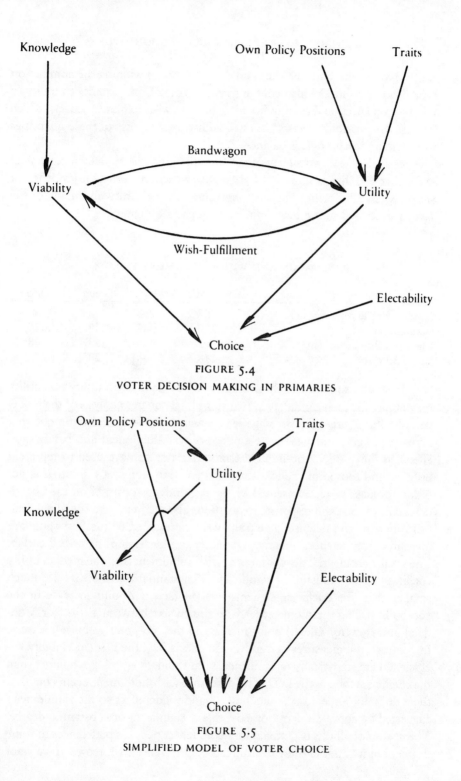

FIGURE 5.4

VOTER DECISION MAKING IN PRIMARIES

FIGURE 5.5

SIMPLIFIED MODEL OF VOTER CHOICE

(utility) for a candidate and the candidate's chance of winning the nomination (viability). This model also contains arrows going from viability to utility (a bandwagon effect) and from utility to viability (a wish-fulfillment effect), which express the possibility that voters will adjust their reports of these quantities to maintain psychological balance.[27]

We shall take a two-step approach to estimating this model. First, we shall show that viability is more than simply a projection from utilities; it is not simply wish-fulfillment. Then we shall show that viability and many of the factors described above have important impacts on choice.

TABLE 5.19

BANDWAGON AND WISH-FULFILLMENT EFFECTS

	Mondale	Hart	Glenn	Jackson
Median viability coefficient	.068	.293	.028	.180
(standard error)	(.290)	(.337)	(.482)	(.325)
Median utility coefficient	.192	.485	.597	.488
(standard error)	(.118)	(.144)	(.208)	(.106)

Table 5.19 summarizes the average effect of viability on utility and utility on viability for each candidate in two-stage least-squares analysis of the model described in figure 5.4. Two stage least-squares is a statistical technique that allows us to get estimates of the amount of wish-fulfillment and bandwagon effect. In this model, 100-point thermometer ratings were used to represent utilities, and 100-point chances scales were used to represent viabilities. In addition, policies were represented by the respondent's position on the liberal-conservative scale and responses to questions about government spending, Central America, and defense. The traits were represented by the four summary measures (competence, integrity, empathy, and leadership) described earlier. The results are clear: The measures of wish-fulfillment (i.e., the median utility coefficients) are statistically significant with standard errors that are much smaller than the coefficients themselves. In fact, a 1-point increase in the 100-point feeling thermometer leads to somewhere between a .192 (for Mondale) and .597 (for Glenn) point increase in the 100-point viability measure. In contrast, the measures of bandwagon effects (i.e., the median viability coefficients) are statistically insignificant, with standard errors much larger than the coefficients themselves. This suggests that wish-fulfillment occurs but that there does not appear to be much of a bandwagon effect so the simultaneity suggested by figure 5.4 does not exist to any significant or substantial degree. The upshot of all this is that viability does reflect people's preferences to some degree, but it is not entirely determined by preferences. Moreover, if we want

TABLE 5.20

MONDALE-HART CHOICE

(STANDARD ERROR IN PARENTHESES)

	Full Sample	Only Democrats and Independents	Only Democrats and Independents
Utility			
Mondale thermometer	.0065 (.0012)	.0067(.0017)	.0067[a]
Hart thermometer	−.0097 (.0012)	.0110(.0016)	.0110[a]
Viability			
Mondale	.0057 (.00097)	.0052(.0014)	.0052[a]
Hart	−.00029 (.0010)	.0010(.0013)	
Traits			
Mondale competence	.013 (.039)	.0045(.061)	
Hart competence	.0035 (.048)	−.0051(.070)	
Mondale leadership	−.070 (.029)	−.110 (.037)	−.110[a]
Hart leadership	.048 (.037)	.039 (.050)	
Mondale integrity	−.060 (.043)	−.075 (.067)	
Hart integrity	−.031 (.052)	−.0070(.070)	
Mondale empathy	.037 (.038)	.097 (.057)	
Hart empathy	−.0031 (.045)	.017 (.059)	
Positions			
Liberal-Conservative	−.0093 (.010)	−.0045(.014)	
Government spending	.0026 (.020)	.013 (.025)	
Minorities	−.018 (.019)	−.027 (.025)	
Central America	.020 (.016)	.019 (.023)	
Defense spending	−.011 (.016)	.0025(.021)	
Women	−.0057 (.017)	−.0066(.024)	
Russia	.0015 (.014)	−.0085(.018)	
Electability			
Mondale	.0023 (.0011)	.0020(.0015)	.0020[b]
Hart	−.0017 (.0011)	−.0029(.0015)	−.0029[a]
Intercept	.59 (.20)	.56 (.26)	
R^2 (adjusted)	.4570	.5147	
(N)	(398)	(219)	

a. Significant at the .01 level (one sided) in both regressions.
b. Significant at the .05 level (one sided) in at least one regression.

to assess its separate effect on choice, we need only include preferences in our model so as to partial out its effect.

THE DETERMINANTS OF PRIMARY VOTES

Figure 5.5 presents such a model, and table 5.20 presents estimates of it using multiple regression. This technique allows us to determine the separate impacts of various independent variables, such as viability or utility, on a dependent variable, such as choice. In this equation, the choice was represented by a dummy variable with the value of 1 if the respondent's first choice was Mondale and with the value of zero if Hart was the first choice. The 100-point utility and chances scales described above were used to represent preferences and viability. Traits were represented by the four summary measures, which each ran between 1 and 5 (with 1 indicating that the trait was very descriptive of the candidate); an expanded list of policy positions included the 7-point liberal-conservative self-placement and responses to 5-point questions about aid to minorities, aid to women, increased defense spending, getting tough with Russia, intervention in Latin America, and government spending. In every case, the scales were recoded so that a high number indicated that the respondent had a conservative position. Finally, electability was represented by the 100-point chances scale.

Two separate regressions are reported in table 5.20. The first includes the full sample and the second excludes all Republicans. The two produce similar results, but we focus on the second regression. To simplify our exposition, the third column is left blank in all places where a coefficient was clearly statistically insignificant because it was not much larger than its standard error. (In many cases where this was true, the coefficient also had the wrong sign.) Because many of the measures used in this regression are highly intercorrelated (e.g., the viability measures for Hart and Mondale), it is not surprising that many of the standard errors are rather larger. Nevertheless, several results seem clear. First, utility and viability have very significant effects. It is true that Hart's viability does not seem to be statistically significant, but this may be partly caused by the correlations among the two viability measures and the electability measure. More important, Mondale's viability has a very strong effect—its impact is more than three-fourths of his thermometer rating. The equation predicts that a decrease of 10 points in Mondale's viability—a change that is well within the range of what was observed—would change Mondale's vote by 5 percent and increase Hart's by 5 percent. This 10 percent swing is more than enough to change the results of a large number of close primaries.

None of the policy positions and only one of the traits seem to be significant in this equation, although electability does appear to be significant.

TABLE 5.21

DETERMINANTS OF UTILITIES

Twelve Traits-Four Areas	Mondale		Jackson		Hart	
Competence						
Hardworking	$-.49$	$(.88)$	$-.88$	$(.79)$	-2.64	(1.15)[a]
Intelligent	-1.22	(1.13)	-1.26	$(.93)$	$-.29$	(1.35)
Knowledgeable	$-.20$	(1.03)	$.78$	$(.73)$	1.44	(1.24)
Leadership						
Commands respect	$-.72$	$(.83)$	-2.70	$(.76)$[a]	-1.66	(1.09)
Inspiring	-2.60	$(.74)$[a]	-2.27	$(.70)$[a]	-3.26	$(.88)$[a]
Strong leader	-3.74	$(.77)$[a]	-1.13	$(.72)$	-2.68	(1.00)[a]
Integrity						
Decent	-2.80	(1.10)[a]	-1.05	(1.03)	$-.41$	(1.49)
Moral	$.80$	(1.01)	1.46	(1.05)	$-.93$	(1.29)
Good example	-2.77	$(.87)$[a]	-1.63	$(.85)$[a]	-2.77	(1.20)[a]
Empathy						
Compassionate	$-.20$	$(.98)$	$-.65$	$(.95)$	$.61$	(1.29)
Kind	2.19	(1.09)[a]	$-.34$	(1.08)	2.66	(1.47)[b]
Cares about you	-1.76	$(.78)$[a]	-3.69	$(.66)$[a]	-3.31	$(.89)$[a]

Policy Positions	Mondale		Jackson		Hart	
Liberal-Conservative	-2.25	$(.43)$[a]	-1.90	$(.43)$[a]	-1.59	$(.47)$[a]
Government Spending	-3.13	$(.67)$[a]	$-.61$	$(.68)$	-1.55	$(.74)$[a]
Minorities	$-.61$	$(.68)$	-1.13	$(.69)$[b]	$-.56$	$(.74)$
Central America	-1.94	$(.56)$[a]	-1.02	$(.56)$[b]	-1.40	$(.63)$[a]
Defense Spending	-1.35	$(.59)$[a]	-2.00	$(.58)$[a]	-1.08	$(.65)$[b]
Women	$-.29$	$(.62)$	$-.61$	$(.63)$	$-.59$	$(.68)$
Russia	$-.54$	$(.52)$	$-.28$	$(.52)$	$.08$	$(.58)$
Intercept	34.58	(5.06)[a]	37.88	(4.93)[a]	40.08	(5.63)[a]
R^2 (adjusted)	$.457$		$.468$		$.383$	
(N)	(736)		(750)		(541)	

a. Significant at the .01 (one sided) level.
b. Significant at the .05 (one sided) level.

The small impact of policy positions and traits is not surprising because it seems likely that these factors do not operate directly on choice. Instead, they operate indirectly through utility, as indicated in figure 5.5. Table 5.21 shows that when utilities are regressed on these factors, a significant number of policy issues (government spending, Central America, defense spending, liberal-conservative self-placment) and traits (decent, commands respect, inspiring, sets a good example, cares, and strong leader), produce substantial effects. These results confirm the model of figure 5.5 where viability, electability, and utility act directly on choice and where issues such as policy positions and traits act indirectly through utilities. Thus issues do matter in a voter's choice, but so does the horse race, through evaluations of the candidates' viabilities. We now turn to a summary of what that means for the nomination process.

8. Conclusions

We started by asking whether citizens are informed about candidates, and whether they know anything or learn anything during the course of a primary season. The answer to both questions has to be yes. Citizens are informed during the primary season. There is a substantial amount of serious coverage of the candidates. Moreover, citizens know something and learn during the course of the campaign. Consequently, a critique of primaries based on the ignorance of the electorate seems wrong to us.

The real problem with primaries is not that citizens do not eventually learn about the candidates. Rather, they learn too slowly about every aspect of the candidates except their viability. And one of the major reasons that citizens learn quickly about viability is the enormous emphasis placed on the horse race by the media, especially right after the Iowa caucuses and the New Hampshire primary.

It is all too easy to formulate homilies for the prospective candidate based on this analysis: First, the only advantage of being well known is that it gets you over the hurdles of name recognition and viability, but it will then vex you as some newcomer temporarily captures the imagination of the public. Second, if you are a newcomer, do not try to create a clear-cut image, as Jesse Jackson did. Remain vague and elusive. Third, as a newcomer, you must find some way to gain name recognition and become viable. This must be done without creating a vivid image. The best way is to plot and scheme to be second (or even first) in some early caucus or primary. The lesson, then, of this analysis is that being the favorite is a mixed blessing, and one might better be a newcomer with media appeal and a little luck in Iowa or New Hampshire.

Notes

Sections 1, 3, 4, and 8 of this chapter were written by Henry Brady alone; sections 2, 5, 6, and 7 were jointly authored with Richard Johnston. The research on which this paper is based has been supported by the National Science Foundation, the Survey Research center of the University of California, Berkeley, and the Data Center of the Department of Government, Harvard University. The authors are pleased to acknowledge the enormously helpful research assistance of Michael Hagen, Lisa Martin, and Stephen Ansolabehere.

1. Conventions may also distort the nominating process. Our paper on "Conventions versus Primaries: A Canadian-American Comparison" in *Party Democracy: The Politics of National Conventions,* ed. G.C. Perlin (Scarborough: Prentice-Hall Canada, 1987), presents a thorough comparison of Canadian conventions with American primaries and may be profitably read as a companion to this chapter.

2. The case for reform is made by W.J. Crotty, *Decision for the Democrats: Reforming the Party Structure* (Baltimore: Johns Hopkins University Press, 1978). The case against reform is made in James W. Ceaser, *Presidential Selection: Theory and Development* (Princeton: Princeton University Press, 1979); and Nelson W. Polsby, *Consequences of Party Reform* (New York: Oxford University Press, 1983).

3. Nelson W. Polsby, *Consequences of Party Reform.*

4. The relevant works are F.C. Arterton, "Campaign Organizations Confront the Media-Political Environment" and "The Media Politics of Presidential Campaigns: A Study of the Carter Nomination," and Donald R. Matthews, "Winnowing," in *Race for the Presidency: The Media and the Nominating Process,* ed. James David Barber (Englewood Cliffs, N.J.: Prentice-Hall, 1978); John Aldrich, "A Dynamic Model of Presidential Nomination Campaigns," *American Political Science Review* 74, no. 3 (September 1980); John Aldrich, *Before the Convention: Strategies and Choices in Presidential Nomination Campaigns* (Chicago: University of Chicago Press, 1980); Thomas E. Patterson, *The Mass Media Election: How Americans Choose Their President* (New York: Praeger, 1980); T.R. Marshall, *Presidential Nominations in a Reform Age* (New York: Praeger, 1981); Larry M. Bartels, "Expectations and Preferences in Presidential Nominating Campaigns," *American Political Science Review* 79 (September 1985); Henry E. Brady, "Knowledge, Strategy, and Momentum in Presidential Primaries" (paper presented at the Weingart Conference, California Institute of Technology, Pasadena, 1984); and Henry E. Brady, "Chances, Utilities, and Voting in Presidential Primaries" (paper presented to the Annual Meeting of the Public Choice Society, Phoenix, 1984).

5. Steven Hess, *The Presidential Campaign,* rev. ed. (Washington, D.C.: Brookings Institution, 1978).

6. Polsby, *Consequences of Party Reform.*

7. Ibid., 67.

8. Ibid., 71.

9. Patterson, *The Mass Media Election.*

10. James W. Ceasar, *Presidential Selection;* and *Reforming the Reforms: A Critical Analysis of the Presidential Selection Process* (Cambridge, Mass.: Ballinger, 1982).

11. Henry E. Brady, "Conventions or Primaries? A Book Proposal," Occasional Paper 85-9, Center for American Political Studies, Harvard University, 1985.

12. Brady, "Knowledge, Strategy, and Momentum in Presidential Primaries."

13. Walter Lippmann, *Public Opinon* (New York: Macmillan, 1922), 341-42.

14. Michael J. Robinson and Margaret A. Sheehan, *Over the Wire and on TV* (New York: Russell Sage Foundation, 1983).

15. Ibid., 40.

16. As this discussion suggests, a completely acceptable statistical analysis of media coverage requires some in-depth thinking about news gathering and news writing as a stochastic process in which one day's stories affect the next day's news and in which the coverage in one medium, such as television, affects coverage in another, such as the wire services.

17. Robinson and Sheehan, *Over the Wire and on TV*, 80.

18. Ibid., 94.

19. Ibid., 94-95.

20. Ibid., 94-96.

21. These seven periods were first used in Merrill Shanks, Warren Miller, Henry Brady, and Bradley Palmquist, "Viability, Electability, and Presidential 'Preference' " (paper presented at the Midwest Political Science Association Meetings, Chicago, 1985).

22. Brady, "Knowledge, Strategy, and Momentum in Presidential Primaries."

23. Donald R. Kinder, "Presidential Traits" (pilot study for the 1984 NES Planning Committee and the NES Board of Overseers, 1983).

24. A more complete discussion of distinctness and stability can be found in Henry E. Brady, "A Few Tricks for Those Intrepid Souls Analyzing the 1984 NES Rolling Cross-Section" (paper presented to the Annual Meetings of the American Political Science Association, 1985).

25. These relationships are discussed in more detail in Henry E. Brady and Michael G. Hagen, "The 'Horse Race' or the Issues? What Do Voters Learn from Presidential Primaries?" (paper presented at the Annual Meeting of the American Political Science Association, Washington, August 1986).

26. Brady, "Chances, Utilities, and Voting in Presidential Primaries."

27. Henry E. Brady and Paul Sniderman, "Attitude Attribution," *American Political Science Review* 79 (December 1985).

By the Numbers:
A Statistical Profile of
New Hampshire

PETER M. YU

1. The Basics

Population 1980: 920,610; 1984: 978,000 (est.). Area: 9279 square miles. Ten counties; two congressional districts. Cities larger than 50,000: Manchester (90,936), Nashua (67,865).

A. THE STATE ECONOMY

Leading industries: manufacturing, service industries, retail trade. Leading agricultural commodities: dairy products, greenhouse, cattle. State and local government direct general expenditures (per capita): $1723 (38th in nation).

B. DEMOGRAPHICS

	New Hampshire	United States
Residence		
Urban	52.2%	73.7%
Rural	47.8	26.3
Age		
Under 18	28.0%	28.1%
18-29	21.7	21.9
30-44	20.1	19.1
45-59	14.7	15.2
60 and over	15.5	15.7
Voting-age population (1984)	722,000	173,000,000

	New Hampshire	United States
Race/Ethnicity		
White	98.9%	83.4%
Black and other	1.1	16.6
Hispanic	.6	6.4
National Origin		
Naturalized citizens	3.1%	3.1%
French spoken at home (persons 18 and over)	8.5	.8
Education (persons 25 and over, years of school completed)		
Less than 8	14.7%	18.2%
9-11	13.1	15.3
12 years	37.2	34.6
College, 1-3 years	16.9	15.6
College, 4 years	10.8	8.6
Postgraduate	7.4	7.6
Income Distribution (household income, 1979)		
Less than $5000	10.6%	13.3%
$5000-15,000	32.4	31.2
$15,000-25,000	30.3	26.6
More than $25,000	26.7	29.0
Per capita income (1983)	$9866	$9496
Poverty rate (1979)	8.5%	12.4%
Occupation (1979)		
Managerial/professional	23.0%	22.7%
Technical/sales/support	29.1	30.3
Service	11.5	12.9
Farming/fishing/forestry	1.5	2.9
Precision work/craft	14.5	12.9
Operators/laborers	20.3	18.3
Unemployment rate		
1979	3.1%	6.5%
1984	4.3	7.5

SOURCE: 1980 US. Census; *State and Metropolitan Area Data Book; Almanac of the Fifty States.*

2. New Hampshire's Political Characteristics

A. PARTISANSHIP (see figure A.1 on p. 189)

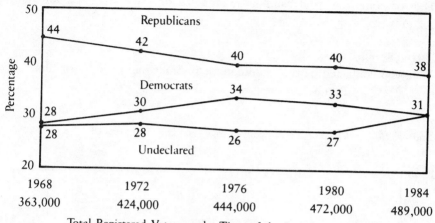

FIGURE A.I

PARTY REGISTRATION, 1968-84

B. POLITICAL PARTICIPATION

1. *Registration, General Election Turnout, Presidential Primary Turnout* (as percentage of voting-age population; see figure A.2 on p. 190)

2. *Participation in the Presidential Primary* (as percentage of registered voters)

	1968	1972	1976	1980	1984
Democratic primary Turnout[a]	60,519 (30.0%)	88,742 (36.0%)	90,340 (34.2%)	111,930 (35.9%)	102,180 (33.6%)
Republican primary Turnout[a]	108,273 (41.4%)	117,863 (40.0%)	112,576 (38.1%)	147,157 (41.8%)	78,399 (23.3%)

a. Since state law allows "independent" (undeclared) voters to vote in either primary, the turnout rate represents the proportion of *registered* voters eligible to vote in that party's primary (including both affiliated and undeclared voters) who actually cast ballots. The relevant section of the *New Hampshire Election Laws and Political Calendar, 1986-87*, reads: "A person desiring to vote at a presidential primary election shall, at the time of anouncing his name, also announce the name of the party to which he belongs. If his name is found on the checklist and if his party membership has not been before registered, it shall then be registered; and he shall be given the ballot of his party" (p. 86).

SOURCE: *New Hampshire Manual for the General Court; State and Metropolitan Area Data Book*.

3. *"Retail Politics" and Personal Contacting*
THE 1984 DEMOCRATIC PRIMARY:
Have you met any 1984 Democratic presidential candidate?   Yes   34%

Did someone from your candidate's organization ask you to vote for him?
  Yes 25%

THE 1980 PRIMARIES:
Were you contacted by this candidate or by someone working for him?
                Republicans (Reagan)   Democrats (Carter)
                Yes   33%   Yes   40%

SOURCE: *New York Times*/CBS exit polls in New Hampshire (1980, 1984).

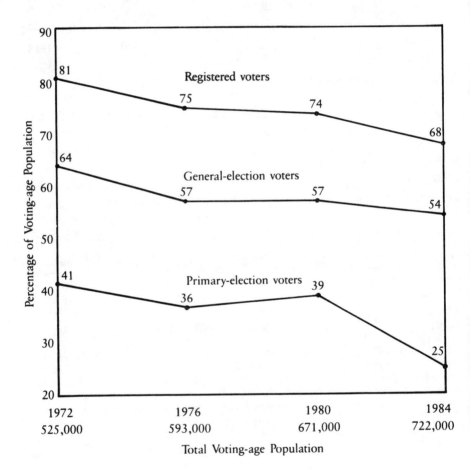

FIGURE A.2
ELECTORAL PARTICIPATION, 1972-1984

C. PRIMARY-VOTER CHOICES (in percent)

Democrats

1952		1956		1960		1964		1968	
Kefauver	55	Kefauver	85	Kennedy	85	Johnson	95	Johnson	50
Truman	44	Stevenson	15	Fisher	14	Others	5	McCarthy	42
Others	1			Others	1			Nixon	5
								Others	3

1972		1976		1980		1984	
Muskie	46	Carter	28	Carter	47	Hart	37
McGovern	37	Udall	23	Kennedy	37	Mondale	28
Yorty	6	Bayh	15	Brown	10	Glenn	12
Others	11	Harris	11	Others	6	Jackson	5
		Shriver	8			McGovern	5
		Others	15			Others	13

Republicans

1952		1956		1960		1964		1968	
Eisenhower	50	Eisenhower	99	Nixon	89	Lodge	36	Nixon	78
Taft	39	Others	1	Rockefeller	4	Goldwater	22	Rockefeller	11
Stassen	7			Fisher	3	Rockefeller	21	McCarthy	5
Others	4			Others	4	Nixon	17	Others	6
						Others	4		

1972		1976		1980		1984	
Nixon	68	Ford	49	Reagan	50	Reagan	86
McCloskey	20	Reagan	48	Bush	23	Hart	5
Ashbrook	10	Others	3	Baker	13	Others	9
Others	2			Anderson	10		
				Others	4		

SOURCE: *New Hampshire Manual for the General Court; Almanac of American Politics, 1982, 1986; Guide to U.S. Elections.*

D. PROFILE OF THE NEW HAMPSHIRE PRIMARY ELECTORATE

	Total Eighteen and Over (1980)	Republican Primary Voters (1980)	Democratic Primary Voters (1980)	Democratic Primary Voters (1984)
Age				
18-29	30%	18%	32%	20%
30-44	28	33	38	39
45-59	20	27	20	22
60 and over	22	21	10	20
Gender				
Male	48%	n.a.	n.a.	49%
Female	52	n.a.	n.a.	51
Religion				
Catholic	47%	27%	53%	51%
Protestant	44	57	25	n.a.
Jewish	1	1	3	n.a.
Education				
Less than high school	28%	6%	8%	n.a.
High school	37	24	28	n.a.
Some college	17	25	20	n.a.
College graduate	18	45	44	36%
Family income[a]				
Under $15,000	33%	31%	36%	18%
$15,000-$25,000	34	36	38	31
Over $25,000	33	33	26	51
Ideology (considers self)				
Liberal	22%	10%	29%	28%
Moderate	41	45	49	50
Conervative	32	39	15	18

SOURCE: 1980 U.S. Census; *New York Times*/CBS exit polls in New Hampshire (1980, 1984); *Boston Globe* poll in New Hampshire (March 1987).

a. In 1984, the income categories were less than $12,500, $12,500 to $24,999, and $25,000 and over.

3. City and County Profiles

	Manchester	Nashua	Belknap County	Carroll County	Cheshire County	Coos County
Population	90,900	67,900	42,900	27,900	62,100	35,100
College graduate	13.3%	18.4%	16.2%	20.7%	18.0%	8.2%
Median household income	$15,600	$19,300	$15,200	$13,600	$16,000	$13,700
French spoken at home	21.9%	14.5%	7.2%	2.1%	2.5%	30.1%
Unemployment	5.2%	3.5%	5.0%	7.2%	4.3%	10.9%
Party registration						
Republicans	28.5%	21.7%	44.9%	55.1%	37.7%	31.8%
Democrats	54.3%	33.3%	22.2%	15.6%	29.3%	37.0%
Undeclared	17.2%	44.9%	32.8%	29.3%	33.0%	31.2%
Voted for Reagan (1984)	70.7%	64.6%	75.0%	75.8%	63.8%	71.4%

	Grafton County	Hillsborough County	Merrimack County	Rockingham County	Strafford County	Sullivan County
Population	65,800	276,600	98,300	190,300	85,400	36,100
College graduate	21.9%	18.5%	19.9%	19.1%	17.6%	12.5%
Median household income	$14,500	$18,700	$16,700	$19,000	$16,100	$15,300
French spoken at home	2.8%	14.3%	5.7%	3.4%	9.1%	4.8%
Unemployment	6.2%	4.1%	4.2%	4.3%	5.4%	4.4%
Party registration						
Republicans	42.7%	33.4%	42.9%	38.4%	30.2%	38.1%
Democrats	25.8%	38.1%	24.6%	29.2%	36.1%	34.8%
Undeclared	31.5%	28.5%	32.5%	32.4%	33.7%	27.1%
Voted for Reagan (1984)	67.8%	71.0%	67.4%	69.3%	61.6%	65.0%

SOURCE: 1980 U.S. Census; *County and City Data Book, 1983; New Hampshire Manual for the General Court.*

Notes on the Contributors

GARY R. ORREN, born in 1945 in Kansas City, is associate professor of public policy and associate director of the Joan Shorenstein Barone Center on Press, Politics, and Public Policy at the Kennedy School of Government, Harvard University. He served as an adviser to the last two Democratic party commissions that designed the rules for the presidential nomination process, and he has conducted public opinion polls for the *New York Times, Washington Post,* and *Boston Globe.* Professor Orren is the co-author of *Equality in America: The View from the Top* (1985), *Elites and the Idea of Equality: A Comparison of Japan, Sweden, and the United States* (1987), and *New Media Technologies and Democratic Values* (forthcoming, 1988).

NELSON W. POLSBY, born in 1934 in Norwich, Connecticut, is visiting professor in the Frank Stanton Chair of the First Amendment at the Kennedy School of Government, Harvard University, for 1986-87, on leave from the Department of Political Science at the University of California, Berkeley, where he has taught American politics and government for the last 20 years. He is a former managing editor of the *American Political Science Review.* His books include *Congress and the Presidency* (4th ed., 1986), *Consequences of Party Reform* (1983), *Community Power and Political Theory* (2d ed., 1980), and *Presidential Elections* (with Aaron Wildavsky, 6th ed., 1984).

WILLIAM G. MAYER, born in 1956 in Chicago, is a teaching fellow and Ph.D. candidate in government at Harvard University. His writings on politics and popular culture have appeared in *Commonweal, Boston Magazine,* and the *Boston Globe.* He is currently working on a dissertation examining the sources of electoral change in the late 1970s and early 1980s.

WILLIAM C. ADAMS, born in 1948 in Chilton, Texas, is professor of public administration at George Washington University. He has edited *Television Network News: Issues in Content Research* (1978), *Television Coverage of the Middle East* (1981), *Television Coverage of International Affairs* (1982), and *Television Coverage of the 1980 Presidential Campaign* (1983). Professor Adams is co-author of *An Assessment of Telephone Survey Methods* (1977).

EMMETT H. BUELL, JR., born in 1941 in Longview, Texas, is professor of political science at Denison University. He is the author of *School Desegregation and Defended Neighborhoods* (1982), and of articles published in *American Politics Quarterly, Social Science Quarterly, Urban Affairs Quarterly, Election Politics,* and other journals.

DAVID W. MOORE, born in 1940 in Honolulu, Hawaii, is professor of political science at the University of New Hampshire. He has written numerous articles analyzing public opinion, media effects, and voting behavior. His work has appeared in *Public Opinion Quarterly, Foreign Policy, American Political Science Review, Public Opinion, Military and Society,* and *Polity,* among others.

HENRY E. BRADY, born in Yonkers, New York, in 1947, is associate professor of political science at the University of Chicago and has taught at the University of California at Berkeley and Harvard University. He is the author of many articles on political behavior and political methodology that have appeared in journals such as *American Political Science Review, Psychometrika, British Journal of Political Science,* and *Political Methodology.* He is now working on a book entitled *Conventions or Primaries?* which compares Canadian and pre-1968 American nominating conventions with the post-1968 American system of caucuses and primaries.

RICHARD JOHNSTON, born in New Westminster, British Columbia, in 1948, is associate professor of political science at the University of British Columbia. He is the author of *Public Opinion and Public Policy in Canada: Questions of Confidence.* He is a contributor to *Party Democracy in Canada: The Politics of National Conventions* and has published in the *Canadian Journal of Political Science, Explorations in Economic History,* and other journals.

PETER M. YU, born in Worcester, Massachusetts, in 1961, is a doctoral candidate in government at Harvard University. Most recently a fellow and research associate at the Center for the Study of Social Policy in Washington, D.C., Mr. Yu is the author of several articles and monographs on American income support and health policy.

Index